ANOTHER
YIN OAN
A WAN WAY TICKUT

A personal diary documenting the rise from
Belisha Boy signalman to the giddy
heights of 2nd Lieutenant in the Royal Corps of Signals

ANOTHER
YIN OAN
A WAN WAY TICKUT

MEMOIRS

Cirencester

Published by Memoirs

MEMOIRS
PUBLISHING

25 Market Place, Cirencester, Gloucestershire, GL7 2NX
info@memoirsbooks.co.uk www.memoirspublishing.com

First published in England, August 2012

Book jacket design Ray Lipscombe

ISBN 978-1-909020-75-7

Printed in England

DEDICATION

This book is dedicated to my wife Bette
and my two daughters Anne & Lee.

ACKNOWLEDGEMENTS

With thanks to George Haddow for his comradeship throughout our internment in the Prisoner of War Camps, his manuscript 'One Parent's Answer' and his daughter's permission to reprint the pen drawings.

CHAPTER 1

1939

1939 was in many ways a good year. I was well established in Forbes & Co and enjoying my greater responsibility. My mother was slowly coming to terms with being left a widow; life was more peaceful in the house. She turned down a proposal of marriage from an old family friend, the family lawyer - the same lawyer who had manipulated my father's will by foxing the Revenue to believe that my father had intended to retire to England, thus the will came under English not Scottish law and I was cut out. Probably correctly so; aged 19, I might have squandered my inheritance fast. If the lawyer hoped this might help his courtship, it failed; neither was the refusal on my account, I assure you. She was a one-man woman. I married the same.

Bette and I still rowed fiercely but not so often and we did have a lot of good times, perhaps due to the high spot of that year being that I bought a motorbike. A 1932 250 cc side valve BSA AXV65479 (vague memory); it had been hard used by a telegraph boy and eventually I replaced or refurbished almost every bit of it, but it gave us mobility. Poor Bette - all I could afford was an inflatable pillion which did not stay fully inflated for too long. Bette, as game as ever, travelled with a wee pot of Iodex. The bike cost £8 and we had hundreds of pounds of pleasure from it. I carried wire, string, pliers and a knife, as bits tended to fall off, particularly if I went over 35 mph. I bought,

1

it, licensed it (Insurance probably with the lorries), took out a Provisional Licence on a Saturday and passed my test on the following Saturday. Fortunately the Examiner did not look at the date on my Provisional licence until after he had passed me. He told me that he would not have passed me if he had known that I had only driven for a week. The test consisted of driving round Blysthwood Square, giving all the correct hand signals, down across St Vincent Street to Bothwell Street, right-hand turn, then another and back up to Blysthwood Square with a stop and start on the steepest bit. That was quite exciting. Dorothy, as we named her, was well past her youth and protested, but we managed.

Nothing would do but collect Bette from her office, off India Street, and take her home to Dowanside Road. She was wearing a green tweed suit with a tight skirt and game as ever hung on to me as we wavered along Sauchiehall Street. The trams looked enormous, but the real danger was the tram lines. They could get greasy in a smirr of rain. Once, we skidded, turning left into Byres Road from Great Western Road and landed in the gutter, the engine still running. A crowd of spectators materialised out of nowhere. Realising this, I righted Dorothy, got Bette back on and we rode back to Dowanside Road, looking neither left nor right, our eyes firmly fixed to the front. Bette had quite a tear in her trousers and had to sidle into her bedroom so that her mother did not find out. That was the worst joint episode with 'Dorothy' and regularly served up to me.

Not so much walking with the dogs at the weekends now; we could get far away. Petrol, Russian, was half a crown a gallon and she went a long way on a gallon. We covered most of Ayrshire, Perthshire and Argyll. Reliable she was not, but we were young and carefree.

There was a wonderful camaraderie among motor cyclists in those days. The roads were not congested as now; a wave was exchanged as you passed; if you saw one at the side of the road, you stopped to offer assistance. At her maximum safe speed (35 mph), i.e. when things were not liable to fall off, it was exhilarating to feel the air rushing past. The Kilmarnock Road was something special in the early morning. Our greatest disaster was on a Sunday evening when we had gone up east of Loch Lomond and back across to Crianlarich. The road to Oban was being rebuilt and the surface was hellish. Bette needed the Iodex! We hit a dreadful pothole just outside Crianlarich and I found that I could not change gear, using the hand change on the saddle tank. A fellow biker in the railway cottages opposite us saw that we were in trouble, came across the road, used a Birmingham screwdriver (large hammer) and off we set. We were late so I pushed on, down the winding road to and along Loch Lomond and got Bette home a bit late but the roast beef and apple pie was still warm in the oven. I left as usual about 11 p.m. and was trundling up University Avenue when the steering went woolly; I pushed Dorothy into a car park and walked home. One of the coal lorries picked her up the next morning and brought her back to the depot, where we found that the front down tube had broken and the only steering was through the barrel spring. Once again we had to strip her down, bore out the broken bits and get a new tube at Rattray's cycle shop in Parliamentary Road. What would have happened if the tube had gone while going down Loch Lomondside, I shudder to think.

Nothing daunted, we decided to go down to Bette's uncle and aunt in Rhwbina near Cardiff at the Glasgow Fair for a week. Bette had always gone there for her summer holidays. Even in the days when she was put in a corner seat of the Cardiff train at Central Station, Glasgow with a label, her name and destination on it, hanging round her neck and her ticket in her purse; a responsible adult in the compartment asked to keep an eye on her. You would not dare to do that nowadays. She was collected by her uncle Gwess at Cardiff. He was in charge of the Goods Depot there, which helped. Probably she was treated better than, if not as well, as royalty.

This trip was a great adventure. Having promised to come for Bette at 6 in the morning, I slept in and in a state of panic, hared off forgetting to lock the communal garage, for which I was severely censured on my return. My late reception by the Thompsons was, to put it mildly, frosty. Off we set, a little late, after I had swallowed a hasty breakfast. Near Bothwell Dorothy seized up; I had forgotten that we had just had her rebored and oversized piston rings fitted and I should have put in some upper cylinder lubricant along with the petrol. It was drizzling and life was not much fun. However, along came a big commercial lorry; the driver leaned out of the cab and in a Yorkshire accent asked what was wrong. He thereupon produced a very large, long-spouted oilcan, took the plug out, squirted a liberal amount of oil into the cylinder and off he and we went. Apart from being rather damp with the drizzle we tootled along past Carlisle. The sun came out; we stopped at the side of the Carlisle-Penrith road, then three lanes, and had a sandwich and something to drink while my socks dried on the cylinder. Dorothy was so designed that, in the wet, the bow wave off the front wheel was carefully directed to the top of my (ex-Ski) boots.

Outside Penrith the clutch cable became detached. Fortunately this happened just outside a smiddy and the blacksmith kindly sweated on a new nipple, charged me sixpence, and off we set. He, of course, was another motor cyclist.

Having chugged down and up Shap with considerable trepidation, we very slowly negotiated with great care the 40 miles of alleged wooden causeys between Lancaster and Warrington, and reached Tarporley, where we decided to stay the night. Graham, Bette's elder brother, a powerful, not to say overpowering, personality had repeatedly made a big thing about these causeys on which he had frequently travelled on his ex-TT (with him of course it had to be ex-TT) 350c.c. Velocette, while courting a Cardiff girl; this was before he met and was conquered by his Bette, a very different character to my Bette.

Landladies were pretty suspicious then, so we agreed that it was better for Bette to go and negotiate, making it plain that it was to be two single rooms, a disappointment for me, but not unexpected.

After demolishing a High Tea to remember, Bette decided to bathe first, saying she would knock on my door as she passed and if I came along 5 minutes later, I would find the door unlocked and would be allowed to scrub her back. Daring Stuff! Bliss! Unfortunately I laid myself down, fell asleep and missed out. This also was served up to me regularly through the years.

Next morning we had a good breakfast and set off for Hereford, finally arriving at Rhwibina, Bette and I safe and sound, but not Dorothy, who was shedding ball-bearings from her front wheel like shelling peas. I pushed her down the garden path and left her there with no regrets. I had to buy a new front hub bearing in Cardiff and fit it. Bette's aunt was appalled at how covered in oil I got. I was amazed that I fitted it.

We spent a wonderful week in Rhwbina. Bette's uncle and aunt were so good to us; I was very touched. I was even allowed to take Bette's morning cup of tea to her in bed. Sadly it took another 56 years before I was allowed to repeat the process. I married a very independent lady.

We could come and go as we pleased. The sun shone, except for one spectacular thunderstorm. There was, nearby, a wonderful place covered in high bracken called the Wennault, where we could go and have privacy; we were both really sorry when the week was over. I shall never forget their kindness to me, considering they had never before met me. Bette took the place of the daughter they never had. Their only son was an oddbod, ate all sweets offered but never did his own see the light of day; no change from Bette's childhood there. He eventually reached, in his career, the dizzy heights of internal postman for the Cardiff Inland Revenue Offices.

Once again, sadly, off we set at 6 a.m. All went well until we crossed the hump-backed bridge in Hereford, when I nearly lost my passenger. She had fallen asleep and left the pillion when we hit the hump, woke up suddenly in mid-air, made a grab for my belt and hauled herself back on. I decided it was a good time to stop and we had a memorable breakfast of ham and eggs in an Italian cafe. On a Sunday too.

We negotiated Warrington to Lancaster with its wooden (??) causeys and Shap again and all went well, apart from occasionally having recourse to string or wire, until darkness fell about thirty miles from home. Dorothy's headlamp could not be numbered amongst her virtues. I was not accustomed to riding outside of street lighting and could only afford a very cheap battery. All you could say about her full beam was that at six feet a faint glow was just about visible. We were determined to make Dowanside Road that night, so we pressed on; fortunately another motor cyclist overtook us near Lesmahagow and asked why we were going so slowly. On hearing the reason he sat behind us, on full beam, until we came to the street lights when with a wave he soared off and I got Bette home safe and sound.

It had been quite an adventure. Bette's mother was very glad to see her daughter back safe and sound and was gladder still to be informed that we had not called in at the Blacksmith in Gretna, as I had threatened, nor had her precious daughter suffered "a fate worse than death". She really should have known her own daughter better. The next day I heard about leaving the garage door open and was very nearly expelled from the garage commune. I apologised profusely, was let off and life went on, regardless of the political storm clouds.

All good things, verily, come to an end; working a 50-hour

week and winching hard four nights a week, I had little time to read the papers or listen to the wireless. Thus, I was completely caught out by the arrival of Conscription for my age group. This had been ever so cleverly put before Parliament by the same Hoare Belisha, who had introduced the first pedestrian crossings, and meant that my age group was to be called up for military service. It was the first peacetime conscription ever in Britain. The Government had finally realised that appeasement of Hitler just fed his ambition to create a Pan European Reich. We had suffered from years of Pacifism and unwillingness to pay the price for essential rearmament post-W.W.1. Kipling's poem "Tommy" very accurately portrays the British public's attitude to the army. After Chamberlain's fatuous remark about "Peace in our Time" (perhaps not so fatuous, he may well have been buying valuable time for preparation for the inevitable war) on his return from Munich, people, even some of the squires from the shires who had never forgotten the catastrophic Dardanelles campaign of W.W.1, began to think that that upstart Winston Churchill was not so wild in his statements after all.

Peacetime Conscription, a dirty word to this day in this country, was thus surreptitiously brought onto the agenda. Shadow Factories started to be built, quietly, not to say clandestinely, in the most unlikely places—green field sites they would be called today. These were destined to manufacture armaments and particularly parts for aircraft. Named Shadow Factories, they, very probably, were one of the saviours of the country after Dunkirk. I don't know what happened to them; I can't remember them being mentioned after I came home. What seemed to exercise most people at that time was to prove that their bomb was much bigger than yours; Britain was very war weary by then.

The clever move was to introduce Conscription by the back door under the subterfuge of giving British youth, male only of course, some good healthy exercise, a little military training and discipline and only for six months at that. They were not to be treated the same as the brutal and licentious soldiery of liberal propaganda. To soothe and reassure the formidable mothers of Britain that their little lambs were not so to become, it was decreed that it would only apply to twenty-year-old males and that they were to be called up in batches, one batch every two months. We (yes, I was one) were not to wear Khaki for walking out like the common soldiery, but were instead to be issued with grey flannel trousers and a blazer to distinguish us. Never actually saw mine.

You should remember that Britain was painfully crawling out of an enormous Depression and the unemployment figures were frightening. The Labour Party, hawking their consciences as usual, had touted disarmament through the years. The Tories (recruits and equipment cost money and taxes cost votes) were too scared of losing the next election to do the right thing. *Plus ca change, plus c'est le meme chose.*

In my total ignorance of the media, as it was not yet called, this passed me by. I was having a good time. I had my girl, the love of my life, my motorbike, was doing well in my job and having the odd game with Whitecraigs 3rd on a Saturday. I played rugby for fun and Saturday afternoons were the high spot of the winter week. First a good physical game, obliterating last week's frustrations, then leaping into the communal bath, all thirty of us, while the water changed colour; mud, I assure you. Sandwiches and tea were provided by wives and girlfriends; finally meeting up in Rogano's later for a pint; also I enjoyed the odd round of golf at Killermont or Glasgow Gailes. The latter was reached by train from St Enoch Station. To get to Killermont entailed taking a tram to Killermont Bridge, (the Council was, as ever, nervously deliberating moving the locker rooms downstairs and the public rooms upstairs) and walking up the drive, clubs on your shoulder, to the clubhouse. I vaguely remember that the drive was made out of or patched by railway sleepers. It was a good club then, a strong representation of the best of the city. Glasgow Golf Club, as I remember it pre-W.W.2., drew its members from businessmen of all sorts from shopkeepers to Company Directors. It did not much matter how much money you had, it was your character that mattered. Pity, I think, that this has been reversed. Nowadays I think that money does not talk in the club, it shouts. Along with its strong Protestant ethics came its faults. Jews and Catholics, I must admit, were scarce but there were some and once accepted, everyone mixed in; once a member, everyone was equal. Glasgow Gailes' clubhouse was very different then. I remember a large room, a bar, lockers on the walls for your clothes, communal dining tables in the middle, and the magnificent leaded panoramic window. Good healthy plain food (poached eggs on mince and hot buttered toast remains a favourite for me to this day) which you ate to a backdrop of hairy backsides as men changed round the walls into grey flannel trousers, hand-knitted sweaters and spiked shoes, to face the weather and the heather. Golf then was much cheaper to enjoy than today. What about the ladies, you ask? There was a suggestion book; I read one suggestion that ladies would be allowed to play Glasgow Gailes on two weekday afternoons with very restricted tee times. It received two signatures. The next suggestion in the book was forcibly to the effect that ladies should never ever be allowed to play. There were so many signatures that I could not count them. I recall also, a wild Annual General Meeting immediately post-W.W.2, when the Council recommended that the annual subscription (for two courses!!) be raised from 6 guineas to 9. You would have thought that the end of the world was imminent.

Suddenly I realised that I was in great danger of being conscripted and sent to an unknown destination. At Fettes almost everyone served in the O.T.C, and like most I had acquired Cert. A, a piece of paper entitling me to an instant Commission in the T.A. So after work, I found my way to a Cameronians' T.A. unit at the back of Sauchiehall Street, proffered the Certificate and my services. The C.O. fell on my neck, coal dust and all. The T.A. was expanding fast and there was a desperate shortage of officers. Unfortunately, while they were confirming my qualifications, the Conscription Act was passed and I was too late. Thus I found myself destined to become a "Belisha Boy", so named after the then Minister for War. Nobody took us very seriously. There was no chance, according to the *Express*, of us actually having to fight. Hitler was a nice man and Mussolini made the trains run on time. Dictatorship worked and even could be envied. Conscription was all a bit of a joke and a great way of reducing pressure on the Dole numbers for a wee while. As it turned out, this might well have saved my life. The life expectancy of a subaltern in the umpty ninth battalion of the Cameronians was not great, although the promotion prospects could well have been excellent but probably not lasting very long.

Eventually, however, the buff envelope arrived, instructing me to report for a medical one summer's afternoon to a T.A. Drill Hall in Dumbarton Road. The Drill Hall was dreary, dirty and dusty. The M.O. fitted the picture and assaulted my privacy in ways hitherto undreamed of by me and peered up at and even handled parts of me that I had always regarded as very personal. I was then introduced to the glass bottle and told to go behind a screen and fill it. As I was stark naked at the time I could not see the point of the screen. Then dressed, I, first, but not by a long chalk the last time, heard the order, "Drop your trousers; head and eyes to the left; cough!" The M.O. cupped your testicles in his hand; this caper was called "The short arm inspection" and became a regular ploy for the common soldier in my day.

Ostensibly a test for hernia, actually I think that it was a regular test for venereal, now called, sexually transmitted, diseases. Officers of course never caught the latter. Like Hell they didn't. When I got home I felt so unclean that I spent half an hour soaking in a hot bath until I felt that I owned myself again.

In my total ignorance of the media, as it was not yet called, this passed me by. I was having a good time. I had my girl, the love of my life, my motorbike, was doing well in my job and having the odd game with Whitecraigs 3rd on a Saturday. I played rugby for fun and Saturday afternoons were the high spot of the week. Suddenly I realised I was in grave danger of being conscripted and sent to an unknown destination. I was a little disappointed and to be honest was not too keen on starting my army career as a humble private soldier. However I buried my head in the sand and just got on with what was one of the happiest times of my life.

What really surprised me was that I was one of the very few who still had his own teeth. I was appalled at the state of the teeth of my generation. The army dentists must have been kept busy sorting mouths. I had been wary of army dentists; silly really, as most of them were civilians, called up like myself, but a lot better paid. I went to the family dentist when I got my call up papers. He, quite a butcher in his own right, passed me on to his newly qualified assistant. This bold lad, just out of Dental College, informed me that I must return within a year and have all my teeth extracted. There was a craze, almost a fashion, for this at that time. I never went back, but on my return from P.O.W. life, visited three dentists, where I learned it would have been madness to have all my teeth out.

After this I was interviewed by a dugout Colonel, whose job was to allocate us to the various regiments. Walter Borland, a long standing friend who must have been a month or so older than I, had been assigned to the first batch. Being an apprentice

Surveyor, the army always so expert at fitting a square peg into a round hole, allocated him to Signals and not the Engineers. I decided to join him. After reading my C.V. the old boy promised me an instant Commission in the Infantry. I was not for having that and told him I was for Signals. He pointed out that a classical education was no recommendation for such a high tech unit and that I would have no chance of getting a Commission in Signals. I stuck to my guns and eventually the old buffer said that he would do what he could. Possibly the first time the name Fettes did me a bit of good. Interestingly enough, when Martyn's turn came to join up, he opted for Signals hoping to meet up with me. None of the three of us ever met up. Signals was where I landed up and I have never regretted it. I learned much that I would otherwise never have known. Anyway the tabloids were absolutely certain there would not be a war, so I settled in my mind to enjoy six months of something different on the principle that a change is as good as a holiday.

However, I did start to pay some attention to the newspapers. Increasingly it became obvious that either Hitler must be faced up to or we would go under and that there was no way that I would not be involved. This gave me time furiously to think. I was very much in love. I still am. In the circle in which my mother and Annie moved there were a lot of "aunts", i.e. older spinsters. Their sweethearts/fiancés had been killed in W.W.1 and though they put a brave face on it they did not have much of a life or money. It seemed but right to me that, if I got killed, Bette should fare better. If we got married then Bette would at least get a widow's pension. I never had any doubt that I would marry her. In those days 20 was rightly considered far too young to get married, but the war changed all that.

Things hotted up. I received my call up papers and a railway warrant for the Signal Training Centre (S.T.C.) at Catterick and the media worked itself up into a crescendo. When Hitler set off his Blitzcrieg and marched into Poland, I knew that that was it. I proposed and was accepted on the Balcony of the Regent Picture House in Renfield Street. Bette was on my left and my mother on my right. It was conducted in a whisper though no doubt my mother had a good idea of what was going on. Space restricted me from going down on one knee, not that I would have been only too glad to. The film was called "Rhodes of Africa", very dull; I do not remember anything about it. Mother by then knew her son well enough to realise that Bette was the only one for me. On the principle that, if you can't beat them, join them, she supported us strongly against the united front of disapproval from all the Forbes on both sides of the Atlantic. She even lent me the money to buy the engagement ring, until I could cash my meagre stock of Savings Certificates.

We put mother on the tram for home, bought a bottle of sherry and headed for 7 Dowanside Road. As we burst into my future in-laws' sitting room, my fiancée, clutching the sherry bottle, blurted out "We have an engagement to announce"—a slip of the tongue. Whereupon my future mother-in-law burst into tears and my future father-in-law, in his LDV (later to become The Home Guard) uniform plus rifle (doing his duty guarding the docks) looked none too happy. It transpired later that he felt that I should have asked his permission first. We had courted for so long and so definitely that we thought that to make the engagement official was more important than the normal courtesies. However the sherry helped to smooth things over and we parted good friends. By that time, with a string over one shoulder, we civilians were all carrying little cardboard boxes containing alleged gas masks. Looking back, I think that they were useless against gas attacks and were more of a propaganda device to deceive the population. I certainly swallowed it whole and dutifully collected mine from some municipal building near Paisley Road Toll. Library?

War was declared against Germany the next day,

simultaneously with all-out war by the Forbes against my mad action. Strangely, from that day on, nothing I ever did met with their approval, (always excepting my mother and my ex-guardian). The Forbes knew that the whole affair was a ghastly mistake and that if we were stupid enough to get married the only consolation was that it would not last. (57 + years not too bad?) They were consistently wrong in their assessment of every move I ever made. I must admit that the truth was that I never could afford any big step, I took, but somehow we always managed. They never could understand that it was my life, not theirs. If I had waited to do anything until I could afford it I would have never done anything.

CHAPTER 2

2nd STC

THE DECLARATION OF WAR stirred the country, particularly the press, into a frenzy. They were sure that the war would be over before Christmas. It could not possibly last more than a few weeks. This put me into a tizzy, in case I missed out. I was so thick that I tried every way to get some unit to accept me. No joy. I had to wait a whole ten days until the date on my warrant. The power of the Press! It was like a fever.

Comes the great day and with my warrant in my hot little hand, I presented myself, as ordered, at Platform 2 in Central Station, Glasgow to be greeted by the Ticket Collector lugubriously chanting "Another Yin Oan A Wan Way Tickut" as he took my warrant. Taking my allocated seat, I encountered for the first time "Haversack Rations". This turned out to be a paper poke just as in a Sunday School Treat, even to the inclusion of the statutory apple. The train wended its leisurely way across Scotland, picking up more Cannon Fodder as it went east through Falkirk to Edinburgh, then South to North Berwick, Berwick, York and Durham, arriving after dark at Catterick, where we got our second *soupcon* of army life. This was travelling at high speed, standing up, packed tight like sardines, in a three-ton truck.

Arriving at our destination we learned our third and most

important lesson in army travel. Complete and continuous chaos! Nobody knew what to do with us; we should not be where we were; they had no orders; get rid of the problem, stick them anywhere. This turned out to be a freezing cold empty Barrack Hut, which we reached after a meal in an equally cold Mess Hall; my introduction to army cooking; no Michelin stars; hungry youth can eat almost anything however badly cooked. I think that, if we had not been given a hot meal, there would have been a mutiny.

Told to stay there for further orders, the rumour mill went into overdrive and stayed with me throughout my army career. We were being sent back home; tents were being erected for us; we were going straight to France; we were to await another train to who knows where. That proved to be true eventually.

Clearly, in retrospect, the army staff were totally overwhelmed by the number of T.A. and Reservists returning to their units and could not cope with us as well. I learned a lot about the army and its limitations in a very short time that evening. In the meantime we were very cold and seeing pot-bellied stoves in the middle of the hut but no fuel, the wooden fitments in the showers were liberated (not looted or vandalised, please note, but early signs of initiative/leadership) and set on fire. Presumably everyone in authority was in such a state of chaos that the little matter of the fire, the smoking stove and the disappearance of the shower fittings was not noticed by the time a fresh train had been commandeered and we had been hurtled back to the station and "entrained"—another new word to learn. Thus was demonstrated the most important of the Ten Commandments. Being the army it was the eleventh of ten. That was: "Thou shalt not be found out and all will be forgiven Thee, and if Thou art found out make damned good sure that it cannot be proven against Thee and all will be well."

Another slow journey took us in the dark across England into Wales and we arrived at Prestatyn, where we were to become the first draft for the Second Signal Training Centre or 2nd S.T.C.

The Government in line with their policy on Shadow Factories had cleverly offered to subsidise the building of a Holiday Camp at Prestatyn which was to be operated jointly by Thomas Cook and the L.M. & S.R., but hidden in the fine print was the proviso, that if a National Emergency broke out, the Camp would be handed over to the army immediately.

The camp being no more than six weeks old, if that, the army had quickly installed an extra bunk in each chalet. I was allocated to a two converted to three bunk chalet. We were three total strangers, a Cockney, Angus Pilton by name, would you believe?, a Midlander and a Scot. We got on extremely well during the six months that I was there. Perhaps the greatest single benefit of Conscription, at that age and at that time of limited travelling facilities, was that it brought home to each of us that Britain contained a vast variety of people, all with different backgrounds, education, religion and upbringing and that if a man wanted a peaceful life he had to learn cooperation and tolerance.

This was not too easy for those who had been brought up as Mummy's boy or had run wild and had never accepted discipline. Ten years at boarding school was as good a training for the army as any. You had already learned that rules, whether just or unjust, had to be obeyed or rather on occasion to be seen to be obeyed. Injustice had to be tholed until there was a chance to get even. Food however badly cooked had to be regarded as fuel and no more. Outrageous injustice from above had to be suffered and a complaint lodged through the proper channels afterwards. Much courage was needed to do that; you travelled via your sergeant, to the C.S.M., to the O.C., then via the R.S.M. to the C.O, each of whom reminded you in a rising crescendo, describing your fate, if your complaint proved faulty or frivolous. Very intimidating.

For your interviews with the O.C. and C.O. you were marched in, marked time (knees up to the chin), halt and hat off.

The chalets were arranged in rectangular groups. Each chalet contained a washbasin, cold tap only. In the middle of each rectangle were two sets of ablutions   (a delightful army word), designated male and female. Unfortunately there were none to be seen of the latter so each half of the rectangle tended to use the nearest set. The ablutions contained w.c.'s and urinals, (I never investigated the female side, never had time to blink), washbasins and showers H&C. Real luxury by army standards. We even had sheets for the first ten days, until the very obvious necessity of laundering them was brought to the notice of authority; they then disappeared. Ammunition boots and white sheets are not good bed mates.

You could call it a rather cosy set up, three 20-year-old total strangers, hormones in full flow, sharing a tiny chalet. This was no problem for me. I was well used to communal living and bare hairy bodies. It was a big shock to the other two who had never been away from home, but luckily for me, they had grown up in good homes. They maybe took their tune from me and soon tumbled to the need to work as a team. I cannot remember any problems. Having a common enemy, the hierarchy, helped. We all had problems there and lessons had to be learned.

The biggest problem was that having been designed as a holiday camp, there was no heating; it had been built below sea level at high tide and was inadequately protected by low sand dunes from the sea, only fifty yards away. The former made it desperately cold in what turned out to be a very hard winter; the latter made the plumbing more than suspect at high tide. What should have gone down often came back up, sometimes very forcibly, not an ideal prescription for a camp whose planned adult population had suddenly increased by nearly 50%.

The camp was exposed to the Irish Channel and that winter

was so cold that the spume from the sea froze on the beach like frosted snow. It does not need a great stretch of imagination to visualise the scene on a morning in January. Snow on the ground; the doors to the ablutions wide open. Coke braziers vainly trying to keep the pipes running and even with their own distinctive pungency failing to kill the pong. Not a lot of privacy. Not a lot of showering. Pale bodies heading for the showers met scarlet ones headed for their chalets. Not a lot of class distinction either. Bare bums look much the same, whatever the rank. Here Fettes was a help. Lack of privacy was no great shock to me. I had already learned at Elie O.T.C. camp that the army's research had persuaded them that three sheets of paper was the correct allocation of bum paper per man per day. One wet wipe, one dry wipe, one polish. I prayed hard that I would never get the trots. Unique to the army, it was brown, hard and glazed on one side.

The next morning, army life began in earnest and we learned right away that the best of ingredients can very swiftly be turned into the most unappetising food. I have to admit that there was plenty of it, and it was not long before I became so hungry that I swallowed anything, which did not come straight back up. The worst was mutton stew. A dirty grey in colour and lukewarm, this was planked on the table in large rectangular metal serving dishes and consisted of roughly chopped meat and bones trying to fight their way out of a thin grey soup, through a thickening skin of congealing grease. It was as if a psychopath had hacked to pieces an elderly sheep's carcase, and thrown it into a cannibal's cooking pot and boiled it and boiled it and boiled it for several days. A close runner up was boiled—kippers, bloaters to the English, for breakfast arriving in the same dishes floating under a similar skin of grease in lukewarm water.

Having cast a jaundiced eye over the A.T.S. in the cookhouse, I decided that discretion was the better part of valour and refrained from comment. They had to be seen to be believed and I can assure you raised no thoughts of lust in our eyes. One would have to be really brutal to be licentious over them. One afternoon on cookhouse fatigue as we were unloading potatoes, a Brunnehilde on the lorry, round about, and I mean 'roundabout', 14 stones with brass curtain rings in her ears that you could have swung from, picked up the cwt. bags of potatoes as if they were pokes of sweeties and threw them at us over the tailgate. One of my mates, caught unawares, buckled at the knees and collapsed on his back clutching the sack, arms and legs flailing like an upturned beetle. None of us really felt like entering into a meaningful dialogue with them, either pro or con, the standard of cooking. There is no doubt that boarding school is the finest preparation for the army or jail. Eat what is put in front of you, keep your mouth shut, hope for nothing, stand still and do what you are told, however stupid it may seem.

After breakfast we drew our kit. Here it was every man for himself. All that interested the C.Q.M.S. was my signature on the form and I had to battle hard to get a decent fit of battledress, socks and boots etc. He just looked at you, made a calculation in his mind, went into the store, brought out a pile of kit and stacked it on the counter. First you checked that everything was there and then entered into a fairly one-sided negotiation about the most glaring misfits. Perseverance was necessary, because once your signature was on the form, you had had it. This widened my army education considerably. The materials, of peacetime manufacture, were top quality. My battledress was made of such excellent cloth that I had the greatest difficulty in damaging it sufficiently in order to exchange it for a new one, when I knew that a Commission was nearly a certainty. Finally I resorted to rubbing the knees with a brick and it took a lot of hard work to do any damage at all. Eternal Vigilance was from then on the watchword. If someone is short of a sock and your back is turned you could well find yourself suddenly short of a sock. Not a good idea on an inspection. The cost of replacement was charged to your meagre wages. The boots, impregnated with grease to make them waterproof, never gave a moment's discomfort but created problems, getting the high standard of polish demanded by the C.S.M. We spent hours in the evenings with the handle of a toothbrush and lots of spit and polish. Originally toothbrushes would have had bone handles, hence the army term "boning up", a nightly chore. If the C.S.M. could not see his face reflected in your toecaps at the morning inspection, you were in trouble. That and the length of your back hair seemed to be his main preoccupation. As he passed behind you, you would hear, "Get your hair cut, is it not hurting? I am standing on it!" This meant that it was at least a quarter of an inch long. The heels of your boots had to have a mirror finish too. All brass polished with the aid of your issued button stick, (a flat strip of brass with a slot, so that it could be slid under the button and thus ensure no marks of dried polish on the battledress or the forage cap). Puttees I hated; finished up with the vee pointing backwards on the outside and directly over the ankle bone, trousers tucked inside, but leaving a fold over the puttees. What all this had to do with the prosecution of the war, we were none too sure, but if you wanted a quiet life there was no alternative. Of course we realised later that it was really all to do with breaking down your resistance to authority prior to building you up into the army's special pattern.

Our C.S.M., Shardlow by name, had but one eye, and could spot, like nobody's business, something not correct at a great distance. His greatest moment came one day when one of my chalet mates rushed on parade to discover that he still had his mug in his hand. He quickly stuffed it in his battledress blouse leaving him with the look of a raffish lopsided Amazon in heavy spectacles. This kept Shardlow going for days and took some of the pressure off the rest of us. Shardlow's language was scatological and explicit; like a lot of fire eaters he was a good bloke at heart. I learned a lot from him and I know that he genuinely regretted that the loss of his eye prevented him from being posted on active service, unlike some of the regular N.C.O.s I met later, who would have given their back teeth for a cushy, safe number in the U.K.

Having recovered from our first midday meal we were interviewed. Marks were awarded according to school, educational qualifications, sporting interests, experience in the Scouts, B.B. and so on. This was an attempt to assess leadership potential. Fortunately the officer who interviewed me was a Scot, who knew of Fettes. I had many problems later on with English interviewers on this subject. On establishing that I was Scottish and had been at a public school, they would look down their noses and say, "Of course what you call a public school in Scotland, we call a Board School in England." I never learned. This really got me on the raw. It was such a tedious business disillusioning them. The net result of the interview was to be repeated ad infinitum. An offer of an instant Commission in the infantry and told that I had no future in Signals.

Reliably (!!) informed by the *Daily Express* that the war would be over by Christmas, I gave my stock reply: "Sir, I would rather be a L/Cpl in Signals than an officer in the Infantry." You see, the *Daily Express* was as accurate in those days as it is now, or should the word rather be inaccurate.

The next day, after our morning boiled bloater, (The way the English cook a kipper makes the word bloater most apposite) we were mustered into squads for square-bashing. Here I found myself at a disadvantage. Since my leaving school some idiot Minister for War had decided that all drill movements would now be carried out in three ranks instead of two. Ministers for War felt that the only way to achieve immortality was to make some small alteration to the drill manual. Usually this was something to do with arms drill, but this particular Minister had gone way over the top. All my hard earned skills in forming fours and learning the esoteric mysteries of the blank file went for naught. The Senior Drill Instructor or S.D.I. as we learned to call him was the epitome of charisma, though that word had not yet become fashionable. George Crawford, good as he is, is not in the same league. Having got us all on parade and facing the same way, a considerable achievement itself at that moment, he proceeded to indoctrinate us, saying that we had joined the Elite Corps, henceforth to be referred to as the "Royal Corps". It was *la Creme de la Creme* of the British Army. All bullshit in hindsight, but we all—I certainly did—swallowed it whole. After the usual guff to the effect that if we played to his tune he would look after us but if not "Gawd help us", he finished up with the immortal words, "Gentlemen, I am a Bugger for Pride. Be proud to be a member of the Royal Corps." His complexion pointed to him being an Anglo Indian. Clearly the army had no colour bar as far as O.R.s (other ranks) were concerned. The same did not seem to apply to Commissions. Hence he revelled in the name of "Inky Udell". First class at his job, in the short space of six weeks he brought us up to giving a passable exposition of the General Salute, quite a tricky manoeuvre involving several foot and arms drill movements, all carried out with no orders given after the first. We worked hard at the drill and at being properly dressed, knowing that we would not be allowed outside the camp perimeter until we had passed out in both aspects.

During this period the enormous and rapid expansion of the army brought huge pressure to find potential officers. Our Camp Commander, a full colonel, later to become a Brigadier, who rejoiced in the name of Le Fanu, decided to form an O.T.C. squad, of which I became a member. This was a disaster waiting to happen. Owing to the aforesaid expansion, N.C.O. promotion had been equally rapid and we found ourselves under the command of a young red haired Acting Lance Sergeant, who had most probably been an unpaid Acting Lance Corporal the week before. He was a nice young man and keen; he never stood a chance. How he could be expected to control a squad, all of whom were convinced they would be commissioned next week if not sooner and bung full of their own ideas of leadership was a clear demonstration of the lack of imagination in the higher echelons. The basic problem was that we all came from different O.T.C.s and had been taught our drill by retired R.S.M.s from different regiments, each with their own little variations in squad drill. No sooner did the poor chap start to instruct us in sloping arms than he was flatly contradicted by various members of the squad. One would say, "But sergeant I was at Harrow and our R.S.M. was from the Grenadier Guards or similar and this is the correct way." No sooner were the words out of his mouth than another would pipe up to say that he had been at Eton or Marlborough and his R.S.M., also from some prestigious regiment, did it quite differently. I stayed in the rear rank and kept my mouth shut, you will be surprised to read. I had very happy memories of being instructed by a wee kilted sergeant of the Gordons, whose uninterrupted flow of words when the improperly fixed bayonet of the cadet in the rank in front of me fell backwards onto the parade ground at my feet was memorable to say the least. Fortunately we were in open order. Otherwise my military career would have been truncated there and then. The result of all this was that the squad fell further and further behind, until one day the C.O. walked round the corner and saw the hassle The next day we were back with the common herd. This was no bad thing. The formation of a small elite squad based on schooling had caused a lot of bad feeling for obvious reasons. Shardlow's welcome back was short and to the point.

Having eventually passed out on the square, we were allowed

outside the camp gate in uniform having been instructed in "salute" and "give the eyes right/left" ad nauseam—"Hup one two three, head and eyes to the right, Dahn one two three…" The problem was that in those days, only Officers and R.S.M.s were permitted to wear KD uniforms, collars and ties. God help you if you saluted an R.S.M. dressed in a raincoat on the other side of the road on a dirty night. This I learned the hard way in Rhyl on a murky night. The fact that his raincoat was the same as that of an officer and that it hid all badges of rank was no excuse.

A Signalman was paid two shillings a day or fourteen shillings a week. Four shillings were withheld for some pretty specious and obscure reasons like cleaning materials and barrack room damages, with the remote possibility of getting the surplus at some unspecified date in the future. All we got in our hot little hands on pay parade was a ten-shilling note. Once a week we attended pay parade, where we carried out the manoeuvre dinned into us on the square. As in alphabetical order my name and number was called out, I marched smartly up to the table from the left, halted, stamping hard, left turn, shattering salute, one pace forward, extend the left hand for the ten-bob note, one pace to the rear, shattering salute, repeat left turn stamping the heels and march off smartly. Otherwise no pay. Many then repaired to the N.A.A.F.I. to lose the lot in a card game called Brag, where only a chosen few prospered. Fortunately I did not know how to play the game and took very good care not to learn. Instead, with thoughts of matrimony, I restricted myself to half a crown pocket money per week and sent a fifteen-shilling postal order to my fiancée once a fortnight. She too was saving hard for the wedding. The Savings account in the Clydesdale Bank in Great Western Road was in her name. Not daft, was she? One shilling of my half-crown bought an ounce of Three Nuns tobacco and a box of Swan Vestas. The other eighteen pence went on riotous living such as mugs of N.A.A.F.I. tea at a penny a time or occasionally, madly, I would splurge out on a penny bun to go with the tea. We were so full of all the bullshit about *la Creme de la Creme* that we did not feel deprived, but rather privileged to serve in such an elite corps. Once a fortnight my *fiancée* sent me a tin containing a large fruit and walnut cake of her own baking. It could have stood in for caviar as far as I was concerned and caused much envy. No chance. The empty tin went back in plenty of time for a refill. I can taste it to this day.

Once we had passed out on the square, we discovered there were three battalions in the camp, each commanded by a Lt. Col.: the Depot Battalion, from which we had just graduated and which would now deal with the next draft, the Trades Battalion and the Operators Wireless and Line Battalion, to which, I was posted. Training was held in huge marquees. First the Morse Code had to be learned and then used for sending and receiving messages using the buzzer on the handset of the sturdy D 5 field telephone. This was a remarkable machine and could stand any amount of punishment. If it failed at any time the first remedy was to use "the kick and throw test" literally. This nearly always worked. There was also some very superficial training on Semaphore, quickly forgotten, and an amazing day with the heliograph. Not a lot of sun in North Wales in December. However, that apparently prepared us for active service against the Pathans on the North West Frontier. Very necessary, I am sure. We were also introduced to the Sounder, the original method of sending Morse. This depended on reading the back clicks and was rather confusing. Our first target was 7 (?) words a minute sending and receiving. We achieved this in three months and were then classified as Operators Wireless and Line Class D. Then we aimed at 18 words a minute in order to become Ops. W. & L. Class B. This was the big one and qualified us for active service.

The whole course took six months. Looking back, it was a

strange life. Up at six, wash and shave in cold water, breakfast at seven, bring your own mug and eating irons. Get cleaned up, boots and brasses polished, chalet clean and tidy, beds properly made and surplus kit displayed; on parade with Shardlow for Inspection at 8.30; off to the marquee, find your own D5 and settle down to practise your speed. This all on slats, seated on wooden benches with wooden tables in the freezing cold; drainage carried no priority; it was a very cold winter. The guy ropes of the marquees were sleeved in an inch of ice for weeks on end; if there was a drop of water in your mug left from rinsing it out, the water would be frozen between the chalet and the Mess Hall. Being under training, fatigues generally passed us by, but on one occasion the local G.O.C. (General Officer Commanding the region) decided to inspect the camp. Panic ensued. All training ceased for three days while every cigarette end and match stick was picked up. It was raining icy stair rods; the whole camp was under two inches of very cold water; we used duckboards to get to the marquees. The lack of drainage seemed to escape the notice of the General, but I can tell you that picking cigarette ends out of two inches of semi-frozen water does not lead to lily white hands—blue and chapped more like. I only sensed the Presence at a distance, just a blur of officers keeping firmly to the duckboards and tarmac. Either we were kept deliberately in the background or he refused to leave the tarmac. A pity really, as to see a real live General might have inspired us, indoctrinated as we were. Also, it was rumoured that he had the V.C. ribbon on his chest.

The best fatigue, I missed. I think we must have been at some critical stage in our training. There had been a heavy fall of snow and Prestatyn was immobilised. Young men with shovels were in big demand. No snowploughs in those days. A rum ration was issued. We, to a man, promptly volunteered for the next day but the thaw came overnight. Par for the course. Guards were on the main gate. Indeed I spent all of my 21st birthday on guard. No presentation of the key of the door but plenty of saluting at the slope, slapping the butt. You developed eagle eyes for S.D. uniforms and pips on shoulders. I spent my hours off in a top bunk, thinking of what might have been. The floor was reserved for the never ending game of Brag being played on the floor on an army blanket. I do not remember any day guards at Prestatyn.

We did plenty of night guards and a few 24-hour ones. Night guards were fun if looked at in one light. Eerie too at 2 a.m. peering through the murk as you listened to footsteps approaching, when you went into the "Halt Who Goes There" routine all set to ram one up the spout if the reply was not favourable. It never occurred to me that it would have to have been a very thick Hun to answer Foe, but I was ready for him if he had. If the faltering footsteps betrayed one of your mates returning slightly the worse for wear, it was vital to get him past the lighted area in front of the guardroom before the sergeant of the guard heard him. The army was pretty tolerant of minor inebriation. If you could manage to proceed under your own steam, however erratically, you usually got away with it. If however you suspected that it was the Orderly Officer trying to catch you out, you had to shout out the challenge loud enough to alert the rest of the guard, give them time to roll up the blanket, money, cards and all, plank it, and then shout out "Stand to the Guard, Guard Turn out", when some bleary eyed characters would stumble out feverishly doing up their buttons and equipment and fall in for inspection while you stood smugly at your post.

Quite frightening it must have been too for a stranger to hear a round being shoved up the spout, the bolt slammed shut and the safety catch pushed forward. Any practical jokers sobered up pretty fast. Who would want to steal a few battered old D5 field telephones escaped my imagination. That winter was cold enough in the chalets but in the marquees it was Arctic. Not only were the ropes covered in a solid inch of ice, but, if you spilt a drop of cocoa, it froze instantly, even before it hit the duckboards. Yes, the big-hearted army allowed the wretched marquee night sentry a paraffin stove and a tin jug of cocoa to sit on top of it. For that duty I wore everything I possessed, even including both pairs of long johns, cap and cap comforter on top of two shirts, two vests, two pairs of pyjamas, a greatcoat and four blankets (an extra blanket was issued—Big Deal!) and it was still too cold to sleep except in fits and starts. No excuse was accepted for being unshaven, late or improperly dressed on parade the next morning. Fortunately that duty only came round once every three weeks.

There was much excitement when a wee two-seater plane crashed on the beach and both occupants were killed. The plane would be iced up no doubt. An ambulance appeared crewed by a couple of F.A.N.Y.s. Unfortunately named, they were a very superior lot and looked down their noses at everyone below the rank of Field Officer and would be very affronted if you called them A.T.S. County definitely and not much appreciated by us. Thus we had a not so quiet smile when they stepped out of the ambulance, caught sight of the two stiffs in the plane and promptly fainted on the spot. They were quickly stuffed back into their own ambulance along with the two corpses and two of our lot drove them off to hospital. Not quite so snooty after that.

I had a short spell in an alleged army hospital, actually a converted villa, and suddenly realised how uncomfortable army life was. I had no desire to be discharged; it was so wonderful to have nurses regularly bringing you cups of tea. Unfortunately German Measles (Rubella) does not last too long. It all happened because I had gone on sick parade with a sore throat. The army was not too keen to encourage you to report sick so they made it as unpleasant as they dared. The wait in the queue down the long draughty corridor, which was seething with germs from all the bodies, standing, waiting their turn, changed my mind about ever reporting sick again. If you were not ill when you went sick, you sure as Hell contracted something there. The other deterrent was that if the M.O. decided you were malingering, he marked against your name, on his form, M.& D. (medicine and duty) in red ink. Not only was your pay stopped but you were put on a charge. This was worse for a married man as his wife's or mother's family allowance also ceased. So going sick was a gamble on the M.O's frame of mind. V.D. was ruled to be self-inflicted and also resulted in red ink and no pay or allowances for the period of treatment. This took a bit of explaining to the wife or mother. The reasoning behind this action was that at the guard room, packages called dreadnaughts were freely available. These contained a sturdy condom and some barrier cream. So I was told. If you had sex in mind you drew your dreadnaught at the guardroom and signed for it. If you had done that and then contracted V.D. you had a better chance of avoiding the dreaded red ink; if not, you were in big trouble and no pay and no family allowances for some considerable time. No Penicillin then. If your wife or mother enquired why she was getting no allowance, she would be told the truth. I never saw a dreadnaught open but was told that they had a considerably negative influence on Romance.

We did eventually qualify for a week's leave and were issued with travel warrants. A weekend pass was not a lot of use to me. Train travel was slow and uncertain. No excuse was accepted for reporting back, late. One minute past your time for checking in at the guardroom and you were A.W.O.L. and in deep trouble. I had to change trains at Crewe, where the W.V.S. did a sterling job, providing stretcher beds, cups of tea and wads (buns and sandwiches). You were given a label on which to write the time of your train. This was tied to the foot of your bed, and you were woken five minutes in advance. All free. They were the unsung heroines of the war. They were everywhere to assist servicemen, even providing guides in the big railway stations. I was proud that my mother worked as a guide in Central Station Glasgow. Britain after Dunkirk was packed solid with all sorts of uniforms, the Free this and the Free that. Many knew little English and depended on these ladies to see them to the right train. Their strange uniforms were a problem to us squaddies. We did not know who to salute and with redcaps standing about, you had to be very careful. Nothing a redcap enjoyed more than putting a poor soldier on a charge. They were definitely the forerunners of today's Meter Wardens. Some of the uniforms were very odd to our eyes. The watchword was, when in doubt, throw one up. You could always claim that the salute was aimed at the guy behind.

The spirit in the country was wonderful. If you were in uniform people could not do enough for you. Particularly after Dunkirk, but they were good before that. Train travel was highly complicated, especially if you had to change trains at one of the smaller stations. The names of stations were blacked out to confuse enemy fifth column agents. We were indoctrinated to expect hordes of enemy paratroopers dressed as nuns, with sub-machine guns concealed in their habits, dropping from the sky at any moment. So, approaching your destination, you had to listen at the ventilator window and try to make out the name being shouted. Not easy in the dark for a Scot in Wales or rural England. What it must have been like for a Cockney in Aberdeenshire I cannot imagine. Once again you got help from the locals in the compartment.

It was a wonderful leave. So good to be back in civilisation, though rationing was beginning to bite. We were each issued with a week's ration card. The Forbes's took us to the Alhambra where there was a sort of Cochrane show complete with a magnificent high-kicking chorus. We had good seats and I must

31

confess I enjoyed it. My fiancée was working of course, so mother and the Forbes's saw more of me, during daylight, than she did.

Back at Prestatyn the hunt for potential officer material had resurfaced, but this time it was approached more tactfully. Forty of us were chosen and appointed Squad Leaders, a totally fictitious rank, but operating as sort of embryo L/cpls. We were issued with blue and white, (R. Signals colours), ribbons to put round our epaulettes, posted to a separate squad, and given a small amount of responsibility. Not all of us ex-Public School this time. Four more interviews ensued, one with each Lt. Col. and one with the Brigadier. All followed the same pattern; idiot Brown again refusing the offer of an instant Infantry Commission, standing rigidly to attention and enunciating the immortal words: "Sir, I would rather be a Lance Cpl in the Royal Corps of Signals than an officer in any Infantry Regiment." I was barking mad of course, but had by that time been totally indoctrinated. The sentiment went down well with the regular Signals officers but I was given no reason to be optimistic. With hindsight it probably did not do me any harm with dyed-in-the-wool career Signals officers.

CHAPTER 3

O.C.T.U

A SIGNALS O.C.T.U. had been set up in Aldershot to progress the half-trained Gentlemen Cadets from Woolwich; their course accelerated, they were coming to the end of this course so the net was being extended to suitable candidates from the two S.T.C.s. Weekly three aspirants were sent down alternately from each S.T.C. I had just qualified as an Op W. & L. B, and was awaiting a posting, and was pleasantly surprised to be included in a later trio.

The reception at O.C.T.U consisted of the C.O. and a Major Moberly (Senior Instructor); they had in the past sent the odd aspirant back as unsuitable, but had got too big for their boots and had returned *en bloc* as unsuitable the previous trio from Prestatyn. There was the most unholy row and a furious letter went hurtling down to the O.C.T.U. asking "who the Hell a Lt. Col. and his 2 i/c. a mere major thought they were" to overrule the recommendations of three Lt. Cols. and a Brigadier, threatening to take the matter to the War Office if there was any more of this disgraceful insubordination.

As it transpired, I was one of the next three to go down from Prestatyn. If it had not been for the foregoing, I would certainly have been on the first train back from Aldershot. I was so full of bullshit that this would not have bothered me one bit. Ten days earlier I had been made up to acting unpaid lance corporal and was pretty full of myself, so much so that I spent many happy hours sewing my stripe on anything in sight. I was so pleased that I had earned the stripe by myself with no help from the school name or anything else. I would not have called the King my cousin and fair revelled in the little authority and responsibility; already I was aspiring to further promotion. However, down we trundled in the train while I feverishly tried to get the hang of Ohm's Law, the fundamental principle in Electricity and Magnetism theory, something to the effect that $I = E/R$. I am still none too sure; in the end I got it wrong. I did not even know what the letters stood for.

On arrival at the O.C.T.U., we were sat down to two exams, one on Maths and one on Electricity and Magnetism. I got 100% in the former and zero in the latter so all my work on the train went for naught. It would have been much better the other way round. The interview with the C.O. and his Senior Instructor ran the usual course even to having to explain that Fettes was the Eton of the North. Probably, with hindsight, they were taking the Mickey out of me just to gauge my reaction. That was fine until it came to E&M (Electricity & Magnetism). I had tumbled to the fact that here I was not dealing with dugouts but real pros and so answered the questions absolutely straight, thus quickly revealing my total ignorance of the subject. I soon knew how the missionary felt, standing in the cooking pot while the water heated and the cannibals danced round. The only light relief came when I hesitantly vouchsafed that all I knew about E&M was a little Ohm's Law. This had them rolling in the aisles. It was the best joke they had heard in years. I can still hear them chortling away: "A little Ohm's Law!" That of course is the first item on the first page of the beginner's primer on E&M and they knew I had got it wrong in the exam. Well it was a 50/50 chance and the coin came down wrong. They looked down their noses and said that, after all the snash from Prestatyn, they were forced to let me start but that I, even with the highest Classical qualifications, did not have a cat in Hell's chance of completing the most difficult and longest O.C.T.U. course in the army at the time, all eight months of it; one false step, one exam failure and I would be R.T.U.ed i.e. returned to my previous Unit on a single ticket with a small piece of paper stating that I was unsuitable to become an officer; they further emphasised that I would be much wiser to take the offer of an instant Commission in the Infantry; all thoughts of stripes went out the window. That did it. They had clearly never encountered a Forbes before. I made up my mind to prove them wrong and much to my surprise and even more to their amazement, I did. The reader must bear in mind the extreme pressure for officers due to General Conscription and the consequent immediate enlargement of the Army.

Off came the blue and white ribbons and the stripes and I became an Officer Cadet, still in a Signalman's uniform but now garnished with a broad white ribbon round my forage cap. This made me stand out amongst the troops; I became a special target for the Redcaps, who hated all Cadets except the Gentleman Cadets, ex-Woolwich and destined for a Regular Commission. They were addressed as Sir and had all the privileges of Commissioned rank. We were possibly headed for Emergency Commissions and addressed as Cadet So-and-So. We were only allowed to drink in two bars in Aldershot, where the prices were extortionate. We felt like hunted animals; out of camp, one button not properly done up, one salute missed and you were handed the single ticket back to your Unit with the terse message from the C.O., "This man is not suitable to become an officer." There was no appeal. The complaint against you could come from any member of staff or Redcap. One day the Cadet was there. The next day he was gone. I saw it happen more than once. I had eight months of this. I stood to attention to all and any, from foulmouthed London Bus Drivers to Electrical Eggheads, and answered, "Yes Sir. No sir. Three bags full Sir." What I thought had nothing to do with it and was carefully suppressed. Any comment favourable or otherwise had to be accepted without hesitation. No excuses; a very strange life almost like living under a malevolent Dictatorship. It was worse for me as I felt the word had gone out to get this idiot and put Prestatyn in its place; not a lot of fun either for the rest of the squad.

The nearest that I came to the dreaded R.T.U., apart from scraping through some of the technical exams, was when I refused my pay on pay parade. We were paid according to our previous rank; some had come down from higher ranks, but as far as our uniforms showed, we were all equal as Cadets. Some idiot in the Pay Corps (one Pay Corps private, arriving as a neighbour post-war, on being asked what sort of war he had had, replied "Hellish—for three days I never even got to put on my pyjamas!") had me down as having been an R.S.M. (Warrant officer class 1) and I got a huge shock when I looked at my pay. Initially I was pretty pleased at the large sum of money in my hand instead of the humble 10/- shilling note. As the week wore on towards the next pay parade, I had second thoughts. My Scots blood said to me, "Now hang on a minute. What about when they find out? Even the Pay Corps will find out eventually and I will have to pay the whole lot back; have no money and be in debt for the rest of my life." At the next pay parade my heart was in my mouth. Sure enough there was this pile of money again on the table. I took a deep breath and refused my pay because it was not right. The officer looked totally confused. This had never happened before. The sergeant went bright purple and ordered me a second time to take my pay. "Take the money, boy!" I stood my ground with a sinking heart. This was only my second pay parade at O.C.T.U. I got a right rocket and was put on a charge or "fizzer" as it was called. Next morning no lectures for me. Marched in front of my Company Commander: "Mark Time, left right, left, Halt, Cap off, Cadet Brown Sir refusing to obey an order from a superior officer contrary to Section 40 of the Army Act." All this in the stentorian voice of the Orderly Sergeant. Section 40 was a portmanteau section of the Act referring to conduct prejudicial to good order and military discipline. I thought to myself, "This is it. Prestatyn here I come." Much to my surprise my O.C. looked up and said, "What have you got to say for yourself, Cadet Brown?" I was not going to back down and explained that no Scotsman was going to put himself into debt, particularly due to someone else's stupidity. He, much to my surprise, establishing that the pay offered was that of an R.S.M. and that I was indeed only a Signalman, dismissed the charge. It might even have brought me some Brownie points. The squad had written me off and were amazed to see me appear at the next lecture. I was pretty surprised myself. I think with hindsight that that was about the bravest intentional thing I ever did in the army, or was it just foolhardy?

Each squad was allotted to one leg of a spider, a wooden roofed structure with a hub and six legs. We had two coke burning stoves in the middle of our hut, as we called it, a couple of kitchen type tables, benches, and for each of us a tubular metal bed in two sections, with a small shelf above it, a small locker, not lockable, as I remember. Each bed had three small horsehair mattresses, (put end to end, they made a mattress of sorts) called from their colour, biscuits, a pillow and three blankets. The bed had two positions. First thing in the morning after a wash and shave, strip the bed; push the two halves of the bed together; stack the three "biscuits" flat at the foot of the bed with two exactly folded blankets on top; the third blanket folded lengthways and wrapped round the whole contraption making it look like a flattened section of a Swiss Roll; all exactly placed and neat. At the other end of the bed and exactly central, your pack sat upright with all your spare clothing and kit in it.

For a full kit inspection everything had to be laid out on the bed in little piles so that the correct numbers of everything could be checked. Your rifle almost vertical was clipped to the wall alongside your respirator. The rifles were W.W.1 Canadian, Ross .303 Sniper rifles. They had to be cleaned every day for inspection and left with a thin film of oil on all metal parts. Ammunition was only issued for Guard Duty. All this was in addition to the usual spit and polish. A brush and shovel used by the Orderly Cadet of the week for cleaning the wooden floor was also inspected, the ablutions too. The stoves gave little or no heat until they glowed cherry red and were roaring well. As they were our only heating, we were fortunate to arrive in March and leave at the beginning of November. Handy as ash trays, they had to be clean and polished for inspection. Cleanliness was next to Godliness and a bit in front. Personal cleanliness was catered for by the ablutions at the far end of the hut.

Aldershot was a garrison town, and Salisbury Plain, one enormous army camp. The original brick-built Mons Barracks was occupied by the 2nd Canadian Divisional Signals. The Canadians, we suspected, had a fair complement of men, who had been given the option by a Judge of jail or army. This was the time of the phoney war and they were very bored. They wanted action and if it was not provided, were prepared to make their own. They were wild, and I mean *wild*. It was not unusual to see a man with three stripes up one day and no stripes but two black eyes the next. One morning there appeared to be a mutiny of some sort. One of them had got a kitchen chair jammed on the ridge of the barrack hut with its back to the chimney. His inflammatory address to a fair crowd below would have done credit to Hyde Park Corner. He vanished and was never seen again. Another evening as we wended our decorous way back to barracks from one of the only two bars we were allowed to frequent, we saw a couple of three tonners backed onto the pavement outside a pub and a squad of redcaps. (With our give-away white ribbons on our forage caps, we carefully kept to the other side of the road.) The redcaps formed two lines facing inwards and as each body came out, it was slung forcibly into a truck. You could hear the thumps of the heads hitting the metal cab wall.

They deserved some sympathy. They were very frustrated. They had been filled up with stories of their forebears' bravery at Vimy Ridge in W.W.1 and were desperate to prove themselves their equals, but were rightly held in reserve and in fact only landed in France in time to be brought back out at the time of Dunkirk. Never fired a shot in anger. Then as a sop they were used in the disastrous Dieppe Raid. Some sop! On one Guard Duty I shared the Guard Room with some of them including a bunch of French Canadians. I did not dare to close my eyes. I learned some new colloquial French which, in later life, I felt it wiser not to use.

Our training classes were held in modern wooden spiders of similar construction to our hut. Considering war conditions, we were well off. The food was not too bad for army food, but our table manners needed to be improved considerably. Big Brother was always watching. We were young and healthy and could eat anything remotely resembling food. Meals were taken at a gallop, so much swotting, so much bullshit. Every minute was precious. The N.A.A.F.I. was handy and cheap, but I was still getting my fortnightly fruit and walnut cake from my beloved. Tea and a wad was about all most of us could afford.

A few were still getting their pay being made up by their ex-employers and could lash out a bit. One in particular, Hallam by name, a bit older and a bachelor, seemed to have money to burn. He was a C.A. and came from Wales via Birmingham. He had played Rugby for some strong English and Welsh sides. Llanelli comes to mind. He had to have his six or seven pints every night and, loudly singing Rugby songs, would roll into the hut after lights out full of beans and beer. Having made so much noise that we all woke up, he would fall flat on his back on his bed and snore like no man I have ever met. With hindsight he had all the signs, high colour and glistening eyes, of an incipient alcoholic, although he would no doubt be reckoned to be a moderate drinker alongside his Llanelli club mates. Our remonstrances fell on deaf ears. Perhaps we were a little envious of his comparative wealth.

Many of the squad are shadows in my memory now. Amongst those who stand out, of course, is George Haddow, dead now. I still kept in touch with him from time to time, post Liberation. We seemed to be posted to the same units a lot. He was a good friend, utterly reliable; cleverer than I, he already had a degree in Commerce and went on to become a C.A. and then senior partner in a well-respected Glasgow firm of Chartered Accountants. There was a pair of identical twins from Muswell Hill, London. Qualified Post Office Engineers and direct entries into our squad, they had never been away from home and phoned Mum every night. We took a fiendish delight in occupying the phone box, which reduced them to a form of St. Vitus dance, hopping from foot to foot. We thought this hilarious. Permanently glued together, they rushed about and were commonly referred to as "Tear Arse and Panic". This was because they spent their time breathlessly purveying rumours of doom and gloom, usually false. If it was humanly possible to get the wrong end of the stick, they would. The snag was that, if they did get a genuine piece of information, our instinct was to disregard it. The memory of the pair that sticks in my mind is of an occasion when we were suffering the field cable laying section, physically the hardest part of the course. Here Active Service Conditions prevailed; everything was carried out at the double. Their squad had arrived at huge ornamental wrought-iron gates of a large residence. The cable had to be looped from one gatepost to the other, high enough up to allow vehicles to pass beneath. At the foot of one gate stood twin A eyeing the height of the gate with considerable apprehension and saying, "I can't." Our instructor, a large man, at that moment a corporal and working his way back to sergeant. He had been busted already from sergeant three times for fighting and being under the influence of a lot of beer. His knowledge of life in the Glasshouses or Army Detention Centres was considerable. He had in his hand a crookstick, which he waved at the wretched Cadet in a distinctly threatening manner and informed him in succinct but unprintable language what he would do to him with the crookstick if the Cadet was not on top of the gate by the time he finished speaking. A split second later twin A was crouched on top of the gate pillar with his eyes tight shut; twin B wept at the foot, fearing that his brother was too terrified to climb down on his own. Twin A was left behind, chittering, as we went on to the next obstacle. Twin B, horrified to see his 15 cwt. disappearing, had the unenviable decision to make, whether to stay with his brother, who evidently shambled down some time later, still with his eyes tight shut, or run after his squad. He ran, shouting, "Wait for me!" No chance. Poor fellows, they were very much Mummy's boys and could be reduced to tears very easily and often were.

Another direct entry was called Pirie, an "Otis lift engineer". He had come all the way from South America to volunteer. A taciturn chap, he was very clever and I must admit gave me a lot of help with the technical side. I chiefly remember him for how he held on to his watch as a P.O.W., something deviously, forbidden by the Japs. It was a wrist watch with a white leather strap. He wound it nightly and wore it strapped on the wrist behind his scrotum, hidden amongst his pubic hair under his G string. The Japs never found it.

The most remarkable Cadet was a Cornishman from Dawlish, a seaside town in Cornwall. I cannot for the life of me remember his name. He had left school at the earliest possible age to be apprenticed to a joiner. Thus he had had virtually no education compared to the rest of us. He had worked as a joinery instructor in a home for the "mentally retarded" in Dawlish, but his hobby, his passion, was being a Wireless HAM, building and operating his own equipment and contacting HAMs worldwide. Like me he had been told his lack of technical education would preclude him from completing the course. Unlike me, having been brought up under English class distinction, he accepted this as fact. I worked very hard to convince him that if I could do it he would walk the course. He did. Some of the squad looked down their noses at him and his heavy West Country accent, but we became good friends and he was invaluable to me during the Wireless or W/T part of the course. I often wondered what became of him. As I remember, he was posted, on being commissioned, to an Armoured Divisional Signals.

Then there was a brilliant European Jew, whose name I cannot remember. It began with a W and had been anglicised. He had a very large head simply bursting with brains and a totally uncoordinated body. The technical part of the course was a doddle for him, the physical an uproarious joke. No power on earth and certainly no Drill Instructor could get him to swing his arms correctly. His left arm inevitably went with his left leg and his right with his right leg. As soon as he stepped off with his left foot, that is, if he actually did manage to start with his left foot, up would come his left arm, reducing the D.I.s to apoplexy. He could not ride a bicycle ten yards without falling off. He could not even sit on the pillion of a motorbike without falling off, let alone drive one. As for being behind the wheel of a 15 cwt truck, it was not possible to get anyone to sit beside him after the first lesson. He was a bigger menace in a vehicle than a runaway tank. The problem was that he would not give up trying. Finally in the interest of all he was forcibly persuaded to go away and do something else, while we completed the M.T. course. A delightful colleague, the first to laugh at his own physical inadequacies, he could finish written exams in half the allotted time and invariably get 100%. Whether he was a bigger menace on the square as a member of the squad or in charge of it, is a moot point. In arms drill I took good care to keep as far away from him as possible, particularly when fixing bayonets. The sight of an improperly fixed bayonet slowly falling off the end of the rifle in front of you and toppling towards you, as the order to slope arms was given, was guaranteed to increase the heartbeat considerably. His other misfortune was an inbuilt inability to distinguish between right and left and to communicate in those terms to his extremities. His ungainly figure shambling off in the opposite direction to the rest of the squad, after an order to change direction, was no uncommon sight. Chaos would reign as this shambling figure, in thick glasses, a beatific grin on his face, either blundered through the ranks meeting us head on or disappeared in the opposite direction cheerfully swinging his arms along with his legs. He led a charmed life and you could bet that there were no volunteers to partner him in individual drilling. No D.I. would countenance him drilling the squad as a whole. Much as we cursed him for spoiling our drill, passing out from which had become most important to us as a stepping stone to the next part of the course, he was very popular, a sort of mascot. If he survived the war, he must surely have gained a high position in Academe. He had all the brains and intelligence for it and doubtless was sent to some research centre after being commissioned. Far too good a brain to be wasted on active service.

I also remember two red-headed Scots from the east coast, Ross and Reekie. They ran together more than with the squad and quickly learned to ingratiate themselves with Authority. Another lad started with us, a very decent chap. Off farming stock from the North East of Scotland, he, poor chap, contracted Meningitis and fortunately for him, died. In those days survival from that disease condemned you to the life of a vegetable. The real reason I remember him is that he was given a full military funeral. Slow march to a dirge, behind the coffin, resting on a gun carriage and covered by the Union Jack; his white beribboned cap and leather belt on top. All led by a full military brass band to the graveside, followed by a jaunty selection of popular tunes for the quick march back to barracks. Very impressive. I suppose the message to us was that even if the army made our life Hell in this world, at least we would get a good send off to the next.

There was also a most impressive figure with an Oxbridge honours degree and a half blue for boxing, middleweight I would imagine. A sergeant from some top T.A. unit—we all liked him. What happened I do not know, but Plum Warner suddenly disappeared. R.T.U.ed, accused, we were told, of cheating. None of us believed it; there was no appeal; he just was not that kind of man; that was the army for you.

I vaguely remember another one disappearing but not to anyone's regret. It fairly kept "yours truly" on his toes; the speed with which it happened; summoned to the C.O.'s office, handed a one-way warrant and an envelope for his previous C.O. and that was it—Army Career finished. Tough as life was, I was indeed lucky to be still there. Of my erstwhile chalet mates, Pilton had gone to a unit in France and came out at Dunkirk; the other probably went to Narvik. They were both posted while I was waiting for Aldershot, so I might well have gone either way and who knows what might then have happened to me! We must have kept in touch as Pilton came down to see me one Saturday afternoon during the Battle of Britain and could tell me but little about our other chalet mate. We decided that he went to Narvik. While going home on a train for a week's leave I saw some of the poor sods who had got out from that disaster. They looked dreadful, sleeping where they lay in the corridors, toilets or whatever and they were the lucky ones. They got out. Unshaven, some with tin hats, some without, none properly dressed, they looked ghastly and stank of defeat. That was a disaster, one of many still to come; badly equipped, badly trained and not too well led, I was told.

As he and I sat on the grass in the sun, we could follow the vapour trails and hear the chatter of the machine guns in the dog fights and, occasionally, saw a plane spiralling down trailing black smoke. That summer as you went about the lush countryside, here and there you would see crashed planes and the odd trailer loaded with bits and pieces being towed off to be cannibalized. Angus had been doubly lucky, firstly to get off the beach at Dunkirk, after being repeatedly dive bombed and machine-gunned by Stukas while standing up to his waist in the sea waiting for his turn for a place in a boat, secondly by being recalled back to his civvy job as an Instrument Maker by his former employers. He must have been good at it. Not many got out like that. I was happy for him but very concerned with my own affairs.

I, instead, had started eight months of very intensive training just hoping every day to scrape through and prove the Establishment wrong. Drill, P.T., Map Reading, M.T. Driving, Electricity and Magnetism, Cable Laying above and below ground, Cable Jointing, Organisation and Methods, Signal Projects and Planning, Wireless Telegraphy known as W/T., King's Regulations and the Army Act, the most comprehensive and longest O.C.T.U. course in the army at the time. Every day was a new challenge, as apart from Drill, P.T., and Motorbike driving, it was all completely new to me.

We started with P.T. and square bashing and were put through the mill with a vengeance. By the end of the square bashing we could have mounted the guard at Buckingham Palace and shown up the Brigade of Guards. After falling out at the end of the day, we all went into our hut and stretched out on our beds, boots and all, absolutely exhausted, for at least twenty minutes until we felt strong enough to troop along for a mug of tea in the N.A.A.F.I.

In addition to the standard foot and arms drill we had some hilarious sessions drilling each other on a one-to-one basis across the square. Imagine a dozen or so men, ten paces apart, shouting orders at their doppelgangers 100 yards away on the other side of the square. It was bedlam. I learned fast how to throw my voice, something I found very helpful later when handling my dogs on the hill. Finally we took it in turns to drill the squad as a whole. The high spot of square bashing occurred when during a smoke break we were sitting at the side of the square and on came a squad of potential A.T.S. officers to be taught foot drill by a very embarrassed D.I. Poor souls, their uniforms were very different from the smart K.D. of today's W.R.A.C.s and their kind of balletic right and left turns accentuated by the thick lisle stockings and heavy khaki skirts were like something out of a sand dancing Music Hall Act. Male chauvinist pigs that we were, we roared with laughter at their antics. They vanished and we never saw them again. They must have been drilled at a time when it was known we would be on some other ploy. Another red letter day came when we were under an unpopular D.I., each of us taking it in turns to put the squad through its paces. There was a high wind blowing lengthwise down the square, which was about twice the size of George Square and actually, oblong. The D.I. in order to test George Haddow's lungs delayed his instruction of "About Turn" as we marched upwind; we pretended not to hear it and marched right off the parade ground and stood marking time until poor George and the red-faced D.I. doubled up to us. Well, not even the O.C.T.U. could R.T.U. a complete squad. We were made to suffer in other ways, but we knew that we were nearly at the end of that part of the course and trusted that we would never see that D.I. again. The firing range, somewhere on Salisbury Plain, was quite exciting; we were each issued with five rounds of live ammunition. I do not think that the targets suffered much damage, but it did give us the feel of a rifle and the kick of a .303. We then spent the evening pouring a fixed number of pints of boiling water down the barrels of our rifles finishing off by pulling through dry flannel rectangles, measuring 4 by 2 inches, followed by one oily one and cleaning your rifle as normal. Removing the brass butt plate disclosed a regulation pull through, a little metal oil bottle and a strip of 4 by 2s. All rather boring.

The P.T. was tough and the instructors greatly enjoyed making us sweat. There is something peculiarly sadistic about an army P.T. instructor. It was no surprise that their uniform jerseys made them look like perverted hornets. I survived. I was not the worst and certainly not the best. At least I had been broken in at Prestatyn. The Direct Entry and T.A. cadets must have found it absolute Hell.

The last week included route marches short, long and a couple at night. We marched for fifty minutes at the regulation army pace, then ten minutes fallen out at the side of the road for a smoke. Yes, we all smoked. It was the non-smoker who was the odd man out in those days. Our O.C., referred to by me as the Twerp, supervised us intermittently, but on four wheels. He did not look the athletic type, more interested in exercising his right elbow than any other part of his body. He thought that he looked like a film star, always well turned out and highly polished. You will find it hard to believe there was an exact position for our cap badge down to a sixteenth of an inch and every now and then he would appear on parade wielding a foot rule and followed by his batman carrying a stool. He then proceeded to measure the position of each cap badge. How to win a war!

Our last effort was to take part in a scheme or TEWT as it was termed; I think it stood for Tactical Exercise Without Troops. There you could be landed with a blue and white flag and told that you represented a Bren gun or whatever. Our ambition was to be declared dead or a prisoner, when we could fall out, eat our haversack rations, have a smoke in peace and watch the others sweating all over Salisbury Plain. Entering or leaving the square meant marching to attention at the slope and eyes left or right when passing the guardroom.

We had a cursory morning on other weapons, including the Bren gun, the army's new automatic, replacing the W.W.1 Lewis gun. Being at the back of the circle, my normal position, I never got the chance to handle the Bren and was no wiser at the end than I was at the beginning. This was a pity as I could have used one later to some effect if I had only known how. I was indeed glad that my progress in the O.C.T.U. did not depend on my prowess with firearms.

The next part of the course was map reading. We had been strongly advised to buy bicycles. For advised, read instructed. The idea was that you bought one off a member of the squad, which was on the point of completing the course and you hoped to sell it on in turn at the end of your course. I paid a couple of quid and it was the best buy I ever made. On our time off, weekends, we would go touring all round the countryside in pairs. So lush, it was an eye opener to a Scot. There was more hay along the hedgerows than grew on some fields at home and the wild flowers had to be seen to be believed. It was a wonderful summer. The sun seemed to shine all day, as I look back. I knew that I was in a foreign land.

Patriotism ran high and khaki was a popular colour as it always is in war time. Kipling, as so often, hit it off: "It's thank you Mr Atkins when the band begins to play." I am afraid that we capitalised on this after discovering that if on arrival at some little village we, innocently, asked a passer-by where we might get a cup of tea, we would, instantly, be whipped into a house and given a full afternoon tea. If it was a big house we would be directed to the back door to take tea with the cook in the kitchen. Memorable teas indeed! In one big house we were even invited to come back the next Saturday for a game of tennis. That was the second time I played on a grass court. There we were regaled with ginger beer out of stone bottles and cream cakes to boot. We had to be extremely careful not to repeat locations. People were very kind; in that area most folk knew what the white ribbon in the cap meant; this stood us in good stead. I shall always remember the great kindness of the ordinary country folk. These outings were a magical counterbalance to the frenzied life in barracks where you could always feel the presence of Big Brother watching over you.

Back to map reading, which, unfortunately, only lasted for a week. We were under the charge of Lt. the Honourable O.H.P. Lyttleton (I think). Commissioned Lt. largely due to being a member of the Beerage, I am sure. Instantly named by us "Percy the Pathfinder". There were many very odd instant short service Commissions awarded in those days as I had cause to regret later. He had only the faintest idea about the art of map reading. His lectures had obviously been written for him by someone else and his understanding of their contents was vague, to put it as politely as possible. I doubt that we learned much from him except perhaps which way up to hold the map and I am not too sure that he was absolutely clear on that. I can only suppose that "the Powers that be", bearing in mind the powerful family he came from, thought that he would do the least damage to the war effort in that job and I have no doubt he would finish up as an A.D.C. in a cushy billet. On reporting to him in the morning, after drawing our bikes and haversack rations, he would give us a map reference near to a pub where, if we were lucky, he would meet us for lunch. There we could enjoy a pint of shandy and await, without much optimism, Percy's arrival. After a decent interval, we remounted our bikes and wended our way back to barracks to await his appearance. I think he only arrived at the right spot once all week, arriving out of breath just as we were leaving to go back. He always had a new excuse the next day, a puncture, a summons from the C.O. for a meeting and so on. The truth was he could not read a map for toffee. I just followed the herd. The weather was good and it was a wonderful relaxing week after the square bashing and P.T. I suppose I did end up with a rudimentary knowledge of coordinates and so on.

Perhaps, in that context, it was fortunate I was posted to Malaya, where there were really only two main roads running north and south, one each side of the peninsular, with very few laterals. Hardly a demanding test of my map reading skills. How some of my colleagues, who finished up in other spheres of the war managed not to get lost, particularly in the desert, I hate to think. I could very happily have spent the rest of the war lying in the sun on the grass, listening to the insects, in the certain knowledge that Percy was lost again. The birds had too much sense to be out in that heat and enjoyed their siesta in silence.

Having taken a reluctant farewell of Percy we embarked on a fortnight's M.T. course. The technical side rather passed me by, but I did manage to grasp the difference between 2 and 4 stroke engines and the rudiments of the Otto Cycle. This last was a mistake as it led me to try to teach it to an illiterate ex-Horse Transport driver who, in spite of being a very competent M.T. driver, was one of the thickest men I have ever met. It must have been the missionary instinct in my genes that made me persevere in such a hopeless task. The result was total frustration. He had acquired a licence before mandatory testing; never had an accident; could see no point in learning what went on under the bonnet. The motorbikes were much more to my taste although the army 500cc bikes were a lot heavier to handle than Dorothy. We had one memorable day on the firing ranges tackling sand dunes and rough riding. That was one part of the whole course where I could shine having had some previous experience of two wheels.

That day I saw my first modern tank, quite an unusual experience then. The noise was very distinctive, a sort of metallic clatter rising to a crescendo as the monster came over the brow of a low hill. Further down the bank I saw the churned up turf where some driver had tried to turn sharply at too high a speed on a downhill stretch and stripped his tracks. I then realized that although these monsters looked invulnerable they were anything but. In spite of this I still volunteered for an Armoured Divisional Signals on passing out. Fortunately my W/T marks, while good enough to get me a pass, did not qualify for that. My lasting memory of the motorbikes was W being grounded after unwittingly demonstrating wheelies on take-off. He was so keen that he never took in that the throttle had to be opened gently and instead took off at full belt and I mean took off.

We proceeded to four wheels, learning on 15 cwt. Fordson trucks, with no self-starter, windscreen or synchromesh. Close coupled, they were started by swinging the starting handle; it had a vicious kickback, if not swung hard enough; thumbs had to be carefully folded out of the way, otherwise liable to be broken; the canvas tilt gave minimal rear vision; the engine was very powerful, but fitted with a peacetime governor to restrict top speed; the clutch was fierce; the gear lever long and whippy with enormous travel. Hardly the easiest vehicle to learn on. Double declutching was essential whether changing up or down.

This took some learning. Unless the revs were exactly right the protest from the gearbox could be heard at a fair distance even above the vociferous comments of the instructor, usually referring adversely to our parentage. First push the clutch pedal fully to the floor against a very strong spring; not for nothing did we wear ammunition boots; let the revs die down and with a prayer ease into first gear; increase revs delicately just enough to avoid stalling and gently release the clutch or the front wheels left the ground like a leaping salmon; always remember to give the correct hand signals at all times; no indicators in those days. If successful so far, boot the clutch pedal back to the floor and ease the gear lever into neutral; release clutch delicately; long pause while the revs died down, time for a couple of lines of the National Anthem or three Hail Marys; clutch back down to the floor; ease gear lever carefully into second; ease clutch, equally carefully out; increase revs just enough to accelerate away smoothly. Repeat this manoeuvre twice and you found yourself in top and travelling far too fast for your own comfort. Changing down was something else. Foot off the throttle; clutch to the floor; find and enter neutral; a couple of Hail Marys; rev like mad and go for third; if your prayers were answered, you repeated the process all the way down to bottom. Getting into bottom without protest called for luck as well as skill. Getting into bottom by mistake required great strength and the subsequent scream from the gearbox led to scenes not suitable for delicate constitutions. The gearbox and the instructor, a thick ex-London Bus driver with two stripes and a monotonous vocabulary, soon let you know if you had got it wrong. All this time, keep your eye on the road and give the correct hand signals while your ears tried to translate the bellowed Cockney of the instructor into intelligent sense. I bet they grew ulcers fit for a medical museum. I know that I would not care to spend my days sitting beside learner drivers in a vehicle without windscreen, back windows, wing mirrors or synchromesh and a canvas tilt.

At the end of the fortnight, we took our Test. No nonsense about the Highway Code, which still gave diagrams of signals to be given with a whip by four legged, not petrol driven four-wheeled transport operators. We had a whole hour's lecture on that. That was reckoned to be quite enough of that nonsense. Our task was to get the thing started, go up, on a quiet straight road, through the gears to top and back down to bottom without crashing the box, stop on the other side of a crossroads, reverse into the side road, stop, start back onto the main road and repeat the process of the gear changes, until you reached the starting point, all the time giving the correct hand signals. If you managed this without incident, you had passed. Three point turns? Starting on a hill? Pardon?

The real reward came during the second week of the next course. All who had passed and applied were given a certificate to that effect which entitled them to a civilian driving licence. Hence my first red driving licence was issued by Southampton County Council and I was able to renew it, after the war, with no questions asked and no further test.

The next course was make or break: Electricity and Magnetism, presided over by one Captain Palmer, a Post Office boffin and reputed to be one of the six greatest experts in the world on Line Transmission. He had lectured on its theory to all the top people in Europe and America. A typical egghead, slight, bespectacled and balding, he was totally engrossed in his subject, which did not necessarily make him the ideal instructor for those Cadets like me, who were totally ignorant of the subject. He tended largely to talk over our heads and more to the ex-P.O. engineers, who could understand his jargon and who explained it to us later in plain English. Even they could be intimidated by his expertise. As a squad united against the Establishment, we stuck together. This was the part of the whole course which I had been told would finish me off and that I had not the faintest chance of passing. Even the knowledgeable members of the squad were none too confident either. I was told that two years of an Oxbridge degree course had been compressed into six weeks. I still have no idea how I passed. It must have been a close call, perhaps by half a mark. I did work very hard and got a lot of support. The most surprised and disappointed person was Moberly, my interrogator at my first interview. Five weeks of intensive theory were followed by the all-important exams. I must have guessed enough of the answers right to scrape through.

The course started off badly for me. The first lesson told us that originally E&M theory was based on Direct Current flowing from positive to negative, but that it had recently been discovered that it actually flowed the opposite way. I hope that I have got that right, probably not. However as all the textbooks and theory were founded on the original idea and anyway it was of no real importance, it was considered therefore not to be worthwhile going to all the expense and aggro of putting things right; the scientific world would therefore carry on regardless. That was it as far as I was concerned. My grandson David would understand. I found it hard to believe another word the man said and from then on regarded the whole affair as a sort of game played with crooked rules. Maybe "Ladyton Rules"!

Either due to that or to my having swotted so hard, I cannot remember much of those weeks or indeed of E&M. As in a Greek tragedy, a diaphanous veil is drawn over that part in my memory. It was quite an exciting time. First the funeral of a colleague, then the visit from the Minister for War, Anthony Eden, who appeared in the classroom one morning during some abstruse lecture on an esoteric electrical measuring instrument. We had lectures on some very oddly named instruments, much of which passed me by at the time, but came back to haunt me later. Very dapper, leaning on his immaculately furled umbrella, with his eponymous Homburg hat in his hand, very suave, he languidly surveyed us standing to attention in his honour, turned to the blackboard, gave one horrified look, exclaimed " Oh my God!" and passed out of our lives in one minute thirty seconds flat. I cannot say that I was surprised that he was a total disaster as Prime Minister. Suez Disaster. Winston Churchill stayed on as leader of the Conservative Party far too long and kept Eden back. I cannot but see at the time of writing this (5/4/09) that the same thing is happening again with Blair and Brown. In both cases the P.M. outstayed his welcome and his successor caused my country to be disgraced. My prejudices must be declared. I had opined some years previously that Gordon Brown would go down in history as the worst Chancellor of the Exchequer in my lifetime and was now going to rival that soubriquet as P.M. "No more Boom and Bust!!"

During this course one of our squad was R.T.U.ed for cheating. (See above.) I still think that there was dirty work somewhere. He must have made an enemy, or else he was plain unlucky and made a scapegoat in order to impress on us the power of the Establishment, *pour encourager les autres*. I do not understand it. He was in my estimation outstanding officer material and I cannot believe that he was capable of cheating. He certainly had no need to do so, I shall always believe that he had had some encounter with Moberly, where it became only too clear that M. had come up against such a superior intellect that he could not tolerate his presence. There is an interesting tailpiece to this affair. The cadet, now a sergeant again, was posted to India, was approached more than once about going to an O.C.T.U. locally with a view to a Commission but flatly refused to contemplate it. After the war his intellect was so much appreciated that he was appointed a lecturer at the Staff College, Camberley, whither budding Staff Officers were sent on courses to assess their suitability for promotion. Surprise,

surprise, who should appear in a batch of aspirants, but Moberly, who took one look at Plum and said, "Have I not seen you somewhere before?" "Definitely not!" was the reply. The ex-cadet went on to have a distinguished career. There are papers in my desk to that effect. George Haddow had met him in India and kept in touch. The rest of the squad thought the whole affair disgraceful, heaved a big sigh of relief that it was not them and got on with the course. I must admit I kept my head down, determined to win.

Still shaken at having passed the hurdle of E&M, we tackled Cables, underground, overhead, permanent and field. This started with a project aimed at establishing our skills in assessing the materials needed for and the plotting on paper of a complicated communication scheme. After a short concentrated set of lectures on planning, we were each given a map, a clipboard, a chino-graph pencil and instructed to produce a detailed plan of a complete overhead line system of some miles, estimating and tabulating all the stores, men and equipment, needed to put the plan into effect; all to be filled in on the correct army forms, everything from poles to nails and insulating tape. The overall course was so condensed that we were really only going through the motions, as no doubt our raw ideas would have proved highly impractical in real life. We did now know however, what the correct forms looked like, if ever we needed them. Something very important in the army.

Thus the squad appeared blinking in the harsh light of day, highly confused and wandering around Aldershot armed with the above clipboards, pencils, paper and bewildered expressions. The bright spark, who had organized the exercise, had routed the plan past both the V.D. Hospital and the Detention Centre better known as the Glasshouse. The former was largely occupied by Canadians and the latter probably also. Tales told to us by the occupants of the former were hair-raising and did much to keep us on the straight and narrow as far as "horizontal refreshment", as it was then referred to, was concerned. Tender Loving Care has never been an outstanding aspect of the army hospital service at the best of times, but when it came to V.D. that was something else. We heard with mounting horror descriptions of an instrument vulgarly referred to as "the hockey stick"; the shape apparently was similar. This was inserted at regular intervals into the penis during treatment in a raking action and none too gently either. After a sojourn in that Hospital a man would either be very stupid or very drunk to risk a return visit.

I had been forewarned about the Glasshouse at Prestatyn. In any group of young men, there are bound to be the odd tearaways. Early on two had been caught stealing roller skates, of all things. When they returned from the Glass House they looked absolutely dreadful and slept solidly for about 48 hours. Such condign punishment for first offenders was unusual in the army. Normally the book was only thrown at you for a second offence. An object lesson to the rest of us this time. The reason for them being hammered so early on would be "*Pour encourager les autres*".

In the Glasshouse everything happens at the double. This applies to the staff too, all hand-picked sadists, who also have to double everywhere. At the crack of dawn or "sparrow fart", as it was called , the sergeant doubled round the gallery, the cell doors were opened in rotation, and each occupant issued with a razor blade; he completed his circuit and repeated, only this time retrieving the blades; this does not give much time for a shave in cold water. God help anyone not properly shaved on parade. Blood had to be washed off. Definitely not much of a place for the non-morning type. Fatigues, drill at the double wearing full pack and kit fills the miscreant's day. The odd really awkward man might find his pack loaded with bricks. As for P.T. the least said the better. A favourite exercise was to empty the coal store, whitewash it and the coal and then put it back. This could be repeated day after day. No spells for a fly fag, and very plain food. Not the sort of accommodation likely to be awarded stars by the A.A. So the story goes.

Someone, not from our squad, but could have been, definitely not amongst the brightest, either unaware of the foregoing or so wrapped up in his task as to be oblivious, was observed, by a sentry on the gate, to be loitering outside the above Establishment and to be writing on a clipboard. He, poor chap, was drawing diagrams and scribbling notes to do with the scheme, but to the sentry he "appeared" to be drawing plans for the escape of some of the inhabitants, many of whom had been convicted of crimes much more serious than stealing a pair of roller skates. In no time at all the wretched Cadet was arrested and doubled off to a cell via the guard room. His shrill protests, audible at a fair distance, went for naught; after all it is common knowledge that every inmate always loudly protests his innocence. He spent a most uncomfortable night and was doubled about next morning until a none too happy Twerp, our O.C., arrived to establish the Cadet's bona fides and take him back. We all hoped that he too had to double about. It would have done his figure no harm. That Cadet was never seen again. The staff of the Glass House knew fine the truth of the matter but as hardened long service men, they thoroughly enjoyed putting a Cadet, white ribbon and all, through the hoops.

Underground Cables saw us passing a boring week, mostly as observers, I am glad to say. Fibre optics and plastics were still a twinkle in some research scientist's eye. Our cable was a tightly packed mass of copper wires, each individually insulated by variegated coloured and patterned strips of paper, which were wound very carefully round each wire in spirals; all was encased in lead and buried three feet underground. Our main task was to learn how to repair a fault. In pairs we were presented with two pieces of cable, the lead coating, partially peeled back, each looking a bit like a shaving brush whose bristles were thin copper wires. We then had to wrestle with the colour coding, match up the opposing ends, joint them, solder the joints, rewind the paper insulation, bind them in pairs with paper twists and wrap the whole lot up tightly enough to go into the lead covering, which was then rebuilt and made waterproof. This latter was called sweating the joint and was a highly skilled job, by a plumber using a blowlamp. Not much used nowadays. Most interesting it was, to watch an expert at work.

Next came field cable, physically the most demanding part of the whole course. It was a severe test of stamina and guts. Here I reaped the advantage of the heavy physical work on the coal depot. The cable came in two sizes, D 5, composed of 5 strands of steel wire in a rubber sheath and an outer covering of woven fabric wound onto one mile or mostly half-mile wooden drums and D 8, composed of 7 strands of steel and 1 of copper wire, similarly insulated, and wound onto 2-mile wooden drums. The copper strand greatly improved the transmission efficiency of the D 8. The D 5 was used for short runs round a Signal Office or in forward positions. An iron bar, thrust through the hole in the middle of the drum, became the spindle; a couple of linemen seized the ends of the bar and ran like hell from point to point, preferably as the crow flies. A highly hazardous operation, even on manoeuvres; if one carrier tripped, his mate would be catapulted through the air while the drum hurtled on under its own momentum. This was a formidable sight coming erratically at you. Mostly used by battery and battalion signallers, we only used D5 around Divisional H.Q. to set up telephone exchange systems, where there was not normally the necessity to tear about.

D 8 was a very different animal and provided much clearer signals over longer distances. The big drums were very heavy to handle and dated back to the days of horses. In those days, the drum was mounted on a spindle with a wheel at each end and drawn at speed by a pair of horses, rather like cannon in Napoleonic times. Once again the object was to travel in as straight a line as possible however rough the ground.

There was a mounted Divisional Signals in the area. During one of our bicycle runs, I saw the horse lines, looking like something out of a Western film. We understood that it was part of a Cavalry Division destined for Palestine. Now you know why the army differentiated between Drivers H.T. and M.T. and our need to know the hand signals for the drivers of horse-drawn vehicles.

Two methods of laying D 8 cable were in normal use. The simpler and commoner one was to mount the drum on a spindle seated in a cradle in the back of a 15 cwt. truck; make fast the end of the cable and set off with the cable spinning out behind, using the forward speed of the vehicle to do the work. In my experience this was the method generally used. Quick to set up and using a powerful, but small and manoeuvrable vehicle with plenty of space to carry equipment and a small team; it was an extremely flexible and effective method.

The other method, relatively new then to R. Signals, required a 30 cwt or 3-ton truck; and could only be used on good roads or hard open ground. In the back of the truck and bolted to the steel floor was a small 2-stroke engine, started by yanking a lanyard to spin the flywheel. The cable was fed through a double set of rollers, belt driven by the 2-stroke engine; it spewed out over the tailgate of the truck like a jet of water exiting from a power hose; the cable drum revolved freely on a spindle set in the jaws of the frame; this was also bolted to the floor; a cage hung from the tailgate in which stood a man armed with a crookstick, a hefty pole like a shunter's pole, with a double hook on the end, through which the cable was supposed to, but seldom did, flow. With this weapon the poor sod, standing in the cage, was expected to direct the flow of cable in the intended direction. He could bump the cable higher, knock it down into a ditch, or hit it over or onto the top of a hedge. Once again the object was to travel in as straight a line as possible, however rough the ground.

A moment's reflection on the breaking strain of a cable composed of seven strands of steel and one of copper will explain to you why we did not indulge much in running it through the crookstick. It was spewed out at some rate of knots, augmented by the forward speed of the vehicle.

Behind the truck came two 15 cwt. trucks each carrying a team composed of a driver and two to four men plus light poles, hammers, jumpers (heavy steel chisels for making holes in the ground into which the poles were inserted), spades, spunyarn, two types of insulating tape and an assortment of small tools. These teams leapfrogged each other, making the cable fast by tying it back with spunyarn to whatever was handy and generally tidying up. At road crossings out came the hammers and jumpers to punch a hole in the ground on either side of the crossing. Poles already fitted with spunyarn and cable were slotted into the holes to make the crossing safe for traffic. The poles were stayed by spunyarn to iron groundspikes. It was not my idea of fun to be holding the jumper while some other clown tried to hit it with a 14-pound hammer. Miraculously no one got seriously hurt though harsh words could be heard from time to time. All carried out at the double. Just to make sure that we did not enjoy ourselves too much, we did this as if it was the real thing and under fire, wearing overalls, tin hats and respirators in their cases, strapped to our chests. Rifles to hand at all times. You could well imagine me, fully equipped as above, leaping out of a moving 15 cwt truck in order to tackle the next crossing. No chance of waiting until the vehicle stopped. Looming everywhere was one of the two foul mouthed corporals, wielding crooksticks with menace.

For a solid week the drill went thus. No morning parade with the rest of the company. Early breakfast and straight down to the cable store as we eyed the other squads going on parade for inspection. We did not envy them. Formed into two teams; each loaded up three trucks and laid cable at full pelt by alternate routes to arrive at a country pub, chosen by the corporals, for packed lunch. It was a race and the second team was the target of scatological comment from the winning team's corporal. (We changed places every day.) Having arrived at our destination, we lay on the grass outside the pub sinking pints of shandy like camels at an oasis. The first pint turned to steam in our throats and it would be the third before we could enjoy the bliss of lying in the sun feeling the aches slowly being anaesthetized.

All too soon we were off on the return journey. This time the 15 cwts went in front tearing down our morning's work, cutting off the spunyarn and stuffing it in a bag. No litter louts, we. The crossings were dismantled and everything, poles and all, put away, leaving the cable stretched out flat for the big truck to reverse the cable layer and reel the whole lot back on to the drum. All still carried out at the double.

Definitely the toughest part of the course physically and mentally. You dared not show anything less than 100% willing. I suppose this was a test of our stickability. It was after an adverse comment that the bold lad, our egghead mascot, in order to demonstrate his keenness, encumbered by his rifle misjudged the speed of the vehicle, jumped out awkwardly and fell, breaking his arm. He was back out with us, next morning, arm in plaster and a sling. I found jumping off a moving vehicle bad enough but scrambling back on as the driver, exhorted by the corporal waving his crookstick in a distinctly unfriendly manner, accelerated off to the next crossing place was worse.

By far my most frightening experience was when it was my turn to be the unfortunate in the cage armed with the crookstick. As we whizzed along, I was quite enjoying hitting the cable up or down as needed, until suddenly I was horrified to discover that somehow or other the cable had dropped over my tin hat and was encircling my neck prior to leaving the truck. It arrived under my left ear, made a full circuit clockwise and on its second lap exited at my left ear, heading for the road. Many thoughts went through my mind. Firstly I was tempted to shout to the driver or the machine operator to stop. On reflection, this was not a good idea. I would surely have been decapitated by the cable. Fortunately I was wearing heavy protective gloves and whether by reflex or design, I slipped my gloved right hand under the cable at my right ear and slowly widened the loop as the cable whizzed round. I was then able, quietly, to ease the noose over my tin hat and break into a cold sweat. Strangely it was only after freeing myself that I was frightened. Hard to believe, but the red circle round my neck for quite a few days and not from the dye of the cable was proof. Unsurprisingly there was a shortage of volunteers for the cage after that and I only used that method of cable-laying once in my Line Section days. A small aside: When the machine was introduced into India the Sikh Cable Section mutinied. They thought that they were being told to compete in a race with the new machine. I think you will find that almost every mutiny in the Indian Army had Sikh involvement. Great fighters, they were even greater plotters, speaking a language very hard to learn amongst themselves.

Reeling in finished, it was back to camp for a hasty late supper and down to the cable store, where every used drum was run through slowly by hand crank onto an empty drum, every joint carefully repaired, soldered, wrapped with insulating and rubberized tape tightly wound on top to make the joint water proof. God help you if a joint broke while laying cable next day. We slept well, that week.

By a fortunate coincidence it was my week to be acting C.S.M., when I was supposed to carry out all the duties of a Company Sergeant Major, getting the Company on parade on time every morning, following the Twerp as he did his inspection and generally doing dogsbody all day. Of course there was no way that I could do all this and the field cable-laying as well; I dared not miss that. I was safely out of camp before the normal day's routine started and did not get back until the others were finished for the day and even then there was the cable to be run through, checked and jointed properly. I managed to get away sharp from that and do my final and only chore as acting C.S.M., which was to report to the Orderly Officer that my Company had correctly completed the day's tasks, and that all men were present and accounted for. This was a bit hard on my predecessor in the job of acting C.S.M., as he had to stand in for me and do a second week. So I can say that this time an ill wind did do me some good. I was dreading my week as acting C.S.M. and thus not only under the eye of the Twerp but more importantly that of Moberly and the C.O. All I really had to handle was Sunday and the Church parade. Luckily that went off all right.

Having successfully survived Field Cable, I embarked on a week of overhead line construction, something much less hectic; it consisted of erecting wooden telephone poles, furnishing them with arms and insulators and straining on new copper wires. To climb the wooden poles we were issued with spikes, which fitted onto our ammunition boots and heavy leather belts for looping round the pole; by digging the spikes alternately into the wood and leaning out, supported by the belt, we climbed the poles. Heavy gloves were essential to grip the pole, which was a natural repository of skelfs. No sliding down the pole when the task was complete, I can assure you. Once sat on a cross arm up the pole, (a very apt description of me), you very quickly discovered whether you had all the tools you needed. The cross arms, already fitted with insulators, were secured by bolts through the pole before erection. It was a good idea to have a length of cord to hand for hauling up any bits and pieces needed. With the insulators fixed, the next thing was to string the copper wires from the junction pole, strain them tight and fix them. The wires were then attached to the insulators and made fast in a complicated loop arrangement. Similar exercises were carried out, to practise repairing breaks in the wires. This was not an occupation for the faint hearted or those with vertigo even in a mild breeze, let alone rain. In Malaya iron poles and ladders were used; the termites would have made short work of any wooden poles. That made life much easier: just climb the ladder and sit on the arm to do your work.

After the aerobatics we learned how to erect poles using picks, spades and dumpers. The hole was dug in three steps cut at right angles to the intended direction (memory not too clear on that). The pole could then be eased down into the hole by relatively few men. Once lined up with its neighbours and the cross arms facing the right way, heavy stones and earth were packed round the bottom, rammed tight with the dumper and there was the pole waiting for its wires. I have to admit that when I was faced with the real thing, I was more than a little relieved that my sergeant had been a P.O. ganger in civvy life and that one of my signalmen was a heavy duty lineman with an English power company.

Strangely enough the training and practical experience came in handy after the war, when we ran electricity from the garage to the two offices in the depot. Much to everybody's amazement, I was able to show the men how to put a pole (ex-P.O.) up and string the wires thus saving the firm quite a bit of cash. My uncle, convinced that I would make a mess of it, sneaked round the wall and was mortified to find all done and working.

Perhaps I should break in here to describe how the outside world impinged on our little introspective lives. Although it all appeared to us to be happening on a different planet, even we could appreciate the hectic nature of our situation. The phoney war was well and truly over. The impregnable Maginot Line had proved no obstacle to the German tanks. It was much cheaper, in men and materials, to go round the end of it, (why worry about Holland and Belgium?) than to make the expected direct assault. The French army was so badly demoralized that I doubt they would have held the line anyway. The miracle of Dunkirk had been swiftly followed by the Battle of Britain which in turn was followed by the Blitz.

We read the papers at weekends and marked on our maps, with little comprehension, the ignominious rout of the Allied forces as Blitzkrieg and Stuka bombers demoralized Europe. The French had no heart for this war and were the worst of the collaborators. Every country had some, but the French were rotten through and through, with the exception of the Maquis and the few that came over to Britain. There were some collaborationally minded in England too, not just the appeasers, but some of the aristocracy and squirearchy, particularly in East Anglia. Southern Ireland too maintained a false neutrality, which favoured the Germans and caused the deaths of many of our seamen, by denying our Navy the use of their ports while allowing German spies to operate openly on the streets of Dublin. I got a lot of wry amusement from learning after the war that the majority of Germans were against Hitler and Nazism, but much more at learning of the numbers of French, who claimed to have been members of the Maquis. If you believe that you will believe anything.

Graeme Fenton (see above and below) had been interned as a British citizen, not too comfortably, I guess. His English wife, and mother of his three daughters had died; he had married a second wife, a Breton and daughter of the No 1 French Naval Architect. She was called Mad, presumably short for Madeleine. A delightful but formidable Breton lady—quite a match for him; when we met them post-W.W. 2, she was President of the French Yorkshire Terrier Society. They had four, who travelled everywhere with them, each in a sock hung over the back seat of the car. Airing them was a clever drill. He took the lift down with two of them, exercised them and sent them back up in the lift, where she liberated them, put the other two in the lift and sent them down for their outing. After which he brought them back up in the lift. She must have moved Heaven and Earth to get him out of interment into a form of house arrest. I never got to the bottom of that. Generally awkward questions were answered by a knowing wink and a tap on the side of the nose. I do wish I had known the Fenton side of the family better. The other thing that I remember of this highly individual family was that Graeme registered his firstborn as British. She married into a very wealthy French family. Champagne, Brandy and Insurance, I was told. I did meet her, very elegant and soigne. But no children. The other two daughters were registered French. Both married Englishmen. We never met them.

Whatever slanders and muckraking may have been put about in recent years from the safety of not libelling a dead person, Churchill saved Britain, saved Europe, saved the U.S.A. and saved the world from Totalitarianism. Those of us who lived through 1940 and 1941 will testify to the truth. Hitler would have picked off each remaining country one by one. His ambition was limitless. Without Churchill's stand against the Tory appeasers in the government and his wonderful backbone-stiffening speeches, Democracy with all its virtues and frailties would have been destroyed and you would all be dutiful Hitler Youth. Never forget that Britain stood alone in Europe against Hitler from Dunkirk till Pearl Harbour and bankrupted itself in the process. The U.S.A. for the second time came in late and did not seem to have done too badly out of the war. I cannot claim credit here. I was too busy, trying to avoid the one way ticket of R.T.U. and gaining a Commission in Signals. Every day was a fresh challenge. The sword of Damocles was permanently suspended over my head. That turning of a blind eye to real priorities demonstrates powerfully how the army brainwashes its soldiers into accepting artificial horizons. You are moulded to a subtle mix of blind obedience and a leavening of using your own initiative, but only on the army's terms. Without that discipline, ordinary men would refuse to face the harsh reality of war.

No explanation has ever satisfied me as to why Hitler hesitated and failed to push through the Invasion. We lived with the threat for months. He must have believed his Intelligence reports that Britain would sooner or later seek terms for peace. He totally underestimated Churchill. Hitler could not have failed if he had launched an invasion force across the Channel after Dunkirk. Britain was in a state of complete shock and chaos. Yes, an incredible amount of men had been evacuated from France in a miraculous operation, greatly assisted by the weather, the flotilla of small boats and a calm sea, but they were totally disorganized and the immense loss of top rate equipment could not be exaggerated. Now was the time when the Shadow Factories came into their own, pouring out every kind of part for munitions from aircraft and tanks to button sticks and cap badges. Whoever thought up the Shadow Factories deserved to live in the history books. I seem to be the only one who remembers them. The Labour Party, militantly pacifist pre-war, had been so vociferously against rearmament and the gutless Tory Party so frightened of losing its majority in the House of

Commons, that the normal updating of munitions had been neglected. The army and its munitions cost money and that meant increased taxes, which lose votes. Unfortunately the top priority in every M.P.'s mind on being elected is to ensure his own re-election. Both sides had much to answer for. *Plus ca change plus c'est le meme chose.*

We could not avoid noticing the state of the Dunkirk survivors. They were in remnants of uniform; precious few still had their rifles and they were very, very bitter. They looked dreadful to our eyes. As a matter of interest I met a Major De la Poer Tate in Siam, a Regular Signals officer, who had been attached to the Guards Brigade. He told me that he marched his Section onto and off the boat in full battle order. A few of the others could well have done the same. I could believe him. He carried himself with great dignity at all times through the worst of the captivity and was a credit to the Royal Corps of Signals. That was the anomaly of the regular commissioned officers in my experience. Either they were absolutely first class or they were rubbish. There seemed to be no middle way.

The biggest shock was to hear the RAF being booed during the newsreels in the Garrison Cinema. The survivors from Dunkirk were most bitter about the lack of air cover over the beaches; this was understandable coming from men who had been continuously strafed as they stood exposed on the beaches waiting their turn for a place in a boat. They could not know that it was not the pilots' fault, but the result of a strategic decision by Churchill to preserve the RAF for the defence of Britain. A vital and very wise decision too, as it turned out to be. I should explain that the R.A.F. got all the publicity and glamour in those days, and so the Brylcream Boys, as they were called, were not too popular with the P.B.I.

By that time Chamberlain had been made the scapegoat and forced to resign as P.M. Not unreasonably, he might well have thrown in his lot with the appeasers and sued for peace, given the chance. Though there is an argument that by his policy of appeasement Chamberlain gave Britain a year's breathing space to get conscription and rearmament going. If so, it was a damned close run thing, helped by Hitler's inexplicable decision not to invade when he had the ball at his feet.

Churchill was a very different character and stubbornly refused, against all the odds, even to contemplate defeat; his inspiration made Britain stand alone against Hitler for over a year and saved civilization as we now know it. Hitler was not the only enemy. Some of the upper classes believed Hitler to be invincible and thought that he had the right ideas anyway. They would not have been sorry to welcome him and his S.S. That would soon have put the workers in their place and made the trains run on time.

Now we had our backs to the wall and a desperate defence was required from all. Every able bodied person and some not so able bodied was pressed into service. Every weapon, however ancient, was polished and made ready for use. The Home Guard at Killermont were most assiduous, not unconnected possibly with a ration of a bottle of whisky being available in the bar once a day, so I was told. I certainly can remember immediate post war you could see the veteran members drop their clubs where they were playing and migrate to the bar at a fixed time every afternoon, when the daily bottle was opened. 3 o'clock, I seem to remember.

Every unit in Aldershot turned itself into a mini-fortress as best it could, anticipating invasion by sea and hordes of heavily armed fifth columnists disguised as nuns dropping from the sky. This was the confident forecast of the *Daily Express*, the fount of all wisdom then as now!

If the Germans had invaded we would probably have killed more of our own men than they did. Each unit was positioned so as to fire outwards from its perimeter and thus each little mini-fortress was shooting up its neighbouring mini-fortresses. When you realize that a .303 rifle is lethal at over a mile and that few of us were crack shots, you can visualize the mayhem that would have ensued. We got a very clear picture of what chaos a real attack would have caused.

By the Grace of God, Hitler lost his momentum and we were granted enough breathing space to get things into perspective, our army reorganized, modern equipment manufactured and issued. This is not in any way to belittle the courage of our fighter pilots and the doggedness of the Londoners, which was well beyond the call of duty.

The nearest we got to actual action was on a dreich September Sunday with low clouds, almost a Scotch mist. We could hear the irregular beat of a twin-engined plane in trouble and briefly saw a German bomber as it limped very low over the barracks, so low that we could see not only the iron crosses on the wings, but also the pilot's head in its flying helmet. By the time I had tumbled to what was happening and pulled my rifle out of its clip, the plane had wobbled off into the mist again. We could hear it bumbling away and were told later that it had come down just outside Aldershot. What good I was going to do with a W.W.1. Canadian Ross sniper's rifle and no ammo, I don't know. I just wanted to have a go at one of them!

Crashed planes and bits, being ferried about on transporters, were commonplace sights. What interested us most, then, was whether it was one of theirs or one of ours. The weather was so good that summer, that our fighters had a good chance in daytime and were so successful that the Germans took quite a beating and changed to massive night raids. Previously we had enjoyed the daily entertainment of an aerobatics display by a captured Messerschmitt, a Hurricane and a Spitfire having mock dog fights; I believe that an assessment of manoeuvrability and relative speeds was being done. Even a Gloster Gladiator biplane, rescued from Malta, was later involved; it was slower but extremely manoeuvrable.

We could see, on night guard duty at the sewage farm, the searchlights crisscrossing the sky over London and the red glow of giant fires. The monotonous drone of the engines (the engine beat of the Germans was different from that of ours, whether by accident or design I know not), made an impressive noise as the massive squadrons came across the Channel heading for the Thames Estuary, which led them to London. Often they were so clearly silhouetted against the moon and stars that you could count them. Our night fighters were not as effective as the daytime ones. Whether this was due to lack of equipment or training I know not. Radar was in its infancy.

The boffins thought that one of the problems was that the tactic of getting above the bombers and diving to attack meant that the night-fighters were the ones that were silhouetted and thus their soft underbellies were a target for the bomber's tail gunners. The Boulton Paul Defiant was designed and built, almost as a gun platform with all its guns firing upwards. Initially they were a great success and the press and public rejoiced. However the Germans soon tumbled to the fact that if all the guns fired upwards, the Defiants were vulnerable to attack from underneath. They were and the Defiant proved to be a damp squib.

That is really how far the war affected us in the O.C.T.U. Tunnel vision is not the word for it. On the brighter side, I got a week's and a weekend leave and travel warrants during the eight months. My mother turned up trumps as usual and brought Bette down to London for the weekend and put the three of us up in the Regent Palace Hotel. She had even got good seats for the Crazy Gang at the Palladium. It was a wonderful show! The Crazy Gang were unique. None of them knew what line of feed they would get, but the reply was instant. They put on the famous sketch of the painters carrying stepladders and buckets of whitewash. So meticulously rehearsed it was, that it looked hugely disorganised. We were sore laughing. I could feel the spirit of my father beside me. He was a devotee of Variety and the Crazy Gang in particular. It was a marvellous show. The Palladium was a happy hunting ground for him. Once with him, I saw Gracie Fields, just back from a tour in South Africa with highly coloured red hair, saying "Eeh Ba Goom, look what the sun has done to me hair" and singing "Red sails in the Sunset" in a voice which could open sealed tins at a quarter of a mile. Another big hitter was Joe E Brown, the man with the rubber mouth, and I have a memory too of Hutch, in front of the curtain accompanying his wonderful voice on a magnificent grand piano, making much business of flourishing a red silk handkerchief. The rumour was that the ladies of London Society were queuing up to sleep with him. Black artists were not too thick on the ground then, let alone Headliners. The received wisdom was that he was in a class of his own in bed.

Flanagan and Allen sang "Underneath the Arches", "Run Rabbit Run, Run, Run", "We're going to hang out the washing on the Siegfried Line" etc., and for the high spot dimmed the lights, blacked up their faces and sang a pro-American song: "Mr Franklyn D. Roosevelt Jones." For that, the whole theatre was in complete darkness, with just two spotlights trained on their faces. No nonsense about P.C and colour bar then. It was a wonderful show. Such a pity that Variety has died!

The Crazy Gang were always the tops and so unpredictable that they often had to ad lib to keep up with each other. It was a fantastic show and for an hour or so we could forget all our troubles. There was a strong feeling in the country that the only friends we had left were the Empire and the Americans; we appreciated all that F.D.R. was doing to change the Isolationist feeling in the U.S and for this Churchill too deserves an enormous amount of credit.

Sunday morning, my eye was caught by the telephone beside my bed and I tumbled to the fact that Bette would have one too. Washed, shaved and dressed I tried her number, and she answered, a bit puzzled. I said that I was on the way down to wish her "Good Morning". Unfortunately that was all I was allowed to do; probably it was very wise of her, in view of the speed with which Anne arrived on the scene after our wedding. She did not tell me until 48 years later that she had spent the time between the phone call and my arrival at the door, feverishly taking out her curlers.

The week's leave, (Bette taking a week of her holidays), was mostly spent in Mrs Galbraith's Boarding House second from the far end of Oban Bay; carefully chaperoned, as my mother thought. Oban was just as magical as ever. Mother was so good and made her chaperoning as unobtrusive as possible. Bette and I did a lot of walking. Oban and the weather were perfect for that time. Here the white ribbon on my forage cap was a nuisance. Bette preferred to take my right arm and got very fed up with me unhanding her every now and then to throw up a salute at anyone who remotely looked like an officer, even in the most outlandish Free Forces uniform. I was damned sure I was not going to be reported for failing to show respect to any officer in any of the Free Foreign contingents and thus being R.T.U.ed, after having got this far. At one point she threatened to walk behind me! On another occasion we were followed by some revolting small boys chanting "Hey a wounded sodger!" and pointing to the white ribbon round my forage cap. Oban was so special to us. It never let us down and Mr and Mrs Galbraith were kindness itself.

Interestingly the film that we watched one evening was Bob Hope, Bing Crosby and Dorothy Lamour in "The Road to Singapore"—a portent of things to come? Not that we worried about that as we ate our fish suppers on the way back to the

Galbraiths'. A very happy and welcome break to spend with my fiancée away from the ever-present threat from Moberly.

The rest of my leave was spent in Glasgow showing off my fiancée to friends and relations including the redoubtable Cousin Jessie, eighty plus, of whom more later. It was a 'Command Performance' to visit her. She was a great favourite of my father's and I shall never forget her pouring tea with shaky hands from a massive solid silver teapot into her fragile bone china cups. She lived in Great George Street and was a stereotypical mature Hillhead maiden lady with a wicked tongue. My father's joy was to take her out to afternoon tea in Coplands or Pettigrews, both still persevering with all cash being shuttled to a central point on a network of wires on high, and encourage her to make scathing comments about the other ladies present. She was a particularly harsh critic of ladies' hats. He loved it!

After Cable came Organisation and Methods, O&M for short, over which presided the W.W.1 Earl Haig lookalike, complete with cavalry moustache and riding boots. The course was impossible, cramming into two short weeks, the Army Act, King's Regulations and pamphlets galore. He and we knew that the course was impossible. He solved the problem in two ways. One method was, at the end of the day before the exam, to tell our course acting-sergeant to come back after tea and tidy up the room but to bring a pencil and paper, in case he had put some notes on the blackboard. On arrival, our sergeant would find the questions for tomorrow's exam chalked up on the blackboard. These he quickly jotted down, hastened back to the hut and read them out to us. We swotted up the answers feverishly. His other method was to warn us to bring our notes, books etc. with us on the day of the exam. He would arrive, write out the questions on the blackboard, tell us that he had a message to carry out but would be back in 55 minutes, and depart. Back on the dot, he collected our word-perfect papers. Either way he achieved a 100% pass rate.

These spiders (long huts used for lectures and for living in, which lay in the shape of a spider's legs, extending from the body) were built of creosoted wood. One afternoon, crackling could be heard from the hut beside us; later flames, leaping high, could be seen reflected on the walls and the army's own special brand of pandemonium broke out. Men rushed about in different directions, colliding with each other, giving contrary instructions, which were instantly countermanded. Indignant hoses were wrenched from their Rip Van Winkle slumber and when the water was turned on, got their own back, by producing little seepages here and there from numerous perforations, developed through years of idleness. The result was that precious little water fell out of the hoses. Meantime our instructor bumbled on and on; we began to think we were all going to fry. Some even woke up from their postprandial snoozes. Suddenly he broke off and announced "Gentlemen there seems to be some kind of conflagration outside. Collect your books and papers and file out quietly"—which we smartly did and viewed the chaos outside. Conflagration indeed!! The hut had been reduced to ashes. Some disconsolate men were standing about, waiting for the next session of conflicting orders. Himself of course sauntered out last, having assured himself that his uniform, moustache and boots were up to standard. Another side of this remarkable man appeared when, at the end of the course, he gave a talk on Venereal Diseases as they affected the Army. He went through all the penalties of contracting one, resulting in the soldier and his family losing out financially on the grounds that the soldier's inability to put in a day's work was due to V.D. and thus was self-inflicted. He finished up by pointing out that Dreadnaughts were available at the Guard Room and instructing us in its use. "If, gentlemen, you wish to indulge in intercourse with the opposite sex, draw a Dreadnaught at the Guard Room; sign for it; open it; you will find therein Barrier Cream and French Letters (the then colloquialism for condoms). First apply the cream liberally to your member before you put the F.L. on, repeat the process at least once and then, if you take my advice, forget about the whole affair and ask the lady to join you in a cup of tea or something stronger." Personally, I think that by that time, if not asleep, she would have departed. What a delightful man!

During this time the "miracle" of Dunkirk had occurred and we were witnesses of the dreadful state of the men who had survived—most without their rifles and, generally speaking, very demoralized.

It was a very strange time to be alive and try to live an approximation to a normal life. On the roads could be seen flat lorries, loaded with bits of aircraft awaiting scrapping or cannibalisation. I even watched with open mouth an ancient piece of field artillery, wooden wheels and all, being drawn by a battered van through the streets of Aldershot. It must have been of Boer if not Napoleonic war vintage. I wondered if there was still the right ammunition for it. What little pieces of newish equipment the O.C.T.U. had acquired, disappeared overnight and it was a very long time before they were replaced.

Everyone was anticipating "Invasion". It is true that some of the Home Guard had not much more than shotguns and pitch forks for weapons. We were landed with three guards a week, one 24-hour on the main gate. On one of those George Haddow escaped death by a millimetre (see below) and two 12-hour night guards, one on the Sewage Farm. Another unusual and to us superfluous 12-hour guard was to patrol the corridors of the officers' quarters at night as they indulged in their beauty sleep. This was an imposing stone built structure on a small hill. The floors and the corridors were made of concrete. Accordingly we had to parade in gym shoes so as not to interrupt the precious slumber of the residents. All orders were to be given in a whisper. You can picture the pandemonium which followed a member of the squad dropping his rifle on its brass butt plate in the wee sma' hours, on the concrete floor, where it bounced about until he frantically retrieved it. The noise was amplified by the narrow corridor. All this at roughly quarter to two in the morning. Out the residents popped like corks out of bottles, all in different stages of night attire, each one convinced Hitler was there and had made him his own personal target. The Twerp never recovered. It was true as we had suspected and gleefully saw that his hair was not all his own. The last one to stroll out was, of course, the Earl Haig lookalike, immaculate in shot silk dressing gown and red morocco slippers, hair and moustache carefully brushed and as usual totally unfazed. Once he had established what had actually happened, he was the first back in his room

The mind boggles at the thought of .303 rifles being fired in the narrow passage of a stone/concrete building. It also gave us a good idea of how senseless panic can ensue from incorrect information.

We never saw the culprit again. He probably spent the rest of the war in tropical kit as a signalman on 24-hour watch in Iceland. We on the other hand were comforted by the fact that for once in no way could we be to blame. Such a negative life we lived! The eleventh Commandment was far more important than the other ten.

The sewage farm was something else; it was far better to be up wind if possible. I spent many eerie nights in a miasma of insects and an effluvia unsuitable to be bottled by Estee Lauder. The only thing I learned was that tomato seeds are impervious to the bugs in human guts.

The Press was still full of doom-laden prophecies of flotillas of German parachutists carrying submachine guns and dressed as nuns floating out of the night sky. Personally I would have left them in the sewage. As we approached our stations, clouds of dragonflies, looking as big as the bombers, attacked us. All the while we could see squadron after squadron of Heinkel bombers droning overhead as they tried to find the Thames and follow it up to London. Sometimes we could see the flames lighting up our Barrage Balloons in the sky. London was crisscrossed by searchlights trying to point out targets to the night fighters, not with much success; also the pretty, but totally ineffective, display from Bofors tracers. Nice rhythm, pretty colours, but never high enough.

Goering had had to admit defeat in daylight attacks; our Spitfires, Hurricanes and their pilots were too good, in spite of horrendous losses both in pilots and planes. It had been a very near thing but just enough to divert Invasion. Hitler had missed his chance, and incredibly stupidly, turned his attack on Russia. He must have believed that he knew something that Napoleon did not. Wrong, his army met the same fate.

We were not out of the woods, but had got a breathing space during which Roosevelt was able to turn public opinion in the U.S in our direction or, as Churchill so delightfully put it, "The Yanks always arrive at the right answer, but only after exhausting all the alternatives."

Guard on the main gate was carried out in display fashion, open to the road and the public. The old guard paraded in front of the guardroom, awaiting the arrival of the new guard, who were marched up in full fashion and stood to attention to be inspected. Each new guard sentry, in turn, was marched off, at the slope, and halted to the left of an old guard sentry, left turn, much stamping of boots and finally stood at attention still at the slope. This particular evening, George Haddow was the new main guard sentry. As he stood rigidly at attention, the old guard sentry was then ordered to port arms, a move that ended up with his rifle diagonally across his chest with the business end pointing over his left shoulder and to the heavens. The next order was, "Old Guard ease springs." This meant, loosen the bolt and rattle it to and from the firing chamber until the five live cartridges had been ejected and laid on the ground. Finally he slammed the bolt shut and pulled the trigger on an empty chamber with a click. Unfortunately on this occasion, the last chamber was *not* empty; there was a sharp crack and a .303 round whizzed off into the wild blue yonder, missing the rim of George's tin hat by a whisker. George went white, then bright red welled up; the Orderly Officer stuttered; the old guard Sergeant went puce and the R.Q.M.S. started to think very seriously. He had issued five live rounds, but now realised he would only get four back. How was he going to explain this? His whole army career and his future pension depended on correct signatures and all figures neatly matching. It was nearly as serious as when the Brewers delivered the wrong beer to the Sergeants' Mess. He only got away that time by blaming the Brewers. The driver got the sack; yes, he may not have told the whole truth, but no glaring lies either. The eleventh Commandment okay. What the public, watching this, thought I know not, probably just par for the course. George told me later that he had nudged the old guard's rifle up a bit, which doubtless saved his life. None of us slept much that night, not because of George Haddow's near squeak, but because we shared the guard room with French Canadians, a villainous crew.

The next five weeks' course was on Wireless Theory and Practice, one which I was dreading; I knew even less about it than E.&M.; it was the last real hurdle and a mighty tough one at that, particularly for me, who had not the faintest idea how a wireless receiver worked let alone a transmitter. The army with its predilection for Acronyms referred to it as W/T. This was all to do with the army's insider syndrome. They were the first at it; now every big organization follows. Here my friendship with the HAM paid off handsomely. I do not know whether I was the only cadet prepared to work with him or whether he chose me because I had previously befriended him. Whatever, it saved my bacon; he was a delightful companion and knew more about W/T than the instructors. He even managed to implant a little knowledge in me. He could spot faults in a W/T set like nobody's business. It was almost instinctive. Without a doubt, he got me through the course, probably by no more than half a mark. The Army sets (No's 9 and 11) were big, clumsy, but rugged enough to stand up to being jolted over rough ground in army trucks driven by army drivers. Formal education he may have lacked, but a wireless set was an open book to him. While the rest of the squad was laboriously tracing their way through the intricate maze of a circuit diagram in order to establish a fault, he went straight to it as if by instinct. He could read and assimilate a circuit diagram in the time it took the rest of us to get the damned thing the right way up. It was a gift similar to that of some people being able to play a musical instrument without ever having had a lesson. In those days we had to deal with fragile valves, clumsy condensers and wobbly carrier-waves established by resonating crystals. Each set was built on an aluminium metal chassis and all joints and terminals had to be firmly soldered. There were no transistors, nor microchips then. (Probably not invented.) The two sets in common use, i.e. the No 9, the more powerful for longer distances and No 11 for shorter, were fitted all the way across the back of the cab of a truck, with the operator seated on a swivel chair bolted to the floor of the truck. Speech or R/T, another acronym, was possible over a short distance, but only under very favourable climatic and environmental conditions. Morse was the normal practice. The sets worked in groups on a single frequency called a net. (Quite a palaver.) The Command set established the frequency and the other sets had to net onto it *seriatim*. The frequency had to be so accurately defined; this could only be achieved by using a resonating crystal to establish the carrier wave. You can imagine that it took time before all the sets on the net were able to communicate with the Command set and through it to the other sets on the net. Each one had to net on separately. Thus establishing a net was a lengthy business even if every operator was on the ball. Outlying stations wishing to communicate with other outlying stations had to send their message to the Command set which then relayed the message to the designated station. Only one set could transmit at any one time. Just to put the icing on the cake, on active service, Morse had to be sent in code and so involved a cypher clerk at either end. On top of this, every officer, according to his rank, had a signal priority allotted to him, which he invariably used, whether he needed to or not. It was a matter of status. This cluttered up an already constipated system; low priority messages could take days to reach the top of the heap. It was a vicious circle. The greater the backlog, the more the higher priorities were used, the more the pressure on the operators and cypher clerks. In Malaya with its predisposition to electrical storms and thick jungle, W/T was only possible at certain times of the day and in certain geographic and meteorological situations; the main way of getting messages through quickly in active service usually rested on the Despatch Riders or D.R.s, who, accordingly, were vastly overworked.

My mate and I made quite a good team, otherwise I would never have passed. Thanks to my training at Prestatyn and his HAM hobby having been largely voice orientated, I was the better operator on the Morse key, but when it came to handling a wireless set and dealing with its multifarious quirks and faults, he could leave the rest of the squad standing open mouthed; in plain speech working or R/T, as the army had it, he was a pro amongst amateurs.

Having arrived at the designated spot, it was truly amazing how, in spite of Percy the Pathfinder's misinformation, I could get the coordinates right on occasion; he would have the aerial, a great long wire, highly critical of its orientation, slung between two trees or whatever was handy and the set, up, working and on the net, before the others had got their aerials up. The better the position and the more accurately the aerial was strung at right angles to the control set, the better the reception and transmission. Best of all was to be on the edge of a wood facing the control set. Our old friends the hammer, jumper and poles could figure, if there were no suitable trees. After that it was a case of hunt through the frequencies until the carrier wave from the command set came in, fine tune the crystal and lock on.

In such good weather, and in such a luxuriant countryside, the practical side was a pleasant contrast to the theoretical. It was the theory and particularly the fault finding that was a nightmare for me and without my mate's help and a lot of luck I would have failed the whole course there and then. It was nothing short of a miracle for me to pass and I owe him a huge debt of gratitude. It cannot have been easy to deal with such an ignoramus as I. I suppose that having taught backward pupils in civvy life must have helped. Also I suspect that to fail someone so far on in the course on non-disciplinary grounds would not reflect too well on the O.C.T.U.

We also practised eliminating interference, not that any of it worked in Malaya. A few days spent on Direction Finding or D/F, as the army inevitably termed it, were good fun. One truck hid in the woods and sent out a continuous carrier wave. The other trucks spread out in a large circle and tried to establish the direction of the mystery truck by rotating their aerials until the signal was strongest and taking a compass bearing at right angles to the aerial. On a map were drawn these compass bearings and where they intersected should have and usually did mark the location of the hidden truck. Our success rate could be attributed largely to the happy absence of any assistance in coordinates from Percy, the Pathfinder, who would by then be misguiding, in his sloppy way, some other squad. The above procedure was used for ferreting out enemy agents, though it appeared to me that it was such a cumbersome rigmarole that by the time the spot had been established the enemy agent would have, long ago, shut down and moved. It would have been much more effective using powerful fixed installations. Probably, that was how it was handled in real life. The exercise was good fun and the theory interesting, but not to be taken too seriously.

Another day we were issued with No 18 sets, the first man pack set ever in the British Army, and about the first public issue of them, as far as I could make out. It was probably considered a good idea to try them out on Cadets in the belief that, if they could make them work, anybody could. The set was about the same size as a full army pack, fairly heavy, and carried on the back with the usual webbing straps. He was yoked to his mate, who carried a similar burden containing a glass accumulator, also fairly heavy and fragile to boot. The aerial consisted of a series of little rods, like knitting needles, that slotted into each other and fitted onto the top of the set, making life rather difficult in undergrowth. Flexible aerials had not yet arrived. The range of the sets was a little over a mile and only on the line of sight. So what did the bright boys do? They sent us on an exercise in and around the Devil's Punchbowl, a large hollow covered in scrub and small trees. It was good fun and, apart from the weight of the equipment, a delightful way of enjoying the Indian-Summer day.

It was not, however, an outstanding success from the communication point of view, which, after all, was the object of the exercise. Adding to the negative side, one of the sets could not be made to function and the bright or rather dim spark carrying the set decided to use his initiative and found the nearest village, where he handed the set to the local electrician to find the fault! These sets were not just classified, they were top secret and the first to be issued. We never saw or heard of him again. He probably also spent the rest of the war working a Morse key in Iceland, in tropical kit and no gloves. The 18 sets were primitive and unreliable but at least they were a step in the right direction and were followed by superior and more efficient models. We were, of course, still handicapped by having valves and heavy accumulators. Transistors, rechargeable dry batteries and microchips were for the future. Interestingly, mobile phones were preferred in many cases, nowadays, by our troops in Iraq, not good marks for the army sets. Not unexpected either. 2004/09.

An interesting day was spent being shown the No 3 Command Set. This was a very powerful affair capable of spanning the globe; big stuff then. There were only about six of them altogether, placed strategically in vital parts of the Empire. There was also a mobile one, looking like a single deck tramcar, for use in the field by a G.O.C. The fact that there was only one was a damning indictment of the army planners or more likely the Exchequer. I imagine it was destined for North Africa. The above permanent set, with direct land line communication to 10 Downing Street and the War Office was a very impressive affair and heavily defended from air attack. It was connected separately to the receiver or transmitter by underground cables. I later learned that they were called coaxial cables, (very hush hush at the time, but now common for TV), to two sets of transmitters about a couple of miles away. The operators and cypher clerks worked in huge underground bunkers. It seemed very claustrophobic to me. It meant that Churchill could communicate with the Dominions direct or to an Army Corps in the field. We thought it extremely High Tech. Incidentally, Martyn was involved in this caper, but found the whole underground scene so claustrophobic that he threw a "wobbly" and got himself transferred to the Army Photographic side and was much happier thereafter.

In complete contrast to all this high tech. stuff, we spent a day at Odiham Aerodrome, from whence many of the O.S.S. agents were flown into France to work with the Maquis. Here, we were shown the Lysander at work. This was the machine used mostly by the O.S.S. Small and slow, it could operate at very low levels and could land and take off on very short and uneven runways. No Helicopters as yet, except experimental. The Lysander was so slow; could almost hover and hedgehop making it a very difficult target for enemy fighters. Its peculiar design enabled it to do all this. It looked a bit like my idea of a modern Pterodactyl. Another use for it was to pick up and deliver messages behind enemy lines where W/T was too dangerous. A couple of poles were driven into the ground and a contraption made of cable strung over them and running back into a Vee holding a leather pouch containing the messages. Down to about 15 feet comes the Lysander very slowly and lowers a long arm with a hook on the end. The hook snatches the mouth of the cable and hauls in the message bag. A clumsy operation you may think, but the point was that it worked under field conditions.

The pilots of course were very highly skilled at low flying and knew hedgehopping before the word was invented. They could land, disembark or load passengers and be back up in the air in minutes. They often had to. A long Vee of white sheets or small fires made a target for the pilot to aim at. Delivering messages was no problem; the pilot flew in low over the dropping zone, chucked the pouch over the side and got off his mark smartly.

At Odiham we saw some of the Boulton Paul night fighters, which were supposed to be our secret weapon against the Blitz, but turned out to be a disaster. I think that they were trying to modify them and not before time. More interesting were the trials between a prototype Helicopter and an Autogiro. At that time no decision had been made as to which to choose. I think that in our conservative way we did not think much of either of them except as toys. Meccano springs to mind. They were small

There were also barrage balloons, both in- and de-flated. Before sophisticated night fighters and deadly accurate bombsights came along, they were used for the protection of cities. Herds of them floating at the end of very long cables kept the bombers high enough up to make their bomb-aiming highly speculative. The cables too, deterred low level strafing by fighters. It was an interesting and instructive day and raised our eyes above the daily darg in more ways than one.

Towards the end of the W/T course, tailors came down from London to measure us up for our officer's S.D. uniforms. This was a considerable boost to morale and having successfully and surprisingly passed the W/T exam, I was home and dry barring some unforeseen catastrophe. Just to keep us under control, the three per week guards went on right to the end. The last three weeks were composed of highly compressed lectures on Signal Office procedures and wild simulated Signal exercises called T.E.W.T.S, nowadays called War Games. The Signal Office part was fairly straightforward, being concerned with staffing requirements, office procedures, how to indent for stores and general office management. Having spent three summers as office boy in the family firm I did not find this too difficult, although I did think the army's bureaucratic methods were clumsy and seemed to slow things up rather than facilitate smooth running. I took on board one very important rule and that was that Signals Personnel were not at any time to be drafted for fatigues or guard duties, apart from those that strictly applied to the Signal Office itself or its own quarters and transport. The reasoning behind this was that communication was a 24 hour 7 days a week job; if a signalman was not on duty, he was resting, not idle. This was a jealously guarded privilege and the battle had to be fought and won at every new posting to an HQ. My signalmen were always seen by the commander of a new formation as a welcome addition to assist in the necessary, but tedious and manpower consuming business, of round the clock guard duties and general fatigues. It took a fair bit of courage for a green 2nd Lieutenant to give a flat refusal to such a high ranking officer as a Brigadier. I, being an awkward Scot, stuck stubbornly to my guns and landed myself in hot water on more than one occasion. Indeed once the matter went as far as the General commanding the Division, I thought I was heading fast for a Court Martial, but much to my surprise my C.O., a devout coward if ever I saw one, went in to bat for me. I think that sometimes it was a try on, on a subaltern still wet behind the ears, as I would be perceived to be. Perhaps my dour Scots refusal to have my men imposed on did not go down too well with some of the Regular non-Signals Officers. The fact that I only held an Emergency Commission made it worse. In my book these were my men, they worked hard and long hours, sometimes 24 at a stretch, and I was not going to allow them to be imposed upon by whomsoever of whatever rank. It was a strong part of my reading of the duties of a Subaltern that he should always stand up for his men against their superiors, even if he tore them off a strip in private. This was not an attitude which led to glowing reports and promotion, but my men would work their guts out for me and did; that was what mattered.

The T.E.W.T.S were something else and rather difficult to take too seriously. We formed into teams and were supposed to draw up Signal Diagrams to organize all the communications for an imaginary Corps or even an Army and then modify them as a simulated campaign developed. All very interesting but I never visualized myself as a Staff Officer to a Chief Signal Officer at Army or Corps HQ. That would no doubt have led quickly to a Court Martial for insubordination, knowing that, if I knew that I was right, nothing would shift me. The most important lesson

I learned then was that the Golden Rule for a Signal Diagram was that it should work and work efficiently and not that it looked good on paper. This I adhered to rigidly and ran into trouble once again with a Senior Officer, whose plan was grandiose and impractical. He did not like my expressed opinion and it was worse when practice proved me right. Anyone with any grey matter could see instantly the mess he was going to land himself in. I could never claim that my plans were neat and tidy, but they worked under active service conditions, something very different to paper exercises.

Further fittings for our officer's uniforms cheered us up a lot. Mine was made by Weatheralls, presumably the family firm of a later Speaker of the House of Commons. I fair fancied myself in Service Dress and particularly the Sam Browne belt; which without a doubt added a touch of class. Fortunately we got an allowance which covered the cost and I have no doubt that the tailors did well out of the deal. The uniforms were scheduled to be delivered during the last week of the course when we were to be gazetted 2nd Lieutenants as from 00.01 hours on Saturday the 2nd of November1940, but remained Signalmen until midnight on the Friday.

Thus we could not leave Aldershot until the Saturday, which did not suit me at all. We had been granted a week's leave on completion of the course and the wedding had been arranged for Monday the 4th of November. I being in Aldershot and the wedding scheduled for Glasgow, Bette had all the organizing to do, which was not such an easy thing in wartime, what with food rationing and clothes coupons. In her usual competent way she had done everything according to the book, invitations out and acceptances in, even the cake baked and ready.

Panic stations set in when the War Office cancelled all leave, citing the threat of invasion, and Bette had to tell the guests that the wedding was off. Punch drunk as the squad was after eight months of a crammed course and under the constant threat of R.T.U., they were feeling pretty mutinous. I was fit to be tied. The War Office, as I should have predicted, changed its mind again and our leave was suddenly restored in the middle of the last week of the course. Now it was my turn to panic. We only had the time between tea and Lights Out to phone. Telephone boxes were thin on the ground and very much in demand. After tea I hared down to the nearest box and for the first time beat the twins to it. Naturally everyone wanted to phone home with the good news; however I managed second in the queue. Glasgow, on long distance, was not the easiest; there was no automatic dialling—probably not invented by then. I pleaded with the operator to put me through to Bette; after I had explained the reason for the urgency she pulled out all the stops and got me through and I was able to tell Bette that the wedding was back on again.

With all the chopping and changing some of the guests could not make it; in particular Bette's brother Stan, which was a great pity as he was killed in a road accident in the following July. Bill Knight, his great pal and a family friend of long standing was in the same TA Searchlight Unit, and could not make it either. Bette was employed in the office at Colquhouns, the big west end upper class bakers, and her mother, who was, as ever, a gem, was friendly with the Barclays, top class pastry cooks in Byres Road. Both lots contributed to make the purvey amazingly good under such difficult circumstances. The war engendered a wonderful spirit of helpfulness all over. Even my uncle, who greatly disapproved of the whole affair and confidently forecast that it would never last, produced a case of champagne! I have to give him credit for that. Otherwise, it would have been a very dry affair. I don't think I ever did anything in my adult life which met with his approval. We were extremely fortunate in the Minister of Hillhead Baptist Church, a Dr McBeath, who was one in a million. When Bette went back to him in a panic, he just said, "You tell me when you want the wedding to be and I will be there." He was. I shall always remember his kindness to me as I waited for my bride.

I had discovered I had some grounds for escaping early, owing to the distance involved, and made myself such a pest to the Twerp that he finally gave me a pass to go for the 4 p.m. train for London on the Friday afternoon. He was very probably glad to see the back of me; the feeling was mutual. So, full of optimism, I shook the dust of Aldershot from off of the soles of my feet on Friday afternoon, still a Signalman complete with kitbag, but also encumbered with my Officer's valise and the cardboard boxes holding my new uniform. I would have carried double to have come out on top.

CHAPTER 4

WEDDING BELLS

I CAUGHT THE 4 O'CLOCK TRAIN for London, settled in a corner seat and heaved a big sigh of relief. I had beaten Moberly. A sweet victory! Then fate put me in my place. The Air Raid sirens went off. We scuttled into a siding and waited and waited. I thought that the All Clear would never come and wrote off any hope of catching the night train for Glasgow. However it eventually sounded and we finally arrived in London. Burdened with my double kit, I caught a porter. Yes, we still had them then! He hustled me to the taxi rank, got me and my stuff in and told the driver, "Euston, as fast as possible!" We were just moving off when a wee "Glesca Buddy" opened the door and said, "Is youse gaun tae Euston?" When I said yes she, several packages and her brood climbed in, how many I do not know—the blackout was intense and they were wee. It was a horrendous journey, bombs falling, fires burning. We would turn a corner only to be faced by flames, fire engines, their hoses writhing like elongated, drunken snakes. Give the driver full marks—superb is the only word to describe him. All headlamps were masked to throw only the dimmest of lights. He never stopped trying and eventually got us to Euston. After that experience, I take my hat off to the Londoners who suffered that sort of thing night after night.

Leaving me to settle with the driver, and having made no

attempt to pay, the wumman shot off towing her brood behind her, like a tug towing barges. You have to get up early in the morning to be upsides of a "Glesca Wumman". I must have over tipped the cabbie because he said, "Thank you sir." I was too busy getting hold of a porter to haggle.

I asked the porter if the Glasgow train had gone. He said the early one had, but the late one was still at its platform, though the man with the flag and the whistle was getting ready to send it off. We raced up. The porter bundled me and my kit into a 3rd class carriage (my warrant was for 3rd class till midnight). I could have hugged him! I found a compartment whose occupants moved everything to give me a seat. If you were in Khaki people could not do enough for you. I had just sat down when we moved off and I thought, "Great!" However, Fate had not finished with me. We only moved into a siding and sat there through yet another Air Raid.

It was very odd. You could see the searchlights fingering the sky, looking for bombers, kept up high by the herds of Barrage Balloons, making precision aiming impossible; you could hear the crump of the bombs; the A.A. guns were giving it laldy, interspersed with the extraordinary percussion beat of the Bofors guns, which made much noise and threw pretty streams of tracer shells, but did precious little damage, unable to make the range. The strangest noise was the shrapnel falling back to Mother Earth and landing on the carriage roof, pattering like leaves in a storm.

We sat there in darkness for hours, hoping that the Heinkels would not choose us for their next target. Fortunately the herds of Barrage Balloons kept them high up to prevent any precision bombing. What was remarkable was how phlegmatic everyone was. Eventually we slowly moved off. By that time we had lost our spot and meandered aimlessly about England in darkness through the night and crawled into Central Station, Glasgow, about 4 o'clock the next afternoon. The trip had taken 24 hours and my scheme had proved a waste of time. Still dressed as a Signalman and avoiding the eyes of the Redcaps, I skulked down to Boots' corner and mounted a green tram for home. Mother looked a bit anxious. All I wanted, after sitting for so long in a packed railway compartment, was a hot bath, a hot meal (I had been issued with a page detailing my rations for the week) followed by a good night's sleep. I then phoned Bette to reassure her that I had not fled the country.

On Sunday, Bette and I took Stephen for a walk and later on went over to the Beresford Hotel, now halls of residence for students, and had dinner, hosted by my mother.

The strangest things then possessed my mind. I persuaded myself that I would be too nervous to shave myself and that I needed a stiff Brandy to face the wedding ceremony. The first did not live up to my expectations, the second had no effect whatsoever. The best man was late of course; by that I mean I was early and fidgeting, fearing he would not turn up. He finally arrived and Dr MacBeath put us both at our ease by taking us into the vestry and promising to let us know when the bride had arrived at the church. She was late, fulfilling the tradition. By that time I was not fit to hold nor bind. She claimed that, as always, she was on time, but that her photographic family held her up on the steps of the church. The organ burst into the wedding march and up she came, ravishingly beautiful. Not in white of course. This was wartime. She wore a lovely dove grey outfit and carried a huge bouquet of Chrysanthemums, which wavered throughout the ceremony and made the evil minded think the worst.

However all went well and I had the honour of escorting my love down the aisle, seeing in the backmost pew Bette's grandmother glaring at us. A most remarkable lady, she was in a deep huff because her lodger had not been invited, so she was not coming to the wedding reception. I do not recall ever meeting her. Why I know not. Bette's father dutifully had lunch in his mother's flat, once a week, not that it was a lot of fun for him; she was reputed to regale him with his childhood menus, which did not appeal. Having made her point, she did not come to the reception but went home, with her lodger by her side and her nose in the air.

I did later meet her daughter, Bette's aunt, an overpowering lady, very theatrical; her 2nd and considerably younger husband was a semi-operatic tenor. They had orange groves in South Africa. One of her daughters married Emlyn Williams, a noted actor, novelist and playwright, who proved most generous to the Thompson family on many occasions. Bette kept regularly in touch with him. He came out to visit us in Kelvindale after the war, provoking much neighbouring curtain twitching by arriving in a chauffeur driven Daimler with the light on in the back to show how handsome he was. Which he was. He naturally did not pay much attention to me, but was most interested in Bette and our daughters, leaving a ten-pound note for each of them hidden under the cushions of the couch which he had sat on. Departing in his Daimler, with the light illuminating him again, he must have kept the neighbours' tongues wagging for days.

The reception, it being wartime, was held in the Thompson's flat up two stairs in Dowanside Road. I was as impressed as a bridegroom could be, that my ex-guardian climbed the stairs, her last outing ever. My uncle surprised us all by bringing a case of Champagne. An extraordinary man. His wife, my ex-guardian, had contracted Disseminated Sclerosis in the thirties. The GP had told him that she could not live more than a couple of years. She lived for more than twenty and he never forgave either of them. She compounded the crime of survival by him needing to sell the flat, into which he had invested much money, and purchase a bungalow in Bearsden. No stairs. He got his own back by not increasing her housekeeping allowance for the last twenty years of their marriage. He put two tubular electric heaters in the garage for his precious Wolsey car, CGA606. She was forced to install a separate meter in the garage to get the money for the heating. Also in the crowd was the redoubtable "Cousin Jessie", an elderly spinster who lived in Edwardian splendour in Great George Street. She had the real Hillhead piercing voice. With this voice she tried to throw my now father-in- law off his speech, by interjecting "How dull!" while he was stating that he hoped Bette and I would never have a cross word throughout our marriage just as he and his wife had. Those who did not know her were stunned; he however was either too deaf to hear her or too much of a gentleman to appear to have noticed. I prefer the latter.

At last we got away, after a slight contretemps with an ex-lodger of the Thompsons, who was so lit up by the Champagne that instead of confetti he was trying to stuff rice down the front of Bette's dress. I was livid and was preparing to give him a doing, when he saw the look in my eye and vanished. It was the first time I had seen him. It was explained to me later that that was his idea of a joke. I have no idea why he was invited; must have slipped by Bette's eagle eye.

Anyway, down we got to the taxi; the driver, an expert, drove us across Byres Road into Ashton lane, stopped the car and producing the little tray and brush, normally used to brush the crumbs off the tablecloth, proceeded to deal partially with the confetti and then drove us to Central Station to catch the Oban train. We found a compartment to ourselves and in the blackout, our world closed round us. So much so that we had no idea that someone had entered the compartment until he got out at Stirling. No gentleman, he might at least have given a discrete cough.

CHAPTER 5

THE HONEYMOON

ON ARRIVAL AT OBAN, as a delightful compliment from Aunt Lena, we were met by Danny, the Head Porter, who was the one who had the privilege of meeting and greeting "His Grace, the Duke of Argyle" when he came annually to open and preside over the Highland Gathering.

Danny, a magnificent figure of a man, his prominent waxed moustache twinkling in the moonlight, went in front with our baggage on his "Hurley Barra" and we followed slowly arm in arm; the moon and stars shone especially for us as we traversed the bay (how romantic can you get?) to the second end house, where Mrs Galbraith had prepared a supper of poached eggs, toast, home baked scones and tea. It was ambrosia and nectar to us. Such kindness!

Bette, looking absolutely ravishing, went up to bed while I stayed reluctantly for the stipulated ten minutes and followed her, high as a kite, as they say nowadays. You must understand that we had not the least understanding about birth control. The subject was taboo and not talked about in polite society. I have to admit (told that they were thick and sturdy) to not being attracted to what is referred to nowadays as condoms. After some research I persuaded Bette to consider using a pessary, something neither of us knew anything about. We had also agreed to take a bottle of sherry in our luggage and to have a small glass to help smooth over any initial embarrassment. I do not think that it made any difference. She came to me like a fledgling from its nest, warm and trusting. I do not know if it was the same for her as for me. I just hope so. I was woken at 6 o'clock by the sound of ammunition boots clumping above us. We had noticed a ladder leaning against the wall beside our bedroom. We learned later that the aircrew of one of the Sunderland flying boats, moored in the bay, was billeted in the attic above our bedroom and were now getting dressed. I opened my eyes and discovered that I had not been dreaming. There she was, radiant beside me. I took her in my arms and Anne was conceived, not that I knew that at the time.

Sunderland flying boats, (transferred from B.O.A.C.), anchored in Oban Bay and were very advanced for the time; they had their own galley for hot food and could stay aloft for hours and hours. Lying at their moorings like great winged whales, majestic was the only word to describe them and the sight of them taking off will stay in my memory for ever. Their four engines would start in sequence with a roar and they would cast off ploughing a regal 100-foot wide furrow of white foam for a mile and more into the sound of Mull and the Atlantic. I shall never forget them, ploughing through the gap between Kerrera and the mainland to the open sea, leaving behind them a broad path of white water. Just as gracefully, they eased down onto the sea coming back. They were death on German U-boats and on being attacked from the air, they flew down to sea level, became a formidable gun platform and opened up their massive firepower. So you will understand that Sunderlands have always had a very special place in our hearts and we were very touched when Anne organized the wedding cake at our Golden Wedding in the shape of a Sunderland flying boat. So like her to think of that. Lee probably was in on the act.

We may have had only five days, but it was a wonderful

honeymoon, matchless; even the weather was the finest crisp November. Prophetically the film in the local cinema that week was Another Road Film featuring Bob Hope, Bing Crosby and Dorothy Lamour. We did a lot of walking, wrapped up in a world of our own. I quite enjoyed the change in that now I was the one being saluted and could nonchalantly tap the peak of my cap with my swagger stick in return. Bette no longer had to detach herself from my arm as Cadet Brown saluted anything remotely looking like an officer of whatever nationality. She got very tired of that. The Galbraiths could not have been kinder. We fed like fighting cocks. I do not know how the ration books were reconciled. We walked everywhere. Mrs Galbraith even produced a cold roast pheasant, shot for us by her husband, for our train journey back to Glasgow; we ate it with our fingers and nonchalantly threw the bones out the ventilator as we passed round Cruachan, pretending that pheasant was a regular part of our menu.

Mother had arranged bed and breakfast in the Central Hotel for our last night, as being handy for me to catch the morning train for Bakewell and for Bette to get the tram home. The room, high up, looked out on the station concourse, where we could see great puffs of smoke and steam rising from the engines and hear the noise of the trains coming in and out. We had ordered morning tea (big deal), which duly arrived; the maid lifted my pyjama trousers off the floor between finger and thumb and placed them on the bed in a truly disapproving Calvinist manner. Of course it was Sunday! I felt like saying the marriage lines are in my wife's luggage.

It was a sad parting, but we both agreed that the honeymoon had exceeded all our expectations. I have to admit that the anticipation of joining an active service unit was uppermost in my mind at that moment, Chauvinist pig, that I was. Bette had to go home to the normal drag of work. As she sat in the kitchen with a cup of tea all set to go out to work, she burst into tears, whereupon her brother Stan rushed up and said, "Was he bad to you?" "No," said Bette through her tears, "it was wonderful." So I did not have an enraged brother-in-law chasing me with an axe.

CHAPTER 6

K DIVISIONAL SIGNALS

TRAVEL BY TRAIN was quite complicated in wartime. All station names were blacked out to confuse the "parachutist nuns". I had little idea of where I was or whither I was going. All trains were pretty slow, what with bombings and diversions, so it was growing dark after Manchester and as the local train heaved itself from station to station, I had to peer out of the ventilator, in the blackout, at each station and try to recognise the names being shouted out in accents previously unknown to me. I did not feel that it would be a good idea to miss my destination on my first posting.

Arriving safely, I got transport to my new Officers' Mess, and found it to be a requisitioned, stone built villa, and that I was sharing a room with two others. These were known irreverently as Mutt and Jeff, two cartoon characters of the time. One of them was a W.W.1. veteran, with his medal ribbons to prove it. His favourite position was squatting on his hunkers on his bed. This, together with his dark complexion, gained him the immediate nickname of Ghandi. He did not stay long with us, being too old to go overseas; we had been told that we were bound for Kenya; hence the K.

Our Company Commander, Captain Eric Beaver, later to become Major, we discovered was a large, jovial seeming man, in civvy life the Managing Director of Sun Electrics. Obviously very important, he held court every evening, surrounded by us newly commissioned Subalterns hanging on every word. As long as you kowtowed, you were okay. Not a bad man but definitely not one to be crossed. Best to treat him as a surrogate father. He liked that.

Over us all was the finest regular officer I ever met, Major Vickers; such a tragedy that he did not survive captivity. Quiet, competent, kindly, but most of all possessing an amazing faculty for arriving round the corner when you were desperately wondering what to do next. Also there were two promoted quartermasters, one normal, the other technical, called not a Q.M. but a T.M.O. Both wore their 18-year service medals with pride; these were irreverently known as having been conferred for 18 years of undetected crime, not for good service as "the label on the tin" said; both commissioned as Captains. Bygraves, the TMO, was your typical Old Sweat, always reminding me that my number was still wet, meaning that my commission was very new. Underneath he had a good heart along with a good thirst. Goble, the Q.M. proper, was fine as long as the requisite signatures were in place. His priority in life, apart from that, was to ensure that he had a willing woman available at every posting. He must have leapt, precipitately, out of a few windows in his career. I got on fine with both of them.

I doubt that I can remember the names of all the other Subalterns. Here goes. The one that drew your eye was Burrows; he had stroked the Oxford boat the two years that they won before the war and on going down, had gone out to Argentina with a mate to teach the University in Buenos Ayres how to promote the Oxbridge style of rowing "eights". A huge man, his upper body had developed so much by rowing that he could not play tennis. Any attempt at a sudden movement instantly put out the cartilages of both knees. Obviously well connected, Admirals, Group Captains and so on were uncles. Deeply religious and very likeable, he survived captivity, became an Anglican priest and no doubt did much good work. Hancock, just married like me, a nice quiet soul, came from middle England. Lastly, the egregious Murphy, one time Scots Guardsman, later Edinburgh police constable and whole time "no good egg" as P.G. Wodehouse would have put it.

Because Vickers was only a major, a succession of would be Lt Cols descended on us, mostly ex-T.A. Having their business interests nearby made the thought of two incomes most attractive. All apparently, bold, Hell Fire and Brimstone Merchants, they vanished when they discovered we were bound for overseas. No way could they run a second-hand car business in the Midlands from Kenya! The one I despised most instructed that the men be paraded in thick falling snow and turned up half an hour late, making the men present arms for his first inspection as if he was a General and walked ever so slowly round the ranks in spite of one man fainting from standing still in the cold. Then the bold boy ordered that my men should be turfed out of the old Dower House and put to live and sleep on their straw palliasses in Marquees. When I protested, he announced that the men needed toughening up. I was furious and searched my brain. I took our M.O. on a tour and suggested that he might declare the Marquees a Health Hazard, which he was happy to do, having the same opinion of the fire eating armchair warrior as I. This resulted in the M.O. and I becoming marked men, but not with our men. Fortunately, our fire-eater tumbled to the fact that we were headed for Kenya and suddenly developed severe stomach pains resulting in his speedy return to whence he came. Good Riddance!

I was truly grateful that I had been posted to a new unit, as I had been dreading the Mess bills associated with Regular units. On being commissioned, I had lost the weekly 10 bob of a signalman; the balance due from all the £4s deducted weekly seemed to have evaporated into thin air; I had now risen to the giddy heights of £14 a month. The snag was, it was paid in arrears into my new account with "Cox and Kings Bank". To help me out, I received £7, on being commissioned, to see me through the first month and £7 at the end of the first month to see me through the second month. All very fat and fine, but the honeymoon saw to it that I had only 7/6 left to see me through the rest of the first month. These first two months brought out all the best and worst in my Scots canniness. I scraped through.

Human nature is not affected by donning khaki. When a new unit is formed, the C.Os of similar units are instructed to provide experienced N.C.O.s. to stiffen up the new unit. Do they? Do they, Hell! They see this as a great opportunity to off-load their most useless N.C.Os and we got some right brammers. Most of them, if still with us, had to be busted down in rank so that an efficient machine could be created.

For some unknown reason I had clicked for the Signal Office Section, some 90 odd men, containing, to my delight, 27 D.R.s (despatch riders), all volunteers recruited through the Motorcycling Magazines. I had the time of my life organising this lot to be fit to go overseas. The real reason became apparent later. The Section was supposed to have a Captain in charge. He not appearing, Vickers must have thought that I was capable of taking the men out and a Captain would be found later. Of this I was not informed, but in the meantime was happy to have so much work to do.

It was wonderful to have the company of all these D.R.s, slightly balancing the number of Post Office engineers in the section, whose technical knowledge and experience hugely outstripped mine. I decided not to pretend to knowledge that I did not have. The balance between honesty is the best policy and bullshit baffling brains, meant a certain amount of discretion had to be displayed.

On the whole everything progressed well at Bakewell, thanks largely to Vickers's wise guidance. Mother came down for a week, bringing Stephen with her. He accompanied me on a cross-country run, much to the amusement of my section. This was about the time of the Blitz of Manchester and on their return journey, mother and Stephen were thrown out of their train and had to walk miles over broken glass to get into Manchester for the Glasgow train. She said that the contents of the shops, spread out over the road, left a lasting impression, particularly the shoes.

We were given a couple of days leave to buy tropical kit. On learning this Bette went to her boss to get a few days off to be with me on my Embarkation-/Kit-Purchasing leave that we were due. Her boss, Edwardes by name, refused, so she politely told him where to put her job and came down so that we could spend our last few weeks together. Edwardes was deeply shocked and did not repeat the refusal for those who came later. What a girl! Steel through and through! She came with me for the purchase of the Tropical Kit and we spent a couple of days in Manchester. Boy! Did the recommended tailors clear out obsolete stock! I think the only thing I wore in earnest was the Topee. The first thing I did on arrival at Singapore was to commission a Chinese tailor to replace my tropical kit. Much lighter, it fitted, was a whole lot cheaper, not to mention being produced in 24 hours.

With all the talk of nun parachutists threatening daily, it was mandatory to carry your pistol everywhere. Bette did not approve and eyed it with such a baleful look as it sat on the chair beside my side of the bed that it was a wonder it did not curl up and die. On our return to Bakewell, I asked Vickers for a sleeping out pass. This meant that as long as I was present for my scheduled duties, I was free to be with her. We got a room in the local hotel, "Castle and Commercial", and made the most of our time. The weather was crisp and cold; we did a lot of walking, generally landing up for a pint at a handy hotel. Rowsley comes to mind where there was a bobtailed sheepdog which had to be discouraged from coming away with us. Rationing seemed not have weighed too onerously on Derbyshire; ham, Bakewell tarts and cream a-plenty. We lived well and in comfort.

The army had some amazing quirks. One great saying was that there were only two things that they could not do to you; one was to make you pregnant, not relevant perhaps today, while the other was to make you attend a ceremony of religious worship except one of the creed to which you were registered. As an officer you could be detailed to take charge of a church parade, but if of a different sect, you could not be forced to attend the service. The men of K Div. Sigs were predominantly C of E, so when it was my turn to take church parade, I would take over the parade, march it up to the doors of the church and hand over to the senior W.O. or N.C.O, and go down to the hotel; there I would have a game of darts and a pint and be back outside the church to take over the parade and march them back to the parade ground to be dismissed. Shocking! I was never going to Heaven anyway.

We had a front room, which was decorated all over from the wallpaper to the chamber pot with highly coloured roses. I told Bette that this was because she was my English Rose. She had been born in Bishop Auckland of an English father and a mother, really English, but with Welsh tendencies.

There was to be a Conservative Ball in the local big town, Chesterfield, "the town with the crooked spires". We were heavily encouraged to go; there was much discussion about transport; and we finally decided on piling into the doctor's car. I suspected the petrol came from army stores, but did not enquire. The Dance was the real thing, little folding gilt edged cards with small pencils attached by a silken cord for booking your partner for each dance. Bette monopolised my card; there were complaints and I had reluctantly to observe the courtesies. There was quite a whiff of nostalgia about the whole thing and we were glad to get back to our room. Every minute not alone together was a minute lost. A couple of sergeants were bedded in an alcove, just off the passage to the bathroom. Bette found it a little intimidating padding along in her negligee to have her bath. The sergeants did not complain. It must have brightened up their day considerably.

My section was involved in a football match one afternoon, so Bette and I attended in order to show the flag; the pitch ran parallel to the river. As we walked up and down following the game, Bette told me, apprehensively, that I was going to be a father. She did not know how I would take it and the admission was made that the pessary had slipped out and a short game of carpet football had ensued. Male Chauvinist that I was, I was pretty chuffed that I had played my part—completely ignoring the fact that I would shortly be off overseas with an indefinite future, leaving Bette to have Anne and, as a single mother, to bring her up without a father, possibly for ever. In a way things worked out not too badly. As an expectant mum, Bette escaped conscription; a very private person, she would have hated that. She had the support of her parents and my mother in handling Anne; Anne saved Mrs Thompson's reason by arriving practically at the same time that her son Stan was killed by a truck in the blackout. Anne also kept Bette so occupied, that she would not have time to think of her husband being designated "missing believed P.O.W". Mother's idea of heaven was to get all dolled up and push Anne in her pram in the Botanic Gardens. When on occasion she was taken to be the mother while pushing the pram, her cup overfloweth, as the Good Book says!

Thanks, I think, to our M.O., a very likeable man, we were all invited to a party at the factory manager's house. It was a battery manufacturing factory, large batteries for submarines, possibly one of the shadow factories, which nobody remembers now. It was a good night; no rationing, no breathalysers. I faintly remember a game of billiards in the attic where we split into two teams, taking alternate shots. Weird, but most enjoyable!

We knew we were going to Kenya; the whole of Bakewell knew we were going to Singapore—"these stupid civilians believe every rumour." In fact, we did not know that we were going to Singapore until we were sailing down the Clyde, complete with woollen comforts from some well-meaning charity. All too soon we were ordered to parade our sections and march them up to the troop train at midnight on Hogmanay 1940. Bette and I made our farewells not knowing whether we would ever see each other again. It was really hard for her; at least I had my section to keep me occupied; Bette on the other hand had to listen to us marching in three inches of snow past what was our bedroom and then pack, to go home. I could see the bedroom light on as we went by.

The doctor and the daughter of the hotel had got married that morning. They were going to spend their honeymoon on the train. We had reserved a compartment for the pair. I thought our honeymoon was short enough, but 18 hours on a troop train! My mind is blank as to what happened to them. Bette and I went back to the hotel a few years after the end of W.W.2, but could find no one who could tell us anything. Pity, because the family was very good to us at the time.

CHAPTER 7

AT SEA

WE TRUNDLED SLOWLY NORTHWARD until eventually arriving in Glasgow at the dockside on the south bank of the Clyde. Everybody out and crawling slowly up the gangway onto *RMS Empress of Japan*, would you believe? She was crewed by Chinese and officered by Canadians. As far as I know she was C.P.R. from the Pacific side of Canada and so not too suitable for the tropics. The ship's officers were pretty jumpy because a sister ship (*RMS Empress of Britain*) had been bombed and sunk off Southern Ireland fairly recently. They claimed also to have been bombed coming round Ireland and kept pointing out the kink in the rail where they alleged the bomb had bounced off. I failed to notice it.

I found myself in a 2-berth cabin, now converted to 4-berth, by adding "Standees". Total blackout after dark resulted in much discussion about the porthole cover, which could not be opened until the light was out. It became a little stuffy to say the least, but really there was not any argument during the ten weeks we spent on board. The troops slept two-deep everywhere, half on mattresses on the deck, half in hammocks above them. I had to be careful where I put my feet when visiting them at night; it was a good idea too, to cough loudly. I thus gave them time to put everything out of sight. Their main recreation was "Crown and Anchor", greatly practiced. Gambling was forbidden in the army.

I think we were too gobsmacked to say much, transported in 24 hours from a fair representation of an army camp to a ship manned by Chinese speaking an unknown lingo. My batman, ex-T.A., had been left behind as too young to go overseas. He had worked as an apprentice chef in the Caledonian Hotel in Edinburgh; an excellent batman, Scots of course. His *tour de force* was to peel and core a pineapple and present the flesh in rings.

A real Glasgow "peasouper" kept us tied up for nearly a week. It was galling to be confined, knowing that less than half a mile away, across the river, was my beloved, in her parents' flat. I have no doubt that some of the troops shinned down the ropes at night but no notice was taken provided they were back on parade on board in the morning. Not quite the done thing, though, for a white hot, newly commissioned Subaltern, keen as mustard and ready to take on Hitler single handed.

There was also on board a small detachment of Ratings under a Chief Petty Officer, who gave them a Hell of a life, a few Q.A.I.M.N.s, and a larger-than-life RN Commodore, who I learned later was on his way to take over a dry dock in Suez. That was the only dry thing about him. I do not remember ever seeing him sober or not falling off the end of a fat cigar. This he smoked in the blackout, a beacon for a passing U-boat. Being by far the most senior officer on board, nobody dared to say a word. The food was excellent pure white bread, very unlike the brownish rationed stuff at home, but we began to go off roast turkey and Christmas pudding as the weeks went by. The exigencies of the time led to the officers dining in the smaller tourist saloon and the troops dining in the larger first-class saloon. It was a nice change to have our food served to us by a Chinese waiter and eat off spotless napery.

Due to the fog, it was the best part of a week before we moved. Meanwhile the sick bay contained patients, seasick in spite of us being tied up and motionless. There is a certain type of man who turns green and ill the moment he puts his foot on a gangplank and he remains green, ill and uninteresting, until he puts his foot on terra firma again.

Eventually the fog cleared enough for us to move down river and box the compass off the Holy Loch. The Clyde was dredged all the way up to Glasgow; the shipyards were going flat out; the din was horrendous as we made our way down river. Past Dumbarton Rock, it opened out to an amazing sight. So many ships, packed so close together, that you felt that you could walk, dry shod, across the estuary. The compass boxed, the boom opened and we made our way down past Dunoon, Innellan and Toward. As I stood by the rail, the last bit of Scotland that I saw was Ailsa Craig, nearly swallowed up in the deepening dusk. I was not to see Scotland again for the best part of five years. Not that that occurred to me. I was much too keen to begin real life soldiering.

The Convoy contained all sorts of ships, Cunards, Monarchs, Anchor Liners, etc. Well out in front was the *Batory*, Polish and crewed by Poles, carrying German P.O.W.s bound for P.O.W. camps in Canada. I reckon it was decided in cold blood that it would act as the decoy duck and if sunk by a U-boat, they were only drowning their own folk. The Poles did not seem to care. The battleship *Ramillies* was on our starboard side, wallowing well; in any swell you could not see her foredeck as the sea washed over it. It gave us a false sense of security; ignorant were we then that the day of the "Battle Wagon" was well and truly over. A flotilla of destroyers dashed up and down, like dogs working a flock of sheep. All this was monitored by two cruisers and under the overall command of the Admiral, who was flying his flag on *Ramillies*. Overhead flew a Sunderland searching for hidden U-boats. All most impressive.

They escorted us across to Newfoundland, where the *Batory* discharged its cargo of P.O.W.s, and we were left in the tender care of the two cruisers as we headed for Freetown; the rest of the R.N. collected the return convoy and headed for the UK. One small incident occurred. Our top brass was concerned that the troops were not being involved enough and enjoying life too much; I was accordingly ordered to take my Section down into the bowels of the ship and keep them up to speed, practising their Morse. Unforgettable was the diameter of the propeller shaft, slowly revolving beside us.

I found tables, chairs and D.5 field telephones laid out and I sent a message for the section to take down. Hardly had I sent the message when the ship's Master at Arms in full uniform, a very impressive figure, appeared waving a piece of paper, which had come from *Ramillies* giving my message in full and strict instructions from the Admiral never to do such a thing again. Most impressive, they had received my D5 buzzer's Morse over the ether! The R.N. were clearly streets ahead of the army in things electrical. So we had to pack up and think again.

The next ploy was that I should give the Section lectures on all the instruments used in the field by R. Signals. For this I was given the stock issued handbook, which at O.C,T.U. I had only vaguely seen as I peered over someone's shoulder at the various instruments in question, knowing that if it was Technical, it was most unlikely I would ever have anything to do with it. I quickly realised that some of my section were ex-Post Office engineers, who would soon spot that I knew "Hee Haw" about them. I tackled it head on by instructing anyone who had used the instrument in question, to sit at the back of the class and keep his mouth shut, unless I asked for his assistance. They were not daft and obeyed. I have to acknowledge that I knew little more about the things at the end of my lectures than I did at the beginning. The only good thing that came out of it was that the section learned that I was no bullshitter and any orders from me were for the general good.

The weather continued fair and the sea calm as we made our

way back across the Atlantic to Freetown, where we anchored for about 24 hours, but did not go ashore. Like all the ports in the East, you could smell it long before you could see it. The men had a wonderful time throwing pennies into the murky water for the local youths to dive for. How they escaped Bubonic Plague was a mystery.

Big excitement just after breakfast. A wee spotter plane appeared high up. The elderly AA-gun anchored to the boat deck futilely let off a few rounds. The sound between decks was deafening. I realised how my great uncle had lost his hearing on a battleship at the bombardment of the Dardanelles in W.W.1. The Canadian officers panicked and rushed around carrying small cases. The plane, Vichy French, turned round and flew off to report our arrival to Hitler or whoever. Evidently this was a regular occurrence but no one had forewarned us or the Canadians.

Next we were invaded by Bumboat women. It was quite a sight to see them haggling with the Chinese crew. Talk about Greek meeting Greek! Then we had the dispiriting sight of the Chinese crew with difficulty launching lifeboats and paddling aimlessly around. I cannot say this inspired me with much confidence in any future emergency, officers panicking and landlubberly sailors.

A pretty ancient looking gun, fixed to fire over our stern was manned by middle-aged R.A. Reservists. The gunners decided one day, as we passed down the west coast of Africa, to have a practice in mid-ocean, and threw overboard a 40-gallon drum, armed their gun and managed to land their shells near to but not on the target. Not completely impressed, I felt that our best chance, if attacked, would lie with our speed.

Most impressed was I by the two cruisers firing practice broadsides. Fist a puff of smoke, then the amazing sight of these ships practically rolling over on recoil, and lastly the noise. Most impressive. We read with keen interest the Morse messages from the Aldiss lamps, the only method of communication allowed between the ships of the convoy, particularly the terse and explicit messages from the Admiral, when the odd ship zigged when it should have zagged, causing some hairy moments. Admirals do not mince their words. Particularly when dealing with the Wavy Navy, as they call it. I have to confess to a healthy respect for the Royal Navy. Very efficient, it was, in my estimation, how the Admiral marshalled the variegated ships of the convoy. We read with interest one evening that two corvettes would meet us at 6 o'clock the next morning and escort us to our destinations in South Africa and sure as Hell, there they were, waiting at the rendezvous bang on time; two small ships all alone in the vast Atlantic ocean. I was very impressed.

A canvas swimming bath had been rigged up on the foredeck and the pantomime of ducking the first timers to cross the Equator was carried out in full form. I avoided this by pointing out that I had previously crossed the line at least four times.

Finally we tied up safely in Capetown and had three or four days of being feted by flotillas of huge open automobiles, staffed by gorgeous, suntanned nubile maidens (?), caring not a whit if their prey be field officer or Signalman and whisking them away to sample the delights of South Africa. It could not have been better timed; I was not alone in tiring of a constant diet of Turkey and Christmas Pudding.

Hancock and I, as newlyweds, had to forgo these delights and sauntered off to explore, only to discover that white men did not walk in Capetown. We hardly managed a couple of hundred yards at a time before being accosted by a sequence of cars offering us lifts and having to explain that all we wanted was a bit of exercise. This they found incomprehensible. The reason for this hospitality was later explained to us. The white population was divided into the Boer settlers, who were against any involvement in the war, and the British settlers. Not to put too fine a point on it, many of the Boers were Nazis at heart and hoped that Hitler would win the war. It showed. Now the boot was on the other foot. All the Brits wanted from us was to come back after the war and stiffen up the English speaking element of the population. There was a charitable trust, called the "1820 settlers scheme", which attracted settlers from Britain, offering cash aid and land. Very tempting, but Bette said no. How wise she was, as ever.

The critical point was that General Smuts, the anti-Nazi South African President, had decreed that at midday there should be a minute, or so, of silence to remember the South African troops fighting in the Desert to the north. The Boers regularly tried to disrupt this; thus the British were delighted to have a convoy disgorging numbers of troops on the ground. The Boers decided it would be a good idea to absent themselves.

There was a small contingent of QAIMNS (Queen Alexandra Imperial Nurses) on board, who became contested targets for some, who were tired not only of Turkey and Christmas Pudding but also of perpetual male company. The egregious Murphy, full of bullshit, as ever, seemed to have his pick and greatly enjoyed flamboyantly climbing up to the boat deck at night, accompanied by one of them; neither was he backward in regaling us with his exploits next day. Now the boot was on the other foot. Girls do not look their best after weeks of cramped conditions; they were so pale, spotty and uninteresting that they compared most unfavourably with the South African suntanned beauties, bursting with health, not to mention also, sitting at the wheel of expensive automobiles. No contest. The Murphys of our little world were now stuck with their partners, to whom they had doubtless sworn undying love. Not only that, but also they had to pay double everywhere they went, while the rest of us were not allowed to pay for anything. We enjoyed that.

Eventually we met up with a South African naval officer and his wife who were enjoying a week's leave. They could not have been kinder and took us all over from the top of Table Mountain to the wine growing country and the miles of sandy beaches. It truly was a land flowing with milk and honey as the Good Book would have put it. We ascended Table Mountain by cable car. Quite a sight from the sea as we approached Capetown, it provided a stunning seascape from its top. It was a gorgeous day, the "Tablecloth" clouds absent; the view spectacular; the surface not level but covered by huge flat rocks, packed so closely together, that from the sea the illusion of a huge plateau/table was given. As we stood there, we could see a line in the sea stretching out for miles and were told that this marked the confluence of the Atlantic and Indian oceans.

We were also taken to the Club, where we instantly became temporary members. I think each course cost sixpence. Such magnificence in quality and quantity, of food and wine contrasted unfavourably with the rationing we had left at home. A wonderful experience and a welcome break from weeks at sea. We could never thank them enough for their kindness.

Only one of our men disobeyed the strict orders to keep well away from the Black Quarters of the city. He was finally found by the police; handed over to us; carried on board strapped to a stretcher, stark bollock naked and wanting to fight all and sundry; obviously one of those unfortunates, who only need to smell a cork to turn instantly into a mad fighting drunk. He spent the rest of the voyage in irons, down, where my classroom was, beside the Chinaman (also in irons), who disturbed our dinner one night when the door from the kitchen burst open and out popped a Chinaman, going flat out, heels and pigtail, flying, closely followed by another Chinaman brandishing a cleaver, also moving very fast. We only had time to lift our heads to see this pantomime, when the pair disappeared through the exit door, still moving at the speed of light. I was told it was a matter of honour—Chinese honour equals money. I don't think he caught up with his prey; a brandished cleaver at your back does add to your speed. How the pair communicated, broad Glasgow and Chinese side by side in irons, could be fascinating to hear.

Soon we were back on board heading for Bombay, nowadays called Mumbai. The bulk of the convoy, (I was told it was a New Zealand Division) which had gone to Durban for their R. & R., hived off from us and headed for Suez and the Desert.

Suddenly, we were ordered to change course and head at full speed for Mombasa. The most memorable message yet was transmitted from an old coal burner—Anchor Line? She was the oldest and slowest ship in the convoy. Panic stations! A German surface raider had been reported in the area. The old tub, lagging further and further behind, belching out clouds of black smoke, replied to a vitriolic message from the Commodore in the immortal words, "Am trying to increase speed by half a knot." We enjoyed the joke but I doubt if the Master or Chief Engineer of the old tub did. She managed to reach port unscathed, hours after us. Meanwhile our two cruisers set out to find the surface raider and destroy it, which they did. In Mombasa harbour, at anchor, was an extraordinary edifice, like the skeleton of an unfinished factory. We were informed that it was an aircraft carrier. If so, it must have been one of the first ever built; sent out to rust away. Certainly it did not do much to boost our morale.

Next morning we woke to see that the cruisers were back—mission accomplished; soon we were steaming for Bombay, which we smelt long before we saw it. As we entered the harbour, we passed round the *Mauritania*, reducing our estimation that we were big. It was more like a toy dog going round a high lamppost. Also there, was the only ship with two square funnels I have ever seen. French, she was called the *Jean Jaques Rousseau*, so my memory says. We were granted a few hours ashore in Bombay and a bunch of us hailed a taxi, longing for a change of diet from roast turkey and Christmas pudding and found a restaurant, which produced a memorable meal, huge prawns fried in batter followed by a rum omelette, shooting blue flames in all directions as it was carried in. Feeling better and much refreshed, we tamely returned to our ship.

That was the extent of my experience of India *re* army bureaucracy; if I had slept ashore that night, I would have been on the ration strength and so entitled to yet another campaign medal. Makes you think!! Next morning we made for the Straits of Malacca and Singapore, where the cruisers left us. A bit eerie, sailing down the coastline of the country in which I had been born. I had always said that I would be going back, but never for a moment imagined it would be in khaki and no return ticket. I had thought the *Mauretania* huge until I watched her rounding one of the Queens towering over her in Singapore Roads.

CHAPTER 8

SINGAPORE

WE DISEMBARKED, finding that we were walking on jelly legs in a steam bath, and finished up in Bell Tents in a scraggy immature rubber plantation, where we stayed waiting for a C.O. to arrive and for our future home to be built. The humidity and heat after ten weeks at sea hit us hard and we were not much use for a week or two. It rained very hard at the same time every day; heavy squalls, called Sumatras, threateningly dark and thundery, could be seen speeding towards us across the sea; they only lasted for 15 minutes or so, when everything turned to steam and very quickly all was back to the normal Turkish Bath atmosphere.

We were desperate to get some decent tropical kit and were soon at a Chinese tailor, who produced the goods next day. It was such a relief to get rid of the Manchester antiques. I shall never forget those awful trousers, at full stretch not long enough, but convertible into untidy shorts by lifting up the hems and hanging them on a button. Probably designed for the Boer war.

The big propaganda constantly, thrust down our throats, was that Singapore was impregnable by sea and the jungle was impenetrable, thus no attack by land could succeed and any naval invasion would be blown out of the water by the battery of huge ex-naval guns (up to a 16 incher), firing armour piercing shells. It was Goebbels, who operated on the theory that if you made the same point regularly it would eventually become the received wisdom. True, but sad.

Singapore was an eye opener, thronged by every race, creed and colour, in bustling rickshaws, enjoying the "Happy World" and its siblings, Raffles Hotel and the Swimming Club, let alone the dubious delights of Lavender Street, where your rickshaw inevitably went, whatever destination you had specified. A bit of a slur on the Brits, it was, that the rickshaw "wallahs" could not imagine a Brit hailing them unless he was seeking a prostitute. Every taste, every race, every colour of prostitute was available in Lavender Street, all soliciting "business". "Grannie" Gordon, a year or two ahead of me in Kimmerghame, was reputed to be quite a patron. Grannie possessed an open two-seater M.G. and pots of money. He was alleged to cruise Lavender Street at night calling out "Ada? Tada?" until he got what he wanted. He would then take her down to some secluded spot, take the folding camp bed out of the boot and complete the transaction. I suspect that he was the only child of elderly and wealthy parents, at home. "But here, the result of 'Busty Stewart's' ruthless cull of the regular drafts of A&S officer reinforcements. Lt Col Stewart was C.O. of the 2nd battalion of the A and S Highlanders, aka the 93rd of foot." The vehemence with which the battalion denied that it had been posted to India and then Malaya as a punishment posting brought to mind the oft used quotation, "Methinks he doth protest too much." Busty was a rarity in Malaya, a real fighting soldier, who was utterly determined that his battalion was kept up to snuff and fit to face any eventuality. Every convoy that came out brought him some officer reinforcements. Busty promptly went through them with a fine toothcomb, and anyone who did not come up to scratch was thrown out. The Far East was littered with his rejects doing R.T.O., A.P.O. and suchlike jobs. The A&S battalion exercised more days in the jungle than all the other British Battalions did in aggregate, which became very obvious in the campaign.

Here is an instance of the kind of man he was. He had a company of little two-man armoured cars, each armed with heavy machine guns, possibly relics of W.W.1. Just imagine how hot and humid it was to be shut in one of these tin cans on the equator. Standing Orders laid down that all men must wear full kit, even in action. A brave crew complained, after being put on a charge for wearing P.T. kit on the firing range. Busty listened to them, reserved judgement, took one of the cars out onto the firing range and spent two hours trying everything he could think of. When he stepped out, he dismissed the charges and ordered P.T. kit to be the order of the day when in action. He fairly led from the front and put his men through the hoops and it showed where and when it mattered.

Unlike the Australian Division, which got full marks for publicity, he trained his men for the real thing. Hardly a week went by, before the campaign, when the Aussie rat of a General (Gordon Bennet?) did not get a boasting article plus his photo on the front page of the local English language newspaper. I understand that his Division was recruited from the cities and not the boondocks of folklore and I have to say that I did not find them very impressive on the field or in the P.O.W. camps. They were most ingenious, but unreliable and with a lot to say. I have referred below to their poor showing in the campaign.

During the forming up period of the Div. Sigs., we officers, with the exception of the Orderly Officer of the day, were free every evening and thus were able to explore the delights of Singapore City and sample its varied entertainments such as swimming clubs, cinemas, dance halls and so on. Raffles Hotel was a must as was quaffing a Singapore gin sling (a very deceptive, sweet tasting, innocuous seeming fruit drink). If you could consume two and walked out, your manhood was okay. I managed to qualify by filling and smoking my pipe, thus lengthening the timescale, but it was a near thing. I learned that the sweet unassuming taste concealed the alcoholic equivalent of a kick from a mule. A tall Artillery major, in full mess kit, strode in, on his arm a tall handsome Chinese lady in a pencil sheath daringly split practically up to one hip. Very impressive. You could hear the sharp disapproving intake of breath from the assembled memsahibs. The pair looked neither to left nor right but went straight to their reserved table. You could have cut the atmosphere with a knife.

The Happy World and its two lookalikes came to life at night. Transport of a sort was on tap. The kaleidoscope of colours and that was just the humanity, took time for us to adjust to. They were something else. Huge Pleasure Parks, they were unlike anything we had previously encountered. The smells alone were breath-taking in more senses than one, coconut oil mingled with patchouli and the odours of humanity, all competing with the effluvia from the little stalls on every corner selling all sorts of cooked and raw meats. The real killer was blachang. The story was that the Malays gathered at low tide all the small crustaceans and microscopic fish, dug a hole, buried their treasure in the beach for some weeks or months until it decomposed into a paste; dug it up, when it became a pungent delicacy which to them was very desirable; but too strong for me.

A background of hot tropical night, lit largely by small lamps, revealed fire eaters, fire walkers, men stretched out on a bed of nails or broken glass, men having slabs of concrete on their abdomens broken into bits by a sledgehammer as they lay on the ground, sometimes a cocktail of the above, all hoping for a few cents from the gawping crowds. There was the Chinese theatre, with its, to our ears, hideous orchestra, whose main objective seemed to be to make as much noise as possible, particularly on the entrance of some god, an *outre* figure in a splendid costume; throughout the performance, the barely dressed scene shifter with a half lit cigarette glued to his lip moved amongst the caste, placing props. Chinese Opera was much the same, but noisier and more lavishly dressed; on a nearby stage, a bit like an enlarged boxing ring; Malays danced the Rongeng, in which pairs advanced and retreated but never touched. Very sexy for Malays, I was told, but rather monotonous for me.

Once, early on, we had a beer at a taxi-dance hall, where a book of four tickets could be bought for a Dollar, entitling you to four dances with one of the vari-coloured females, who stood smoking sulkily at the far end of the hall. Not a terribly appetising bunch; we curiously watched a depressed couple, gyrating to a wind-up gramophone playing some ancient dance tune. The bold Frankie Goble, always in need of a sex mate (a European one was not possible in Singapore as the Memsahibs were few and far between and anyway looked down their noses at common soldiery) bought a book of tickets and announced he was going to sample the talent. On his return he informed us that he had made his choice, but that she would not be free until her contracted time in the dance hall was up, when she would take him home; he sought support. No takers, so he turned on me and begged me to act as backup. He was most urgent and I must confess I felt a duty of protection, but to be honest, curiosity won. Off we set in a rickshaw, where, having hooked herself a client, she ignored him and turned all her attention onto me, reciting the assets and agility of her sister. Even when I made it plain that I was only there to see that my friend got back to camp safely, she still persisted. We arrived at what I assumed to be the equivalent of a tenement, mounted the stairs to the accompaniment of more tales of the erotic athleticism of her sister. At the top of the stairs was a rectangular landing divided into three by bead curtains. A warm bottle of Tiger beer and a glass was produced for me, while she and Frankie disappeared behind one of the curtains. It was not difficult to discern what was going on behind the curtain and after a few grunts, she came through the curtain, her kimono open, to display her charms and offered herself to me, seductively, as she thought. I thanked her for the offer but firmly declined. By this time Frankie had re-appeared doing up his flies and we departed. What really struck me about the whole affair, was, that there being no transport at that time of night, we had to walk back to camp and far from having to support an exhausted Frankie, he walked me off my feet. Some stamina. I think that if he did not know that I was a happily married man, he would have had dark suspicions as to my sexual orientation. I told him, the next morning, that there would be no repeat. There did not seem to have been much enjoyment for him in the whole escapade, let alone romance.

Slowly we adapted to the climate and evolved into something like a Divisional Signals and were informed that we would be going up country to serve the 11th Indian Division. Finally a Lt. Col. Woodbridge appeared from India. Not a happy man, he had been put on the shelf as a Major, deemed unsuitable for further promotion, not the only one in that position; we had our fill of them in Malaya and in the P.O.W. camps. What annoyed him was that he had been removed from the Indian to the British Army for his pay. He had gone up in rank but down in hard cash. He tried and failed to change it. He then spent two days poring over the G1098 (official list of equipment) for a Divisional Signals, until he found not firearms, but fire irons for the Officer's Mess, missing. Happy as a sand boy he pushed through a demand for Field Allowance on the grounds that we had no pokers, tongs etc.—and this practically on the equator!! He was wasted in the Army. (Should have been in the T.U.C.) I did not complain about the result as we officers got an extra half a crown a day as recompense for this grievous lack of the essentials of civilisation! We of course did not know any different and were quite happy to receive the windfall. Finally we were up to strength, except for my section officer, in men and equipment; and we folded our tents and set off by train to a place none of us had ever heard of, Sungei Patani, the Capital of the native State of Kedah in the North West corner of Malaya. There the 11th Indian Division, charged with the defence of the western border with Siam (now called Thailand) had established its Headquarters in a huge mature rubber plantation under the command of a Major General Murray Lyon, of whom more later.

The big propaganda of our impregnability constantly thrust down our throats led to many of us feeling that we were wasting our time in a Theatre of War where all the action would pass us by. We were also informed that all Japs wore glasses and could not see in the dark. How thick we were! Naive is nicer, thick is more accurate. As I said, it was Goebbels who operated on the theory that if you made the same point regularly, it would eventually become the received wisdom. True, but sad.

Singapore Railway Station was a bizarre sight; its glass canopy, platforms, buffers and ticket office could have been lifted straight from pre-war St Andrews, except for the colour and clothing of the other travellers. The Malays in colourful sarongs and bajus, the men wearing their black Moslem hats, their women with brightly coloured headscarves always at the ready to be drawn across the face if an infidel's gaze became embarrassing, walked a couple of paces behind and one to the side of their Lords and Masters The Chinese, both sexes, in drab blue or black jackets and trousers, worked, and worked, gambled and gambled; but on foot, the same pattern showed of husband in front and wife behind and to one side; both sexes were quite hard to differentiate except for a wisp or two of facial hair on the men. The Tamils, men in white dhotis, their women, gold stud in a nostril, in saris with one end swept over a shoulder leaving a leathery breast exposed.

The station, with its varied groups of nationals, in multi-hued clothing, may have been a surprise to our eyes, but the train was the real surprise. The first class carriages were air-conditioned (this in 1941!); it also provided proper beds, dining facilities and a well-stocked bar for the first class, furnished with comfortable easy chairs. This was my first experience of double glazing, primitive perhaps, but most effective in the prevailing heat and humidity.

Through time, we had begun to see more clearly the mix of races and creeds. At that time by repute and by personal observation, we could see that Malay men did not believe in work, as long as their womenfolk could cope. It was genuinely a male chauvinist society. His idea of a busy day was to sit under a palm tree, smoking and gossiping with his male friends while she organised the family, the marketing and the food. He knew that it was his country and that Allah had reserved for his people fruits and vegetables in abundance and plenty of fish in the canals and the sea. Why bother working? Their hardest work was to penetrate the jungle and find a Durian tree. They and the tiger population would sell their souls for the fruit. I was told a tiger would sit at the base of the tree, waiting for the fruit to fall down. I did see one; it smelt appalling; a bit like a newly opened midden; I was told that it tasted better than strawberries and cream. It may well have, but I did not try it. Definitely an acquired taste and better eaten in a hot bath with a clothes peg over the nose.

To give you an idea of the abundance available in Malaya, the fruit market in the small town, Sungei Patani, we finished beside, was at least half the size of Glasgow's. One big shed alone contained nothing but bananas from pinkie-finger-sized to huge plantains, and ranging from green to yellow to pink.

The water buffalo annually provided milk and a calf on top of working the paddy fields and doing any haulage required.

Death to Europeans they were, but meek and mild to the locals, ridden and bullied by 4-year-old toddlers.

The Tamils, living in a form of almost beneficent slavery, worked the rubber plantations under the control of European Planters, many of them Scots. I knew one from off a farm in Aberdeenshire. Decent bloke, square built, strong as an ox, he was covered in black body hair. So much so that he admitted that on his wedding night, he had to get someone to shave him all over. His new wife must have suffered grievously from stubble trouble! He had lived on half his pay by eating native food, until he could afford a wife and on his next leave, wooed and wed a twin and ever since was quite sure that he had chosen the wrong one!

The planters provided villages, schools, drainage and medical facilities for the rubber tappers, Tamils mostly. Husband and wife, They paraded, at dawn at the factory with their pails and parangs (jungle knives) to milk their allotted trees; an angled slot cut in the bark, a tiny tin gutter placed so that the oozing latex filled a little china pot, which was emptied into one of two buckets, which were carried swinging from each end of a shoulder-carried bamboo pole. He/She pared the fine skin off yesterday's cut to restart the latex flow; the collected latex was brought back to the factory for processing into sheets, which were then packed into bales for shipment. The Planter was God and even was reputed to have *"Droit de Seigneur"*, in that the man had to produce his woman for inspection before permission was granted to marry and the story was that she could be told to stay the night in the bungalow. Possible, but doubtful.

The Planter had to watch his step because it was reputed also that the Tamil women, if sufficiently roused, had been known to throw a Planter into a ditch and urinate upon him, *seriatim*. The women were a surprise to us in that they wore a dress, like, we are led to understand, our male Scots forbears did, a length of cloth making a long skirt and then thrown over a shoulder to expose one leathery breast. Tough ladies, they were reputed to be able, when required, to interrupt their task of latex tapping for long enough to go behind a bush, give birth, clean up and resume their task.

The Sikhs, heavily bearded with waist-long hair piled on top of their heads, were mostly money lenders and in my humble opinion not to be trusted. I understand that their behaviour towards the Chinese during Japanese rule has led to them being scarce to find in post-war Singapore.

The remaining class was Eurasian; a very valuable part of Society holding down jobs in clerical positions of trust and keeping the railways running to a timetable.

The thing that struck me and inclined me to believe that Malaya was a well-run Colony was that each race lived very largely with their own kind, but had open sports facilities, i.e. they socialised on the sports field, but were with their own kin at home.

Malaya at the time seemed to have three forms of governance, Straits Settlements, wholly British and controlled by the Governor, Sultans with an official British Adviser, trying to keep the Sultan in some sort of civilised order and a similar set up with British holding important offices such as Chief of Police. I hope that I have got it right. I found it quite confusing.

This system of government worked pretty well in the circumstances prevailing. It contributed both to the material benefit of Britain and to the physical wellbeing of the native population. In Malaya, as elsewhere in the Empire, the British did not encourage inter-racial integration but adopted the old Roman system of "divide and rule". As a colony, Malaya was probably one of our success stories. Malaria had been to some extent eliminated, the police were in full control and tried to know their own areas inside out. As far as I could see, every decent sized kampong had good water on tap, often a standpipe, and primitive lighting. The main roads, though few and narrow, were tarmacked and well maintained. The telephone system was excellent for the time. Even the Sakai, the aboriginal pigmies in the jungles of the Cameron Highlands, were carefully protected and encouraged to continue living their lives as hunter gatherers in their time honoured way. An interesting side-line on these little people was that they kept some of our folk and in particular their protector, hidden and safe throughout the Japanese occupation. They could only count one, two, three, a lot, but their jungle craft was superb. It would do no harm to read *The Jungle is Neutral* and the biography of Spencer Chapman among my books.

Granted that Britain profited from the rubber and tin industries together with burgeoning palm oil, which was then making a contribution to the wealth of both countries, it seemed to me and I have no reason to change my mind with hindsight, that the country was well run for the time—remarkably so when you take into account the different races and religions involved.

Communism from mainland China had infiltrated some of the Straits Chinese but the police had it well monitored. That did not allay Sir Shenton Thomas, the Singapore Governor's, fears of a Communist uprising. In my opinion, he contributed about as much to the fall of Singapore as the C-in-C. An interesting sidelight how well integrated and law abiding the country was that a tailor's bill for a handmade tie for a few shillings followed me all the way up country from Singapore and in no hurry at that. A Tuan, a Britisher, could sign a chit anywhere and the shopkeeper knew that he would be paid. We were regarded, with good reason, as having complete integrity and there was no need to carry large amounts of money; credit was instant. How the world has changed!

The problem child was the Sultan of Johore, whose latest exploit was reported to be to stuff a champagne bottle up the vagina of a visiting British chorus girl. This caused Diplomatic somersaults. All traffic by road and rail, carrying raw rubber and tin to Singapore ran through Johore. The risk of removing the Sultan and causing native unrest was unthinkable. In the end he was made to pay for a squadron of Fighters as a punishment, which was petty cash to him. We were not told what happened to the girl. Not good, I fear.

We travelled in comfort, but slowly, up the west coast of Malaya, arriving finally at Sungei Patani, the capital city of Kedah, where we detrained, as the army put it, and were conveyed into a large, mature rubber plantation, where 11th Indian Division had set up its H.Q. We were to provide its communication requirements. The mature rubber trees made it a bit like living in the crepuscular gloom of an ancient Cathedral.

CHAPTER 9

SUNGEI PATANI

MALAYA did not seem to have seasons as we understand them. Over about ten days or so, once a year the trees shed their leaves and instantly produced new ones. Rather like birds moulting. The countryside and the jungle appeared to be permanently green.

We were accommodated in new wooden huts with atap roofs. The officers' quarters consisted of a row of single rooms containing a charpoy, a sturdy wooden bed frame; strong string netting made a cool mattress, upon which we unrolled our valises for bedding. So near to the equator, we needed no more than a sheet on top; in fact, after lunch, if in camp, a siesta on your charpoy meant stripping off, laying a towel over your middle, under a mosquito net, sweating like a pig (never seen a pig sweat, now I come to think about it); no double glazing; no air conditioning; no glass in the window. The ablutions were primitive but adequate. The lavatory consisted of a borehole. Quite a clever system, an auger drilled a hole down 18 ft. and an enclosed wooden seat was built on top, sealed and, when not in use, kept closed by a tight fitting lid At the bottom of the shaft was placed some bluebottle larvae, which disposed of the deposits. Because of the depth and the tight fit of the lid, the larvae were kept in darkness and so, never developed into bluebottles. It worked, but anything dropped down the shaft, was lost and gone for ever; a faint staleness emanated but not offensively so.

Our Mess was no more than a hundred yards away from the cookhouse. The villainous Ghulam Hussein ruled there along with his roundabout harem. To be a Muslim then, made married life remarkably simple. As a man tired of wife A, he just told her three times that he was divorcing her; wife B took over and younger wife E was introduced to complete the *ménage*, and so on. Obviously a strong belief that variety is the spice of life and a total absence of Feminism. Back to her family, wife A went. Maintenance? Return of dowry? Doubtful.

He was onto a good thing all round. He drew our rations weekly from the QM, and shopped in the market for extras. He would sell what he dared of the former making a killing in the market. He was in every way a suitable recruit for the Mafia; I have a vivid memory of him chasing a headless but mobile chicken, travelling at speed in ever decreasing circles, spouting gouts of blood like a steam engine going up a steep hill. No need for menu cards in our mess. We could both hear his marital squabbles and see our next meal being prepared through the permanently open Mess window. We fed not too badly but in no way did it match his growing girth and prosperity.

I was kept busy, settling in and getting my Signal Office started. My men knew me well and everything progressed satisfactorily. I soon had the show up and running. We were connected to 3rd (I) Corps back in Kuala Lumpur by two Teleprinters, a sort of line connected typewriter, a precursor of e-mail, but needing a fixed line; its messages had to be coded and decoded; it could not send and receive simultaneously; pretty advanced for the time, but a big heavy and clumsy machine; we were also connected to Div. H.Q. and the two Brigades on line by Morse or phone. The big problem was priority. Every officer had a priority allotted to him according to his rank. By some form of machismo, each always used his personal priority, whether the message merited it or not Thus messages could be delayed for hours if not days as higher priorities kept coming in and being placed above them in the queue. The coding/decoding did not help. W/T was hopelessly unreliable, due largely to the atmospheric conditions and the frequent electric storms. That only left the D.R.s to deliver messages timeously and safely. They were kept hard at it and, being volunteers, revelled in the lack of speed limits.

For a treat, I organised a rough-riding competition for them, including some water and mud splashes. They had the time of their lives; not so did the C.O. as he watched his mud splattered motorbikes cross the finishing line. I assured him that the bikes would be spotless on parade the next morning. He clearly did not believe me. They were. I thought that that would be a good experience of off road riding in a war situation.

Incidentally I had just realised that I was almost the only man in my section who had not been earning £1000 a year in civvy life. It was a wee while before I tumbled to the truth. One of the D.R.s had been Sales Manager for Horlicks, so he may have been telling the truth.

On another occasion, I organised a jungle operation to collect a large number of suitable bamboos to produce a reserve of poles for field cable. We were involved in a hit and run electric storm, fortunately brief, where I saw a large tree split right down the middle not far from where we were working. Quite spectacular; you could smell the scorched timber. We moved. Once again the troops thoroughly enjoyed a day out in the sub jungle. Once again, the C.O. looked askance at his mud splattered 15cwt. trucks. Once again, much to his surprise, they were bright and clean the next day. I knew that my men would not let me down and felt that a bit of off road driving would provide good training for my drivers in any future emergencies.

Harry Bristow arrived, a Direct Commission, and we hit it off right away. He was a most interesting character, an inveterate gambler, but good enough to win more than he lost. In civvy life, he had owned and run a nice little car business in the Shires, but good citizen that he was, he was mad keen to do his bit in the war. Unfortunately he had suffered Rheumatic Fever in his childhood; his heart was affected; accordingly he was turned down by the R.A.F. and the R.N. A competent skier, he went with a pal to fight alongside the Finns, who not wanting to be taken over by the Russians, were giving them a hard time. All went well, until some diplomatic thing made it necessary to get out of Finland—fast! Probably the brief period when Hitler and Stalin were allies, much to the confusion of the Labour Party and the Trades Unions. Not a club I would want to join. Getting back to the UK was a problem for Harry, as the map will show. Finnish friends smuggled the pair onto a Swedish (neutral) ship as stowaways and told them to keep to the back of the coal bunkers until safely in Swedish waters; the ship was due to call at a couple of ports in Germany; they spent a few days amongst the coal, hidden from the German Inspectors, until they docked in Sweden, where they landed on the British Embassy's doorstep. None too popular there; Russia was on the road to becoming an ally at the time; Labour heaved a big sigh of relief. The pair were housed and fed until an escape to Norway had been organised. He never told even me how he got back from Norway— something to do with the Official Secrets Act, but I suspect it would be by the "Shetland Bus"; they were then hustled down to London, given a bollocking by some Minister, whom Harry charmed into getting himself an Instant Commission and a posting to Malaya. Probably to keep him as far away as possible.

We had a lot of fun together, shared two cars and a bag of golf clubs. The first car was a red fabric Riley Monaco, well past its sell-by-date. Pretty to look at, it consumed equal quantities of oil and petrol and was so clapped out that it was necessary to change down, to navigate any corner; it was not a car to follow too closely; the smell of Castrol was bad enough but to have your windscreen covered in burned and unburned oil was a bit much. Its fabric saloon body proved to be an ideal home for ants. Looked okay but did not satisfy our need for reliable transport, so we traded it in for an Essex Terraplane, a luxury car fitted with overdrive and a three-speed box, but so powerful that, once in top (i.e. third) gear, you never needed to change down on Malaya's flat roads.

Driving was easy in the Malaya of those days: good straight, but narrow roads, not many of them, but enough, with little traffic; licences easy to get—if you were British. Go and see the chief of police, have a cup of coffee and a chat with him. No problem! This did not mean he did not (falsely as it transpired) think that he had the whole state including the Sultan taped. We must have had some form of insurance too. Harry would have seen to that; he seldom missed a trick and was a very good friend.

The biggest hazard to driving was the odd water buffalo ambling across the road with a minute brat sitting on top, swearing at it and hitting it with a bamboo wand, not, I might add, to much avail. The buffalo knew fine well where it was going—either to work, to a bath or home. It never failed to amaze me how these fearsome big beasts posed no terror to the smallest naked mite. A hazard at night, it was, to meet one round a corner, hauling a cart, the grey bearded driver fast asleep on the floor and the lantern extinct.

The Terraplane had been the property of some Chinese entrepreneur, either about to become a millionaire and trading up or just ceasing to be one and liquidating his assets. As gamblers, the Chinese put even Harry in the shade. He introduced the Mess to Liar Dice, which sure livened up the evenings. The idea was that the loser paid for the next round of drinks. Harry seemed to be able to fix it so that no one lost consistently, and that each one of us took our turn. I do not know how he did it, but he did. The Jesuit priest, who had accompanied us to the sights of Singapore, was still with us and partook equally in the Liar Dice and golf. This was quite a shock to me, who had been brought up to believe that the Pope had figurative horns and a tail. The beginnings of scepticism started to surface. The C.O. was conspicuous by his absence. Whether he thought that it was beneath his dignity or it was due to his renowned difficulty of getting his purse open, I don't know. Probably the latter.

We found that if we hurried down to the club after work, we could get nine holes in before it got too dark. Night does not hang about on the equator—one minute daylight, the next black night. Harry was a dedicated hooker, I, an equally dedicated slicer; we shared a bag of clubs. We often needed the same club simultaneously; the caddy, a child of about 9 and costing washers, was kept busy scuttling from side to side of the fairway. It was a very pleasant way of winding down at the end of the day, often enhanced by the sight of a certain planter's wife on an adjacent fairway, who preferred to play solo, wearing what we at that time called beach pyjamas, cool but not leaving too much to the imagination, as she knew fine; it was a bit distracting to catch sight of her out of the corner of your eye as you reached the top of your back swing.

The club was open to officers only. This caused problems, when they challenged us to a rugby match. First we had to negotiate the inclusion of O.R.s to make up our numbers. This was managed reasonably quickly, but a flat refusal to allow them to attend the subsequent meal was only solved when we said that if that was the rule there would be no match. In the end it went off well. You must remember that Malaya was being run by and for folk who were socially about 50 years behind U.K. times. Sunday tiffin was the social event of the week. The planters, mostly bachelors, but comforted by a compliant housekeeper; the pragmatic Japanese were reckoned to be the best; they knew fine that marriage was not a possibility. Something the other races coveted, and were inevitably disappointed. These planters worked really long hours through the week, but, on Sundays, they congregated in the club for a Malay curry tiffin, usually excellent fish along with all the extra side dishes according to Malay custom. This was followed by Gula Malacca, a sort of solid sago covered with burnt sugar sauce—nice and cool after the curry. The meal was preceded by several "pahits" (drinks), translated as whisky suku ayers. Whether the suku applied to the whisky or the water (suku Malay = small English) I leave to your imagination. Whatever, after coffee, we all retired to stretcher beds on the verandah, until suitably refreshed, when we returned to the bar for a game of "slosh", a precursor of snooker. A regular part of the scenery was a stuttering self-professed Teetotaller; his repeated calls at the bar for a "Gin-Gin-Gabeer" rather militated against his Rechabite profession, but cheered him up considerably.

The C.O. discovered that we may have fired a few rounds on the range, but not with a pistol, and decided that we should take a course on pistol shooting. Terrifying and not the fun I expected, running about shooting at targets popping up all over the place. I was glad to get back to my charpoy unperforated. My weapon was a Webley .38, kicked upwards and had a dodgy safety catch. From that day on, I never had a live round in the first chamber; I valued my toes too much.

Murphy had become ever more autocratic and insufferable since being confirmed as adjutant. The C.O. realised that Murphy was the only one amongst us who knew and understood all the forms and customs of the army and would hear no ill of him. As a result Murphy became more and more conceited and so much so that he started to act as if he was the C.O., who eventually tumbled to the fact that his own authority was being undermined and, much to our relief, sacked him. Murphy took it badly and, not realising he was in a hole, continued digging. So much so that he was told to go next day. A railway warrant was issued. He was so conceited that he announced that he would first drink a bottle of whisky to drown his sorrows. His grand gesture only lasted halfway down the bottle, when he became garrulous, verging on comatose. We quickly poured him and his gear into a truck, gave the driver strict instructions to dump his cargo at the station and come straight back. We enjoyed the rest of the bottle.

In fact, life was good; my section was running on oiled wheels and I was pretty pleased with myself, when the blow fell. A redheaded Captain appeared and took over the Section. He was one of the ones who had been in the Woolwich squad of Regular entrants, leaving the O.C.T.U., about the time I arrived. He was white hot keen and desperate to win a medal, any medal. I was not too chuffed to lose the Section I had formed, brought out and set up working efficiently. My men were not too pleased either and unfortunately it showed. I should have put a stop to that, but in my resentment of his treatment of me, did not. He did his best to make my life Hell by trying to cause trouble for me. Unfortunately I helped him on his way.

Being still peacetime in Malaya, weekends were free after midday on Saturdays; the main recreation area for us was the island of Penang. At weekends, transport (trucks, not buses) were laid on for the O.R.s with late passes, to connect with the Butterworth ferry. In Penang there were entertainments of a sort, but not up to Singapore standards. If any officers wished to visit Penang, the Orderly Officer of the day was the unlucky chauffeur; that duty fell on me one Saturday. I was enjoying driving the Ford station wagon, not appreciating that the engine was far too powerful for such a light vehicle. Doing at least 60,

I rounded a bend to find the road suddenly swimming from one of the short sharp tropical showers and saw a Tamil on a bicycle in front; he unfortunately wobbled out into the middle of the road just as I moved out to pass him; I went into a broadside skid, over corrected and broadsided the other way, same again; but by this time the road was suddenly dry, the tyres gripped and we shot off down the monsoon drain and back up into a rubber plantation. I was just congratulating myself on my lucky escape in that we were headed straight through between two rows of trees when my offside front axle hit a concealed tree stump and over we went. Bygraves, who had been sitting in the back, realising something was wrong, got up to peer outside and was catapulted out. Unfortunately he was accompanied by a 4-gallon tin of petrol, the edge of which gashed his bald head. I pulled myself together, got out and found him lying bleeding from a sizeable cut to his scalp. I thought I had killed him. Not so; he sat up, looked me in the eye and said, "You owe me a bottle of whisky." He got it. To say that I was relieved was an understatement. We commandeered transport, got him to hospital; and ourselves and the wreck back to camp. I did not sleep too much that night and lived through the accident for quite a few nights. I was very relieved to hear that Bygraves seemed none the worse and indeed was back with us to claim his bottle in a couple of days. It was a good few weeks before I could twit him on the fact that it was lucky that it was his head that was wounded and not somewhere more important, where doubtless he kept his brains. There remained the question of the repair of the vehicle. The rule was that up to a certain figure, no problem, but if over that figure, it had to be reported to the General. In my favour was the fact that my C.O. discovered that the Orderly Officer should not have left camp, realising that if it came out that he had been a passenger on more than one occasion, he too would have been in the soup. The L.A.D.

(Light Aid Detachment) officer had joined our Mess recently and was very surprised to find the C.O. plying him with whisky. The upshot was that the L.A.D. would put the station wagon back to its pristine form, the official price would be kept below the fatal figure and I would pay the difference of the true price. I was really glad to get out of that. The red haired Captain was not pleased. He thought that I was in real trouble and was sorely disappointed with the outcome.

The bold lad then decided to check everything in the section's G1098. The G1098 of an Office Signal Section, (over 90 men), listing all its equipment, ran to several pages, as can be imagined. Obviously, wear and tear could cover small articles, but an extending ladder had gone A.W.O.L. and was too big to be brushed under the carpet. The Redhead was ecstatic and informed me in high glee that he would see to it that I paid for all missing articles. Equally on my high horse, I announced that I would certainly pay for any missing items that I had signed for. Not a smidgeon of a signature could be found and he was livid. I am afraid, I smirked. Once again the unit had to carry out a cover up. Not that that did my reputation much good in certain eyes. I was in danger of thinking I was untouchable.

Then the Divisional Commander, Major General Murray Lyon, had a rush of blood to the head; a typical Indian Army officer of the worst kind, solid ivory between the ears and always looking as if his batman had just given his face a good going over with Cherry Blossom brown boot polish, he would frequently inform all and sundry that "Johnny Jap" was no problem: "… wears glasses and cannot see in the dark, ye see." How wrong he was! He decided that the Division would have an Exercise, a simulated scheme, whereby a Brigade would attack from the North to test our defences. A mock Brigade had to be made up as a replacement and I with some of my men was posted to it, to provide a Signal Office.

Off I went, bright eyed and bushy tailed, only to find that the acting Brigadier, an Indian Army Lt. Col was one Stokes, a descendant of sorts of the man who invented the Stokes Trench Mortar in W.W.1. This fact he broadcast on an hourly basis. On reporting to him, I recognised instantly his attitude towards Emergency Commissions, said nothing, saluted, set up my Signal Office and got it up and running. A couple of hours later he detailed my men for guard duty. This was a sore point; the battle always had to be re-fought. As a Signals unit worked 24/7, the men were only to be detailed for outside duties such as guards, which concerned themselves, i.e. in my case guarding the Signal Office and our transport. Clearly the idiot thought I was so wet behind the ears that I would not be aware of this. So I girded my loins and politely explained my reasons for refusing to allow my men to be taken away from their duties. He blustered and threatened to report me to the General. I stood firm, but polite, saluted him and returned to my unit. Someone on his staff must have explained to him the facts of life. He rescinded the order, but I was a marked man and decided to watch my back.

He then issued an order, which was contrary to K.R.R.s (King's Rules and Regulations), getting it back to front. My teaching from O.C.T.U. was clear and common sense: "…in the event of an air raid, the men put on their tin hats and carried on working, but in the event of a gas attack, they also put on their respirators and carried on working." Priority at all times was to keep the Signal Office working at all costs; communications were vital. Idiot that he was, he blew his whistle for a gas attack as he thought, but actually by the book, it was for an air raid. Shortly he appeared blue in the face, told me I was a disgrace to my uniform, all my men were dead, appealed to the umpire, who nodded his head, and so on; my men listened, their eyes popping out of their heads. I was of course to be reported to the General. I stood quietly, until he had finished his tirade, when I opened my copy of K.R.R.s: oddly enough it fell open at the correct page and I pointed out to him ever so politely that his signal was the wrong one and that as a new Commission, I was bound by K.R.R.s. He nearly had apoplexy, turned on his heel and stamped out. I was indeed reported to the General who summoned my C.O., who much to my surprise, stood up for me and the General had to dismiss the whole affair. That Lt Col never made Brigadier. It would not do, in a Court Martial, for the top brass to be seen to have flouted K.R.R.s.

Incidentally, the Exercise was a complete washout. While the Acting Brigadier was emphasising what a clever chap he was, and believing all the crap about the impenetrable jungle on our eastern flank, left it naked, whereupon the "invader" saying "thanks very much", went through the "impenetrable" jungle like a hot knife through butter, attacking Div HQ in the rear. Panic stations erupted, until the umpire had a blinding flash of light and declared that there had been a big naval battle in the Gulf of Siam, the enemy fleet had been routed and scuttled back home. Exactly the opposite of what actually happened a few months later. Did the brass hats learn? No.

It was explained to me later that our Government had agreed with the Governments of Australia and New Zealand, that Britain would provide all necessary defences for that part of the world and that an annual amount should be paid, like an Insurance Premium. Thus, when the balloon went up, all the best resources, in men and materials, were directed to this end. As a token to Australia and New Zealand, the *Prince of Wales* and the *Repulse* were sacrificed, as was the Ghurkha Brigade, the two jungle Brigades referred to hereunder, and the 18th Anglian Division, whose ships arrived just before the Surrender. In fact, they never unloaded some of their equipment—the Japs got the lot for free. These troops had arrived with the very latest equipment. Such a loss of men and material can hardly be quantified, particularly at that crucial time in the war, when no bookie would have given odds of less than 1000 to one against our survival against Hitler. The only ray of sunshine was that, locked up with us P.O.W.s were all those Majors, previously passed over as not suitable for promotion to Command, who could now no longer cause damage to the War effort. They were a motley lot, some not to be trusted not to side with the Japs against our troops. Oh yes, it happened in some P.O.W. camps. My O.C., Malins, was one of the worst. General Percival had the nerve to put the blame for the defeat on the Subalterns. Talk about people in glass houses! I nearly burst a blood vessel when I heard his verdict. My conscience is clear on that subject. Granted that I had a magnificent squad of men, I can put my hand on my heart and say that we did our job from start to finish and there never was a complaint lodged against my squad.

I became even more of a marked man, was given a week's local leave and sent to Singapore to be shown its defences, including the famous Battery of naval guns, and came to the conclusion that every time Beardmores had a surplus naval gun lying about, they sent it off to Singapore; they varied from 9 inchers to at least one 16 incher. I was impressed by the way the huge charges were moved mechanically from their underground bunker to match up with the war heads and thence fitted into the correct breech, but much more impressed was I, to find that the officers' bedrooms were air conditioned. I was such a fool that I thought that all this was a reward for standing firm for Signals; it might have been slightly so, but actually it was to put me face to face with the Chief Signal Officer Malaya, for him to assess me and decide what to do with this awkward subaltern who may have been a pain, in the backside but could get things done and was not frightened to stand up for Signals. He recruited his memsahib, a formidable lady; I received a three line whip to attend them for Sunday tiffin, where I was given a good going over. There was a special carrousel for all the little extras, which mark a Malay Curry; to finish, we had a pineapple, which had been emptied, the core removed, the flesh amalgamated with ice cream and put in the fridge—scrumptious!

The pair of them turned out, in my opinion, to be good judges of character, and decided that the best thing to do with me was to give me a small independent command, as far away as possible from any HQ. Probably they knew fine well that Stokes was solid bone from the neck up.

CHAPTER 10

ALOH STAR

ACTUALLY I CAME OUT OF IT pretty well; said farewell to my friends in 11th (I) Div. Sigs and found myself transferred to the 76th Independent Line Section of 3 (I) Corps Signals (fully equipped and manned so that it could operate anywhere in the world) and sent up north with half of the section to Aloh Star aerodrome. My C.O. and O.C. were 200 miles further south and never once appeared. It could not have been better. My orders were to extend the overhead line system all over the aerodrome. With hindsight, this was madness and doomed to destruction in the first wave of bombing, as indeed did happen. It was typical of the whole outlook of Malaya Command. It looked substantial enough, metal telephone poles, chosen as being impervious to termites, with copper wires strung on porcelain insulators, but actually vulnerable to air attack. I thoroughly enjoyed the job; working out in the open was much preferable to being tied to an office and being 200 miles from my C.O. or O.C., was just the icing on the cake. I was even given company commander's powers, which was most unusual for a 2nd Lt. The R.A.F. put my men up and granted me the privileges of their officer's quarters and mess. Excellent!

The men with whom I had been landed were the best. This extraordinary human faculty of looking back and remembering the good times, the laughs and the softening of the edges of the worst experiences, must be the mainspring of our steady progress towards civilisation. Otherwise we would not have been able to survive the horrors, which we endured later and have gone seriously and permanently mad. As it was, when P.O.W.s, we all went a bit 'doolally' from time to time. That was Nature's other way of helping us to survive. Temporarily unbalanced and irrational, as each of us was on occasion; quite understandably so, considering the conditions we were to suffer; the permanent hollow pang of extreme hunger; always on the brink of starvation, never knowing from day to day, whether or when we would get anything to eat; the shouting and the constant bashings.

Sergeant Powner, an ideal choice for the job, having been a Post Office ganger for line erection in civvy life, did as much as any of my companions to help me to survive. His breezy manner, unfailing courtesy, easy efficiency, and staunch unfailing loyalty made him the ideal sergeant in peace, in war, and in the P.O.W. camps. Later, as P.O.Ws, after a really foul patch, of which there were many, Sgt. Powner would say, "Don't worry about it Sir, you will be laughing at it in six months." I could have shot him on the spot. The maddening thing is that he was usually proved correct. Finally, did any newly commissioned subaltern have a better man to say "carry on Sergeant" to? I remember him with great affection and real respect. We were all highly amused when the first of the only two batches of letters arrived on the Railway. In his breezy way, in his last mail home, he had inadvertently put his letter to his wife into his girlfriend's envelope and vice versa. The letter from his wife was, to put it mildly, pointed, the one from his girl-friend, puzzled. He thought the whole thing a huge joke. I often wondered how much hilarity there was when he got home. An added bonus was a heavy-duty-power lineman from a Yorkshire electricity generator, a stereotypically craggy Yorkshireman, he was not only a first class tradesman, but also a natural versifier. Taciturn by nature, almost inarticulate in normal conversation, given a photograph of a child, wife or sweetheart, he could, like turning on a tap, compose a couple of relevant verses for the soldier to send home. Not McGonagallesqe either—some of it was really quite good. It was a God-given talent and he was a great asset to the section both as tradesman and morale booster. One minute he was totally monosyllabic, the next producing rhyming, scanning verse. The rest of the squad were the salt of the earth, almost to a man from Scotland and the North of England; we got on fine. There was an interesting distinction there. If I said to an Englishman from south of the Watford Gap, "Get up that pole and sort the fault," he would be sitting on one of the arms in a flash only to find that he had left some vital pieces of equipment below. In contrast one from the north would say "Yes Sir", methodically check that he had everything he needed, climb the pole and finish the job more quickly.

The return trip from Penang was timed to coincide with the last ferry for Butterworth. Unfortunately the cinemas closed an hour and a half earlier. This posed a big problem for the O.R.s. They had no desire to take an early ferry and hang about Butterworth, until their transport arrived. Butterworth could just about beat Crewe Station without the W.V.S., for an exciting hour and a half, late at night. The European civilians either did not want to invite common soldiery into their homes or feared the social ostracism that would be visited on them if they did. Thus the only available choice open to the O.R.s, after the cinemas closed, was a bar (most were out of bounds for reasons of class or colour) or a brothel, also out of bounds, but less likely to be found in. Whichever they chose they were liable for eventual big trouble. In the first case the Redcaps would appear on their rounds and the probability of a fight developing was good. After a few beers, Redcaps were as a red rag to a bull to most of the men. In the second case V.D. or, as it is fashionable nowadays to call it, S.T.D., would strike sooner or later with the inevitable devastating consequence of pay and allowances being stopped and pointed questions from home. It was very hard to watch decent respectable men fall into this trap out of boredom and the class consciousness of the civilian population.

Eventually a young Corporal, one time Divisional boxing champion at his weight, a once magnificent physical specimen, contracted secondary Gonorrhoea. He returned from hospital, and the sight of this one time perfect physique ravaged by the disease, did more than all the homilies about the threat of V.D. and the consequent army financial strictures, to deter the men from following his example. The brothel's income dropped considerably. The irony was that he was shipped home on medical grounds and thus escaped captivity.

But if found by Redcaps in a banned bar, a brawl would start, which my men relished, resulting in a couple of them being locked up overnight; I got very tired of finding a message for me at breakfast on Sunday mornings to collect a pair from Pokey a.s.a.p. I cast my mind back to Fettes and decided to form football and hockey teams and challenge anybody and everybody to a match after work. I laid down that all my men had to play or attend as spectators. I opted for hockey, but otherwise regularly attended as a spectator. The men loved the contact sports and I think we beat everyone in sight. In fact, we began to run out of teams willing to take us on just before we finished the job on the 'drome. It fairly cut down my Sunday visits to Penang. I had ruled that anyone who caused me to go there was not allowed to play for a week, but had to attend as a spectator. Perhaps I should explain that I had a totally unlicensed agreement with Captain Mason that any man who did not like my methods could volunteer to return to K.L. There was a small queue of volunteers wishing to join me.

Oddly enough, this worked well for me on the Railway; during one of the hockey matches, I fell and grazed a knee. In that climate the graze festered, so I sought out the M.O., who looked at it, produced a packet of powder and said, "This is M&B powder; it arrived from home a couple of days ago, I know nothing about it. You can be the guinea-pig." He then slabbered my knee with it, stuck a large plaster over it and told me to keep the plaster on until it fell off, which I did and the whole thing cleared leaving a small scar. I did not know it then, but I was now inoculated against tropical ulcers and avoided the very real threat of amputation. Nature in its extraordinary way had endowed the vegetation, including bamboos, in certain parts of Siam with sharp thorns; gashed by one, odds on suppuration a tropical ulcer developed with consequent amputation a distinct possibility. These thorns were perhaps Nature's way of protecting herbage.

We were guarded (???) by a battalion of the Bahalwarpur State Infantry. Somehow the Maharajah of Bahalwarpur had been "persuaded" to offer some of his personal private army to the allied cause, and a right Fred Karno's army they proved to be. While we were working on the perimeter one morning, the aforesaid battalion were on their morning parade, when a Lance Naik, (L/Cpl equivalent), announced that some officer had been rogering his pet drummer boy, and therefore he was going to shoot anyone with pips on his shoulder. Suiting action to his words, he released his safety catch, rammed one up the spout and closed the bolt with a loud click. Thereupon, as one man, their officers in the lead, the parade hurdled the barbed wire fence like Olympic hopefuls and headed fast for their quarters. The officers, well in front, locked themselves in their ablutions, while the miscreant pranced around, repeating his threats and waving his rifle in all directions, letting one off every now and then.

The R.A.F. H.Q staff were working away in their offices as normal when they heard the disturbance. The Wingco shepherded his lot into the slit trenches, joined them, drew his pistol and shot the man in the groin. Damned good shot. Whereupon the man fell to the ground, was arrested, taken to hospital under armed guard, still issuing threats. We missed all this but were treated to an explicit account on our return for tiffin. It did not seem to me, on reflection, very sensible to put much trust in the Bahalwarpuris for my personal defence. I was very glad I was absent from the scene of the crime as the thought of being a witness in a court martial under Indian Army control did not appeal to me. Imagine all the cousins and so on, who would give long and contradictory evidence, depending on their blood relationship or not to the accused.

Our work went on successfully and I was introduced in the Mess to the "Blue Nile", consisting of Drambhuie at 7 shillings and sixpence a half bottle, and lime, an insult to Scottish Malts, but a very pleasant after dinner *Digestif*. There was one exceedingly unpleasant character in the Mess, a Southern Irish born, Liaison Officer. He was so obnoxious that at the end of one boisterous Mess night, he was carried down to the river and, in full mess kit, thrown in. I was told that he had previously been on some diplomatic job in Tokyo and was kept under long time surveillance; when the balloon went up, he was promptly arrested, tried for espionage and shot... He had been transmitting direct to Tokyo. So we were told. All the photographic shops seemed to be owned by Jap civilians. This man seemed to spend a lot of time in these shops. Coincidence? I think not.

Every morning a naked tot would appear, seated on the back of a water buffalo, tether it by pushing a peg into the rough grass and disappear. This day the beast was grazing right in the middle of our projected line. Fortunately, while I was geeing myself up to move the beast, in his usual gallus way Sgt. Powner said, "Don't worry Sir, I'll soon move it for you", and set off.

These beasts are like putty in the hands of the smallest Malay mite, but dislike Europeans intensely—probably our strange smell, due to a different diet. The beast saw Powner appear, put its head down, snorted and charged, pulling out the peg on its tether with the greatest of ease, and we were treated to the sight of my sergeant going flat out, his knees hitting his chin, the buffalo's scimitar horns too close to his backside for comfort. Eventually the beast considered it had seen off its enemy, resumed grazing, but was no longer now on our line, so we could resume work after wiping the tears of laughter off our faces. Completely unfazed, Powner rejoined us, ever keeping a wary eye on and a safe distance from the beast.

The RAF treated us extremely well. The men were well housed and fed and I was welcomed into the Mess. The only snag was that the Wing Commander overheard me one evening telling someone that it was my birthday; he immediately ordered drinks all round to be charged to my Mess bill. Altogether they were a first-class crowd, something which did not apply to their aircraft, slow and long out of date. Extraordinary machines. Classed as fighters (by whom?), Wirraways, Brewster Buffaloes and armoured long nosed Blenheims, they were all obsolete or obsolescent. A Jap spotter plane started to appear about midday, very high up; one of these obsolescent "fighters" was then "scrambled." It was so slow that by the time it got high enough up, the Jap had gone. Not that our man could have done any damage in such a clapped out crate. Above a certain height, in some, the pilot had to pump oil into the engine by hand. Incredible but true. Presumably, he had then to decide whether to fire his gun or steer the plane. I was so involved in my work that it did not occur to me that our fighters did not provide any degree of protection. Something I learned very quickly, later on.

Our work went on successfully. We had one W.W.1. veteran in the Mess, very proud of his wings, which he was still entitled to wear. The Mess were getting a little tired of his tales of

"Derring Do" in W.W.1. and being told that we knew nothing about real war. I think it was out of pure mischief that the Wingco put him on as duty pilot while the rest were away on the other side of Malaya on a bombing exercise. When Pop remonstrated, he was reminded that he was wearing wings and drawing flying pay and felt it wiser not to continue the conversation. He was white as a sheet until our planes came back, and did not talk so much from then on about his exploits in W.W.1.

Finally the job was finished and I said goodbye to all my friends at the Aerodrome. I was sorry to learn later that the Wing had been sent to bomb the Japs landing on the east coast. The Japs waited until they returned and landed, carpet bombed the whole place, killing too many of my friends, destroying their aircraft and much of our work.

As I discovered later, the Jap drill was that 27 bombers would fly in formation; and when over the target, the leading pilot would fire a machine gun burst. This was the signal for all to release their bombs. Possibly there was a shortage of skilled pilots and the leader was German trained. It was called carpet bombing. Incidentally the bombers had an escort of 27 fighters above them, until the Japs realised that there was no opposition.

General Percival's (C.I.C. Malaya) defence plan for North Malaya included a pre-emptive strike by an armoured train across the border into Siam up to a railway junction called Hadji. There, about 40 miles north of the border, the East /West and North /South Lines of the Siamese railways intercepted; the idea was to seize control of that 40 miles from the frontier to Hadji, using my new friends, a Punjabi company, whom I was yet to meet, thus denying to the invaders that point of entry to western Malaya. An engine and a couple of carriages were lightly armoured and put on standby. There were four intermediate stations involved. The railway system was similar, on both sides of the border, to the old West Highland line, single track with passing places at the stations. The signalling was of the same complicated design. The driver of the down train had to await the arrival of the up train, or vice versa, at a station, holding a looped passing place, where each handed the other the heavy wire loop holding the key to the section of railway that they had just used and took on the new key for the track to their next station; this, I understood, worked the points and signals for their next piece of track. Padang Besar marked the railway crossing point of the border between Malaya and Siam. There was no road. The nearest road was some miles away through thick jungle.

I was therefore ordered to go by motorbike to Padang Besar, join a company of Punjabis guarding the frontier and be prepared to travel in the armoured train to Hadji, taking control of each of the four stations, in order to deny them to the Japs. i.e. 40 miles through very thick jungle. For this, I was to be provided with one infantry private, one Malayan railway signaller, and one of my own signalmen per station, i.e. one rifleman for defence, one real Signals lineman to deal with any faults on the lines, and one Railway signaller who understood and could work the esoteric signalling methods of the single track railway, for each station. How to mount a 24-hour guard over a railway station in thick jungle with one Punjabi soldier was not explained. It was a suicide mission. Nevertheless I was so Gung Ho that I was up for it. Fortunately I had not seen their idea of an armoured train, idiot that I was. Two further forms of signalling made for more complications, one a primitive and now obsolete sounder system working on back clicks for Morse communication between stations, the other operating the railway signals and points at the passing places. Teams of three were allotted to me for each station.

This then was the solution to the question, "What the Hell are we going to do with this troublesome subaltern now?" Put him in charge of the 40 miles of railway between the Siam/Malaya border and the East/West and North/South railway junction at Hadji, using the armoured train, which would go from Padang Besar, the frontier station cum Railway Halt, seize control of the 40 miles and the four stations as far as Hadji, thereby denying the Japs entry into Malaya. Send the maverick on that. That will quieten him down. There was no road at Padang Besar. The nearest road was miles away through extremely thick jungle.

The famous "Exercise", referred to above, was a washout. I learned later that I had taken the place in this section of an officer, named Dingley, whom the men detested. I did not care for him myself. He walked about with his nose in the air and liked to think big of himself; physically, he was the spitting image of my daughter Lee's brother-in-law. Probably that is why I instantly took a dislike against Des. Captain Mason, my senior officer, was first class and probably was relieved that his problem Subaltern was a couple of hundred miles away. We got on fine and I would not hear a word against him. I only found out seven years ago that the men had nicknamed me behind my back "the Topper". Actually a compliment, and not a reference to my attire at Fettes, I was later assured.

My C.O., I would like to think, detailed me for the job on the grounds that I was the best man for such an escapade of derring-do, but the truth probably was that two of us in one Independent Line Section at Corps HQ in K.L. were one too many and the troublesome one was the expendable one.

CHAPTER 11

PREPARING FOR THE REAL THING

LT. COL MILNER, my new C.O., a very wise man, had quickly tumbled to the fact that the best way to handle me was to keep me both busy and as far away from H.Q. as possible.

The result was, (see above) that I was detailed to seize and hold 40 miles of railway track, defend four stations and maintain 40 miles of overhead lines, not to mention handle 24/7 communications with H.Q. aided by this Fred Karno's army contraption. The whole scheme was crackpot; 40 miles of single track railway through the thickest tropical jungle; one real soldier and one halt/station every ten miles; no reason to believe that the locals would be friendly: Orientals are perhaps even more inclined than Europeans to sit on the fence before backing the winning side, though looking at the numbers of French who claimed from the safety of liberated France to have been in the Resistance, I am not so sure. A typical effort it was, from a High Command that thought the best way to defend Singapore was to have all but two of its heavy guns able only to fire out to sea.

So off I went on my motorbike, using the railway track to reach Padang Besar, the frontier station, inaccessible by road, to live with the Punjabi garrison and get to know them, before joining them in the armoured train with my troops!! For transport I had a 500 cc B S A. and to reach the garrison on this, I had to travel the last seven miles (I don't remember exactly but it seemed a long way), using the narrow laterite strip between the railway track and the monsoon drain, and similarly on the way back to base. The bridges (and there were many of them) were iron skeletons; if I looked down as I crossed, and generally speaking I preferred not to, it seemed a long way down, about 20 feet, to the rocky riverbed. I had to tooter across the skeleton bridges, with my heart in my mouth, on a series of single planks loosely laid on top of the railway sleepers.

To paint the picture properly, you must imagine the terrain. The jungle, through which the armoured train and I were to travel, was so thick that it felt as if you were riding down a lane completely curtained off by greenery on either side. The trace, (a technical term for the bit of land through which the railway ran), extended only a few yards either side of the track. At the edge of the jungle, Elephant grass grew thickly. The laterite strip, on which I had to ride, was very slippery, if wet, and bounded by the monsoon drain. I had to ride very carefully along narrow lengths of laterite, alternating with trips up to and along the planks across the bridges. To add to my feeling of well-being, I had to travel fully equipped with rifle, pistol, respirator in its case, pack and a full tank of petrol on my way to Padang Besar. It was not the easiest thing in the world to balance the machine, a BSA 500 cc side valve Gold Star full to the brim with petrol, dressed like a Christmas tree. A very eerie feeling it was, to be all on my own in the jungle with no chance of help in an emergency. My only companions were the Wah Wah monkeys (Gibbons?), whose ghoulish, mournful cries led me to expect to meet Dracula or Bram Stoker round the next bend, accompanied by the odd Monitor Lizard, about as big as a crocodile. I was always very glad to see the Atap huts of the Punjabi garrison looming in front of me.

My billet was with the Punjabi officers, a very friendly bunch, who welcomed me and invited me to join their small mess, which like all temporary buildings had its floor a foot or so above the ground to deter snakes, scorpions, termites, flash floods and so on. The worst plague were the centipedes, whose scales rattled as they walked over you; if jarred, they would dig their pointed feet into your skin and a nasty bout of poisoning would ensue, sending you to bed for a few days. Their poisoned legs curved backwards, so it was risky, but possible, to sweep them forward, but never back and then stamp on them with a heavy ammunition boot. Not an easy feat, if barefoot under a mosquito net. It was essential, too, before donning them, to shake your boots, upside down; scorpions found their toes an ideal dark cave to relax in. The space between the floor and the ground provided an excellent cellar for each individual officer's bottle of whisky which was kept to the right of your charpoy, very handy for reaching, from a reclining position. Each officer had his own bottle and the Punjabis made great play of each officer, marking his bottle's level with a pencil as he put it back under the floor. This, they said, was to deter this thieving Scot, who had been parachuted into their midst. I made an equally great fuss of marking my own bottle with all these Sassenachs about. They were an excellent bunch and we lived remarkably well in a sort of picnic fashion; they seemed to enjoy being on detachment as much as I did.

I had to go down to Aloh Star once a week to organize my men's rations and pay and receive any new orders. This made me quite blasé about my new transport arrangements, until one afternoon, as I was wending my way back to camp, I became aware of an elephant eyeing me from the edge of the jungle on my left. The grass was so high that all I could see were its ears flapping, its piggy eyes and its extended trunk and tusks pointing at me. That did it; the next thing I knew, I was on my back trapped in the monsoon drain with the bike on top of me. I was so angry with myself for being so stupid as to relax concentration, that I was not frightened. The elephant got the shock of its life and went crashing off through the jungle. Elephants are so big and have such thick hides that they make their own path; it only appears behind them. I have seen one go straight through a clump of bamboos the size of a tennis court, even one with thorns. As I lay there thinking about what to do, petrol started seeping out of the saddle-tank air vent and dripping into my boots. I was jammed tight with the weight of the machine on top of me and was slowly realising the extent of my predicament, when the Miracle happened. Round the corner came a station wagon, bringing the weekly rations for the Punjabis; a standard army issue, it had been fitted with railway type wheels and unbeknown to me, was the detachment's sole link with civilization.

They were most astonished to see a motorbike, wheels still spinning, upside down at the side of the track and stopped to investigate, only to be more astonished to find me jammed under it. However they hauled both of us out, loaded us into the back of the station wagon and took me back to camp. It really was nothing short of a miracle; they only did this trip twice a week; there was only one train a day each way and I had timed my journey to avoid it. Whether I would ever have got out on my own, I do not know; even if I had, I would have had a dicey walk of some miles; the petrol in my boots would not have helped.

Arriving at the camp, I retired, pretty shaken, to change my clothes, only to find my socks soaked in petrol, my feet from the shins down turning a fiery shade of red and starting to itch. In such a small and remote unit, there was no doctor and the only medic available was an Indian holding the grand sounding rank of Assistant Surgeon, but with limited qualifications. After inspecting my feet he took out a big bottle of iodine and a sort of paint brush. I was horrified and thanked him but sent him on his way, not a happy bunny; Iodine seemed to be his panacea. Not a lot of sleep that night. The top layer of skin proceeded to peel off and I was carted off barefoot next morning in the aforesaid station wagon to the 5th CCS (Casualty Clearing Station), halfway between Sungei Patani and Aloh Star, sorry to leave my new friends at Padang Besar but hoping to return after my feet had healed.

Meanwhile I lived the life of Riley in the C.C.S. Apart from my feet, I was in the best of health and much enjoyed the care and attention I received. Each morning at breakfast time, I was asked to choose my menu for the day, which duly arrived, a lot better cooked, than I had been accustomed to for some time. In addition some charming Memsahibs in India had raised a vast sum of money to provide extra comforts for us poor officers suffering in hospital. This ran to a fluid ounce of whisky and two bottles of Worthington's Pale Ale per day. The other three officers in the ward were suffering malaria, rigors etc. and could not avail themselves of this bounty and I was "reluctantly" prevailed upon to help them out. Fortunately there were only three of them; I tried manfully to cope but found the going tougher as the day wore on. It was real hard work, but I did my best, beginning to feel that I had finally arrived at my proper place in His Majesty's Forces and would have been very happy to have spent the rest of the war there. Then the Japs invaded and spoiled everything. That would be when my undying hatred for them started. Still there, always will be.

The Armoured Train, I heard later, pushed a few miles into Siam and retreated back to Malaya, half blowing up bridges and culverts as it went. After all the hurroosh, neither I nor my men even set foot in Siam. Typical! That set the pattern for the next ten weeks. Balls up after Balls up. Cloud Cuckoo Land planning and incompetent leadership. In the retreat, the bridges were never properly destroyed and proved little obstacle to the Japs. The real villain, in the piece, was the Civil Governor, Sir Shenton Thomas, so petrified of Communist infiltration of the

Chinese population that it never entered his bird brain that they were itching to take revenge for the genocide inflicted on their mainland brothers and sisters. They knew fine what would happen to them, if the Japs prevailed. It did. He obstructed all attempts to recruit local labour for mainland defence-construction for fear of alarming the civilian population; he had the ear of the Foreign and Colonial Office, which, prodded, I fear, by Commercial Interests, was more interested in Malaya's production than its defence. All in all, this was a recipe for disaster. Percival had a lot to answer for; he was promoted to C-in-C, due to having shown up well as a desk soldier during the evacuation at Dunkirk; this in spite of him never having been a fighting soldier, as far as I know. Otherwise he would have stood up to the Governor and sacked some of his own subordinates. I never even saw him; he kept himself safe inside the Battle Box in Singapore.

The two Fortress Commanders (Singapore & Penang) were well beyond their sell-by-date; the Aussie Divisional Commander was a paper bag showman, lucky not to have been court-martialled for desertion. He had previously managed to get himself on the front page of the local papers every week to show how well the Aussies were trained in jungle fighting; in fact, they fought for, at most, two to three days and then said, "No Fucking Air Cover, No Fucking Fight." In the last fortnight of the campaign, I saw and heard them, strolling through our lines, fully equipped and shouting the above. At the very end The C. in C. ordered a bombardment of the Japs by every available gun as a final flourish, or was it a devious plan to reduce the amount of ammo to be handed over? The Aussies refused to cooperate, due to having no General! He had flown back to Australia, leaving his whole Division leaderless and facing Surrender. So much for Waltzing Matilda! I gathered it was a Division recruited from the cities and very different from our imagined ANZACs from W.W.1. Our Corps General, Heath by name, was a fighting soldier with a good campaign record, even with only one arm functioning, in Eretria under his belt, but was heavily handicapped by the joint incompetence of the C-in-C and the meddling Governor.

On hearing the news of the Jap landing, my conscience and my sybaritic tendency had a short sharp discussion. Duty won hands down (I was all set to win the war, single handed). Accordingly I commandeered transport and headed for Aloh Star, where, to my surprise, Major the Hon. Patrick Malins (take away the a&t and he was well named) had arrived and was seated at a wooden table in a Corrugated Iron hut, banging his tin hat on the table and shouting down the phone to our C.O., Lt Col Milner, "By Christ Nig, you should hear the shit falling down here!" Nig was short for Nigger, a reference to our Colonel's complexion. I had never seen either of them in my life. I quickly deduced that Malins was a balloon, because the Japs had not even, at that moment, invaded Malaya and when they did, it was on the other side. His most revealing utterance to us later was to the effect that a short service Commission made for an enjoyable and easy career; what between cubbing, hunting, grouse and pheasant shooting, Christmas and cricketing leaves; then a few months soldiering could be endured. Yes, another recruit from the Beerage, not one it should be proud of. He grunted a greeting and ordered me to take my men up to the tiny native state of Perlis and stand by for orders, depending on the result of the battle of Jitra, where a fully equipped Gurkha Brigade would be thrown in to repel the invasion. No one at the top took the Japs seriously until it was too late. I never saw Malins again until just before the Surrender. He always made sure that he never moved far from the safety of Corps HQ.

CHAPTER 12

IS THAT IT?

YOU READ THAT WAR CONSISTS of long periods of boredom interspersed with short bursts of fear. I cannot say that that applied to me. My lot was kept hard at it from start to finish and generally speaking, we were so busy one way and another, that I had no time to be bored or frightened. Also, having the responsibility for the lives and welfare of my men meant that when I should have been frightened, I was concentrating so much on them that I had no time for fear. Also, I would have been black ashamed to show them anything but supreme confidence. Not that I did not take cover when necessary. The other side of the coin was that for the same reason, I did not realize we were doomed. I was always sure that there would be a successful counter attack. The penalty of a one-track mind!

The campaign started for me in the tiny wee native state of Perlis, whose canny Sultan, seeing the way the wind was blowing, barefaced and regardless of Diplomacy, rang our switchboard, got through and demanded a direct line to Emperor Hirohito in Tokyo, in order to negotiate a separate peace. I bet Hirohito would have been thrilled. It says a lot about the state of play in Malaya, that the Sultan was able to access Div. H.Q. telephone exchange.

Arriving in Perlis and finding our location, we stood about

in the heat for hours awaiting orders; none came. I have a vivid memory of the welcome arrival, just before dark, of 6-gallon containers of tea, bully beef stew and biscuits. I have had a soft spot for Army Compo tea ever since and make a similar brew with condensed milk from time to time. Nostalgia! Eventually I was told to stand my troops down and tell them to find somewhere to kip down for the night. There were my men and I, all ready and raring to go, but no orders anywhere, just chaos, confusion and rumours everywhere. I felt like the man who had taken his harp to the party but nobody asked him to play. Being excited about actually being in a real war at last, I slept the first night in the open, thinking to myself this is the real thing and to set a good example used the front doorstep of a planter's bungalow as my bed. He had wisely removed himself and was probably in Singapore by then, wangling a passage to Australia. Later in the campaign and more of a veteran, I would have enjoyed the comfort of his bed instead. The men dossed down as best they could, comforted by the rations and tea. I cannot really recommend a concrete doorstep as a bed, although I later slept many times on worse. I woke at dawn stiff and sore and when it looked as if no orders were in the offing and we were going to spend another night there, I had second thoughts and moved my lot into the Sultan's harem, temporarily bereft of its normal inhabitants, I assure you; they, clearly thinking that discretion was the better part of valour, had vanished. In daylight it did not live up to Hollywood's standards and was pretty tatty, but reasonably dry. A rather second rate Sultanate, I fear. Apart from the quite fine carpets on the floor and hangings on the walls, I did not think that it matched up to my conceptions of a Harem. Pretty tawdry and none too clean, it was also my first introduction to bedbugs. Later I was to get to know them only too well. Not to be recommended.

I was still awaiting orders, which regularly came and equally regularly were cancelled; we hung about for hours, until finally I was ordered to take my men south to the next line of defence and start my proper job of maintaining the lines from the fighting Brigade H.Q. to Advanced Div. H.Q. This was to be my job until the Surrender. The Battle of Jitra had resulted in a fiasco: Shenton Thomas had refused permission for enough local labourers to be recruited to construct the planned defences; the drainage in particular had not been completed and as a result the trenches were full of water; that on top of the chaos forced the Ghurkha Brigade (on whom the defence depended) to abandon their split new equipment and retreat for the first, but unfortunately, not the last time; a fatal pattern of regular retreats revealed itself. It goes without saying that the Japs had cut through the "impenetrable" jungle and reappeared behind us, "nae bother" and nae defence put up by us either, because our staff still maintained that the jungle was impenetrable. When it finally penetrated the bone-headed staff that the Japs were behind them, "Panic! Panic!" ensued and we were ordered to retreat back 30 miles to new Defensive Positions; this rigmarole was to be repeated again and again all the way to Singapore. We were now in full retreat. What a nightmare journey! Lashing rain; total blackout, a shattered brigade of Ghurkhas heading south, barefoot, their boots slung round their necks, all carrying their rifles, kukris and ammo, but nothing else and as usual grinning through their chain smoking. Thought briefly of acquiring a tommy gun through some form of barter. No joy. I might have known better. Chaos continued. Orders were followed by counter orders and followed by yet more conflicting orders until we did not know whether we were on our head or our heels. I think the night of that first retreat was one of the worst nights of my life.

Hardly had I got my men settled into our first billet in order to tackle our job, when I was ordered back to square one to rescue some vital equipment, probably the teleprinters, and their operators, abandoned by Div.Sigs. in the general panic. Black night had closed in; the rain was lashing down; any trucks unable to move in the mud were abandoned and pushed off the road anywhere; the retreat (rout) had started; a fatal pattern had revealed itself.

It was eerie driving north against the spate of traffic heading south: here being on a motorbike was a plus. The most worrying thing was that the Sappers were in the process of fitting demolition charges to the many bridges. This was scheduled to be carried out as soon as the rear guard had passed through. As I passed them, going the wrong way, the general reply to my pleadings to await my return with essential equipment was, "Tough, hope you can swim!" It was a nightmare ride in the dark and the lashing rain. I wasted no time and on reaching the abandoned vehicle, explained the urgency and no time was wasted in loading up. No sign of the Japs yet, but I could feel them all around me. Just as we were ready to go, a signalman pointed to a Singer Le Mans sports car abandoned outside a planter's bungalow and said, "What a pity to leave such a pretty wee thing for the Japs." I jumped in; the key was in the dashboard; petrol in the tank; she started instantly; shouting the immortal words "Follow me!" I roared off.

I later saw a Brit standing at the side of the road, a civilian, abandoned by whoever was supposed to pick him up. Gladly, he accepted the offer of a lift and I dropped him off at some *rendezvous* of his own. He was a surveyor and was working on plans for a new Aerodrome, hush hush, so I did not pursue the matter. Much to my amazement the same man appeared one day, post W.W.2., renting the office next to mine in Blysthwood Square. I think he must have got away on one of the escape boats. Odd sort of person with a social climber wife and an even odder son.

I then discovered that the Singer had a wireless set and on tuning in to the news was horrified to hear of the sinking of the *Prince of Wales* and the *Repulse* in the Gulf of Siam. I could not believe it. I did not want to believe it. I was told in the P.O.W. Camps by survivors, that after their ships were disabled and made powerless by the Kamikaze pilots, the Marines pushed their white hot gun turrets round by hand, and fired over open sights at the Jap Kamikaze planes. They downed many, but the loss of these two capital ships was catastrophic. It was criminal to send them without air cover into the Gulf of Siam; yet another sop to the Antipodeans. Once the Japs had taken out the airfields on the mainland and used them as bases for their aircraft, there was no chance for these ships to survive air attack.

Salvaged motor transport, heading south, met transport carrying reinforcements and ambulances heading north: all this on a not too broad road, with dispatch riders weaving in and out like sheepdogs. Chaos reigned. The skies rained too, not an intentional pun. We were really in the monsoon area and I don't think I was dry for weeks, except immediately after changing my clothes. It was bad enough for us; my men at least had trucks to sleep in, but it must have been pure hell for the P.B.I. The rain lashed down; the road was packed with vehicles and marching troops all fighting their way through unlit bullock carts and swarms of refugees heading for the jungle or anywhere, far enough away from the fighting. They carried all their transportable worldly goods on their heads, their backs or slung on bamboo poles fore and aft. With only one road and not too wide a one at that, you can imagine the chaos in the dark; monsoon downpour; convoys going both ways; marching troops trying to keep formation; motorbikes dashing up and down; lights down to a glimmer and in amongst them the wretched refugees, men, women and children, bewildered and frightened. I think that was one of the worst times of my life up to then. My life and all that I had previously held precious was crashing down about my ears. The British were retreating from the little bandy legged and bespectacled Japanese. I could not believe it. I refused to believe it, even although it hit me in the face. The whole campaign might well have been nipped in the bud, if orders had been given to the RAF to bomb the Jap transports while they were still a day's steaming time from Malaya instead of futile discussion whether we were in a war situation or not. Talk about the Kirk counting how many angels could dance on the point of a pin!

Realising that Jitra was a shambles and that we would have to retreat and regroup and that the campaign would take longer than I had thought, I quickly came to the conclusion that having a 500 c.c. BSA as my issue transport, meant that my kit, including my bottle of whisky, travelled separately in one of the trucks, not much cop in a monsoon. My liberated Singer Le Mans came to the rescue and served me well all the way; the B.S.A. was relegated to one of the Chevs. Miraculously, the Singer's canvas roof kept out the torrential rain and there was just enough room with the passenger seat folded forward for my valise to be unrolled full length and a mosquito net to be rigged up, providing a tolerable bed on the few occasions when I could not find more substantial accommodation. She was a joy to drive, small and light enough to be manhandled even in the thickest mud.

We were soon rocking along at 60 mph; the men, in a Chev were able to keep up; the road was clear by then, except for ambulances. Was I glad to see the bridges on my return journey! I knew that, if I got safely over the first, I was quids in: the sappers would never leave their own on the wrong side of a blown bridge. I then delivered the very relieved men and their equipment to Div. Sigs. and got cracking on my new job A quiet chat with and good advice from Vickers saw me with my half of the section setting up camp in a secluded spot, preferably an abandoned kampong, halfway between Adv. Div.H.Q. and the H.Q. of the Brigade fighting the Japs at that moment. There I teed into the main line connecting Advanced Div. H.Q. to the H.Q. of the fighting Brigade; sat a man listening 24/7 as they say nowadays; the moment he got silence either side, I took a team out to find and sort the fault, sometimes up to the front line. This was the pattern day or night, wet or dry. Corporals commanded each team; I Supervised and whistled up any stores or reinforcement needed.

Fordsons 15 cwts were invaluable; they were fast, worked well off the road, and could carry an awful lot more than their nominated load. My leading truck was so loaded with tools and equipment that there was no room for a lookout at the back; we depended on the follow up 15 cwt. truck to act as point, and any blast from its horn caused a swift swerve under the nearest trees, if we were lucky, otherwise a sudden stop and everybody out fast and into the nearest ditch or whatever cover. We got quite adept after the first time we got shot up. Fortunately, we were going so slowly that the Jap overshot; we learned fast. I led from the front and worked two squads, so that the men got some rest. I thrived on the adrenaline.

No squad ever went out on a job, but I was with them and stayed until the job was satisfactorily completed. I never touched my mess tin until I had seen my men fed. I never laid myself down at night until I had checked the security and seen that the men were bedded down. This may sound as a bit of self-promotion; it was however just simple man-management. I demanded and got 100 per cent from my men, because they knew that I would not ask them to do something I would not tackle myself and that they would be as well looked after as I could manage. Looking back, it was potential suicide, such a small unit and so isolated as we were. I was meticulous, however, about fixing my sentries; tents and vehicles were well camouflaged and I was in touch by phone. Actually the Japs were too concentrated on putting the wind up our staff to bother about a wee unit like ours.

I was very fortunate in my cook, Skillington by name. An absolute gem, he contributed greatly to the excellence of the feeding, so important to men doing hard physical work under pressure. At the drop of a hat and single-handed he could produce hot food and unlimited strong tea 24 hours a day. He never knew when a detachment would come in hungry and thirsty. As long as I provided the raw materials (with my unusual powers, I soon had the RIASC suppliers eating out of my hand; soap, cigarettes and razor blades worked wonders—he delivered the goods). A skinny wee soul with sloping shoulders, dowager's hump; not an ounce of fat on him; never up nor down; slow spoken, he got full marks from me. Before the war, he had made a living, peddling yeast and spices to remote farms all over the wilds of S. Yorkshire. Unfortunately I lost touch with him after the surrender. I hope he came through captivity all right. He was a survivor. I even landed him with extra customers by encouragingly the D.R.s of my old section to use our billet as a place where they could get fed, watered and even kip down on occasion. They were the only sure means of getting messages through, apart from the lines, which were permanently choked with priority messages. Vastly overworked they knew only too well that as soon as they reported in at either end they would be given another stack of deliveries to make. My billets were discreet and well positioned for them to take a breather. The D.R.s were truly remarkable men. Two come to mind. The first hit a water buffalo going flat out, the only speed he knew. The buffalo died, he went sailing through the air, landed on his face and chest. Some mess; he had to be shipped out and so missed the Prison Camp and perhaps had the best of the bargain; the other, (see above), came round a corner to see a column of wee Jap tanks heading straight at him, flattened himself on the saddle tank, turned up the taps and was through them before they could depress their guns and get him. Luck and quick thinking.

My successor in the Signal Office section was so desperate to get a decoration that he had no interest in his men's welfare and would have worked them till they dropped. These D.Rs. were the salt of the earth and it was madness to expect them to keep on driving flat out with no sleep or hot food. I knew every one of them and hoped that by looking after them I might save a few lives. They knew they could depend on my section. We would all have perjured our souls to give them some breathing space.

The Governor and the Commander in Chief share the blame for the disastrous campaign. The Governor was a total wet, so terrified of Chinese Communists that he never grasped the fact that the Chinese hated the Japs and were itching for any chance of revenge for the near genocide and worse that their kin on the mainland had suffered at the hands of the I.J.A. (Imperial Japanese Army) and knew only too well the fate that awaited them if the Japs won (it did), he would not accept their offer of armed help. His influence with the Foreign and Colonial Office in Whitehall, and through it to Churchill, rendered the gutless C-in-C Percival even more useless as a fighting soldier than he naturally was. The defences were never completed in Singapore or Jitra. His fault. He was a total disaster; apparently a good desk soldier in Whitehall; had made his name on the Admin side during the first flurry in France and Dunkirk, but was useless as a fighting General, and was quite unable to make decisions or to enforce any he did manage to make. He was no match for the waffling Governor, who could always claim he had the ear of His Majesty's Government. This could well have been yet another case of the civil servants of the Foreign and Colonial Office interfering to Britain's disadvantage. Margaret Thatcher would agree with that. On that occasion she would have been correct.

The Japs, after the Jitra debacle, disappeared into the still designated "impenetrable" jungle and reappeared behind rear Div. H.Q., let off a few rounds, and some firecrackers; the Staff promptly panicked and we were ordered south. This ploy was repeated time and time again. Thus the Japs simply went round our Division, by disappearing into the "impenetrable" jungle on our Eastern flank and turning it. This was their tactic throughout the campaign. Whenever they came up against any form of resolute defence, they went round it either by sea or through the so-called impenetrable jungle. Having got behind us they would noisily shoot up the rear. Our staff promptly panicked and withdrew the whole Division, 30 or 40 miles further south to a new defensive position; the Japs repeated the process. With hindsight it was pathetic. I was too busy to pay attention to anything except my job, keeping the lines open and my men as well fed and happy as possible. Any General worth his salt would have seen to it that the Jitra position was properly completed and rendered fit to withstand a siege, front, back, and sideways. The correct thing to do was to let the Japs encircle us and sit tight. Supply by air was in its infancy but something could have been arranged. This would have delayed the Japs long enough to have saved Java and the very real threat to Australia and New Zealand.

Having observed the behaviour of the (white) Dutch officers in various P.O.W. camps, I am not too sure of a successful outcome in this scenario, but it would have at least let 18th Division have sufficient time to land, get organised and really give the Japs a doing, instead of which, as happened, a fully equipped and trained modern Division was thrown away, just like the Ghurkha Brigade, many of the men never having landed their stores and equipment let alone fired a shot. The

Hurricanes, which arrived too late, would also then have had secure aerodromes and a chance to be really effective. But no, our staff had us leapfrogging at high speed down Malaya and the whole sad affair was wrapped up in ten short weeks. It was incredible. What was even more incredible was that Major General Murray Lyon, having made such a mess of the construction of the defences at Jitra and being responsible for the reporting and assessment of the disastrous Exercise, on which the whole landward defence of Western Malaya was founded, was relieved of his command and flown back to India, where, wait for it, he was appointed Chief Umpire of all the T.E.W.T.s and tactical exercises throughout the whole of India Command!! That really sums up the Indian Army outlook at the top. They were not fighting the last war, they were still fighting the Crimean War. Much of this passed me by; my nose was too close to the ground, trying to keep some sort of communications going, despite receiving contradictory orders regularly every hour on the hour.

Although I shall hate them to my dying day, I have to admit that the Japs were good jungle fighters. They did not need a supporting train of cooks and rations. As long as the Jap soldiers had a day's rice in their mess tins, designed for cooking over a fire anywhere; anything else they needed they just stole, including native clothing. To Europeans they could then pass as Chinese. One minute they were on foot, the next on stolen bicycles, silent and easily hidden in the jungle, until trouble passed by. They wore "Speedo" boots with canvas tops and heavy welded rubber soles each having a separated big toe, giving them extra purchase on slippery fallen trees in the jungle. Most importantly they were silent compared to our ammunition boots. This gave them the invaluable element of surprise. Thus equipped they could climb a tree in a trice: what could be more natural than a native up a palm tree cutting down coconuts? He could sit there and greet our unsuspecting troops passing under him with a wave; preferably in a Bren Carrier when a carefully placed handgrenade reduced the interior of the carrier to a rather disgusting thick tomato soup. The Carrier, better in the desert, was a light, fastish, open-topped, tracked cross-country vehicle, capable of transporting men and materials over rough ground; great fun to drive or to play at tanks in. It took some time for the P.B.I. to realize that real tanks did not come with a permanently open sunshine roof and the danger that that defect posed. It was a slow and painful learning process, in which a lot of good men got killed. Being surrounded by armour gave the men a false sense of security; unwittingly we made it easy all round for the Japs. Two or three of them in native dress, on bicycles, concealing a bundle of firecrackers and a tommy gun, could mingle with the fleeing refugees, get behind our lines, let off a few bursts and firecrackers, resulting in staff panic, and bingo we were another 30 miles nearer Singapore.

CHAPTER 13

THE CAMPAIGN 2

WE TRAVELLED in 3.15 cwt. Canadian built Fordsons, 2.30 cwt, 4-wheel drive Chevrolets, and a Malayan built five tonner. The latter I dared my men to allow off hard standing. It could bog itself at the drop of a hat like nobody's business. The Chevrolets were alleged to be able to carry only 30 cwt.s, even though their tare was more than 50 cwt.s. They were marvellous machines, built like battleships, their pulling power in the thickest and slimiest mud remarkable. I became very popular as the proprietor of far superior extractors than the L.A.D. lightweight machines. One particular morning sticks in my mind. A 25-pounder field gun, gun-quad and limber had been put under some big rubber trees for protection; it had rained hard over night. Even the GunQuad, 4-wheel drive and all, could not get itself out, let alone pull out the gun and limber. I was called on, took a Chev and a wire hawser, told the driver on no account to take the Chev off the metalled road, ran the hawser out hooked on to the GunQuad set up and winched them out *seriatim*. I was delighted that Signals had helped out the Gunners, who had proved themselves true pros as long as they had a field of vision. Not often so, in jungle conditions. The five-ton Ford was the only one with a proper windscreen, the others had canvas dodgers. Not much chance of a driver falling asleep at the wheel there, particularly in a monsoon.

The Chevs indeed were so heavy that, on an exercise before the campaign, a driver misjudged the width of the road while driving through mangrove swamps and went down four feet into the swamp. The L.A.D. truck was summoned, but instead of winching the Chevrolet out, it was pulled over the top of its own stilts and nearly joined the Chevrolet. I had to go back to camp for TROWELLA winches and ground anchors. These latter consisted of heavy lengths of steel semi-circular sections drilled with holes for long spikes, which were driven by a heavy hammer deep into the ground. Two of them at each end, these ground anchors were attached by chains to the winch and its hand-operated rocking bar; chains were attached fore and aft to the Chevrolet and inch by inch, link by link, each end of the truck in turn was laboriously winched up enough to slip a sleeper under the chassis, until the truck was level with the road and then to winch it across the road. This all took about 36 hours and I kept the guilty driver there the whole time and made him take a little more than his fair share of rocking the winch lever. A tedious job and very exhausting; I was extremely angry; it was a lesson for every one of my drivers; it never happened again.

During my time in the Signal Office section I had tried out (see above) the 15-hundredweight trucks under jungle and plantation conditions and had a good idea of what they could and could not do. As you may have guessed, the first thing the drivers did at the commencement of hostilities was to remove the governor from the engines and let rip. These governors were designed to regulate a top speed of 50 mph and before hostilities, were inspected regularly by the L.A.D., much to the disgust of my drivers. Their powerful engines, once liberated, could propel these vehicles at some speed. Even the Chevs, handicapped by 4-wheel drive, could keep up a steady 60 to 65 mph. It took them a wee while to get wound up, but once there, they could keep rocking along for hours on end. This was all to the good because we often had very little time to move from one position to the next and set up our intercept station. That did not mean that the section did not look after itself. Any edible fresh meat seen from the cab would bring the Chevrolet to an abrupt stop, a leap from the cab by the Navigator, a few squawks or grunts and there was tomorrow's evening meal.

There was a fair bit of what was, euphemistically, called liberation, that went on. Once we realised we were going backwards, it seemed stupid to leave anything behind that could be useful to the Japs. The high spot for me was following one of my Chevs going like the clappers, with four turkeys gobbling at me over the back cape. Thus my section got their traditional Christmas dinner. Where the birds came from I do not know. I knew better than to enquire, but one of my linesmen, a villainous looking Lancastrian by the name of Scrafton, was undoubtedly at the bottom of it. If he has kept out of jail in civvy street, he must be a reformed character. A handy man in the conditions then obtaining, he was also an excellent linesman, fearless, cheerful at all times with that peculiar pessimistic humour of his type, a rogue for sure, but a very likeable one. I found out, only recently, that he helped one of my section during the worst of the Speedo on the Railway into a quieter squad at a fraught time and doubtless saved his life. I only heard this from Neville recently. I was on the phone to him two days ago (30/10/2010). He was pretty far down at that time. Needless to say we inspected a few abandoned native stores as we retreated, to make sure nothing of any value was being left for the Japs, a case or two of Tiger beer for example. Everything was signed for. I have often wondered since, how all the chits signed by a certain lieutenant Joe Soap, Scots Guards, were dealt with after the re-occupation. I was determined that my men would live as well as I could manage. Provided that the lines were okay, the sentries in position, and the men were relaxing, we would have a singsong on the odd night with a bottle of beer a man. I learned some new songs and enjoyed many of the old sentimental ballads which Bette and I had listened to in the old Empress Theatre at St George's Cross. ''Twas an old Australian homestead with the roses round the door... She's an angel of the Great White Way... Danny Boy' and so on. These would be punctuated by 'The quartermaster's stores, My Brother Sylvestre' and a few not very suitable for print. The out and out favourite, sung with much feeling, was the one that began, 'The troopship was leaving Bombay bound for old Blighty Shore...' It was great therapy for all of us, because when the lines were down we worked flat out regardless of time, day, night, or enemy action.

My job never altered. Accordingly I followed Vicker's good advice and made full use of my company commander's powers, and struck up a strong line with the R.I.A.S.C., the Royal Indian Army Supply Corps so that my lot fed as well if not better than anyone else. I soon discovered that razor blades and cigarettes could be swapped for the little extras that made life a bit more bearable.

The Japs just could not believe their luck. Heavily outnumbered, all they needed to do was to outflank us either through the "impenetrable" jungle or by sea, loose off a few firecrackers and rounds behind Rear Div. H.Q., and panic ensued and down the road we were sent. The sad truth was that the Japs bothered not a whit about movement through the jungle, equipped as they were with Speedo boots and an issue mess tin, full of the day's rice and capable of being boiled up over any fire; they were totally independent. They were also Orientals and dressed as locals mounted on purloined bicycles, they could pass for Chinese. Thus equipped they could filter through our lines and cause any damage they wanted. Apart from the Argylls, no unit had seriously practised any sort of jungle fighting. We were inferior in Malaya and it was our own fault. The Aussies in particular talked big and managed to get plenty of front page publicity in the local paper; this might look like the real thing but it was not; it was bags of bullshit and useless when the chips were down.

The Argylls, the 93rd were commanded by Lt. Col "Busty" Stewart, a real soldier. If we had had a few more like him, the campaign might well have ended very differently. He was hard on his men but absolutely fair, and determined that his Battalion would be capable of handling anything. A full Division defended the west coast, another the east; both fell back in retreat. The A&S, only a single Battalion, held the Grik Road, a minor road that crossed the middle of the Siam/Malaya border, for more than a week against three Jap Regiments, each consisting of three Battalions; a fresh Regiment each day was thrown at them; the Argylls were only withdrawn when their flanks on both sides were badly exposed by the retreat of the Divisions. Busty had reconnoitred the position and made sure everything was the way he wanted. Such a contrast to the boneheads either side of him.

Someone must have noticed. Following the debacle/disaster of Jitra, heads started to roll. The first to go was our General and guess what? He was not sacked or court martialled. Jitra, his choice I presume, had not been properly completed. I was told that what trenches had been started were full of water. It is incredible that his reward for a total cockup was (see above). Brigadier Paris, who had a bit to do with the Argylls's magnificent defence of the Grik road, was promoted to Major General and appointed to the Command of 11th Indian Div, but on second thoughts was regarded as so valuable, that he was brought back to India to brief the staff about what went wrong in Malaya. Busty Stewart replaced him first as Brigadier, then Divisional Commander, but was also recalled to India for the same reason. Things were chaotic, but that is how it was, as I remember. I was kept pretty busy at the time.

By that time we were in full retreat and I had lost interest in anything outside my little circle. Either I was too busy and or had my head in a bucket of sand. I honestly believed that we would win right up to the end and even then was sure we would not be abandoned. What a mug I was! It would not have been so bad if we had retreated yard by yard or even mile by mile, but it was 30 miles or more at a time. The jungle was the problem; our troops, saving the Argylls and the Ghurkhas had no idea how to handle it; our staff was defeatist and retreatist.

We actually did make a stand in the tin dredging area between Tapar and Kampar. No jungle, but open ground. Our Gunners and Infantry made hay with the Japs and we held them off for a week. I got optimistic. In the open we were more than a match for them.

The Japs had, of course, overrun Penang, where the hopeless staff, still living in the previous century, had not checked that their orders to destroy all craft had been properly carried out. So the Japs, having failed to beat us in open country, found a free flotilla of boats, unscuttled and launched a seaborne invasion, landing behind our lines at Telok Anson. All we had, to defend Telok Anson, where the Jap makeshift assault craft landed, was a half battery of Malay Volunteers (our TA equivalent but quite a bit older and armed with W.W.1. popguns). They were scratch troops at best and were overwhelmed; no disgrace to them, but completely on the Staff, which moved us back again. Such a pity. Such a wasted opportunity. I blame Percival, C-in C Malaya, and Shenton Thomas. Percival may have been a good desk staff officer over France and Dunkirk; defeat and evacuation were hardly the best psychological training for positive action in Malaya. I admit that this is all written with hindsight. At the time I was too preoccupied to think about anything other than the job in hand and seeing that my men were as well fed and housed as possible. It is possibly impertinent for a mere subaltern to suggest that that was the moment when Britain lost her Empire, but perhaps it is not such a fanciful thought. Our bold staff instead of standing fast, and making the Japs attack on ground of our choosing, retreated, yet again, to a position south of Telok Anson. Things had reached the stage that, when the order was given ("This position is to be defended to the last man and the last round"), we kept everything packed for a swift getaway. We needed to move fast to create and maintain the vital communications at the new defensive position. If we only had stayed where we were, the campaign could have been extended long enough to let the Dutch defences do their job in Sumatra and Java. That is, assuming that they wanted to. Doubtful! The two main problems out East were that vast sums of money were being made out of Rubber and Tin. The civilians were dead against anything that would interfere with their profits. The other was Sir Shenton Thomas, the Governor of the Straits Settlements of Malaya. He, unfortunately, had a direct link to the Foreign and Colonial Office and the Cabinet through its Secretary (see above). Capitalism interfering with Defence is fatal in wartime. I hold the Governor equally to blame with our Divisional Commander for the unfinished defences at Jitra. He made it almost impossible to obtain civilians to work on the defences (you cannot expect white soldiers to navvy on the Equator, when a large native labour force was available, can you?). Busty saw to it that his men could and did. Apologies for the repetition, but I am still very bitter. The Governor obviously had the ear of someone who had influence with Churchill, whose mind would be wholly concentrated on the defence of the U.K. That was the time when Britain stood alone in Europe against the Nazis, and there were enough foreign Royals in and around London to staff a munitions factory. My king, George V1, deserves more credit than history has given him. Strong pressure was put on him to remove himself and his family to Canada. He refused point blank. The Queen got the credit, but I think he was a good king and a man of principle. I was also told that Churchill practically had to handcuff him to stop him from landing in France in the early days of our (later) invasion. Not always the easiest of men, he knew his duty, did it and cared deeply about the welfare of his armed forces.

It was unfortunate too for us that General Percival had been appointed Commander in Chief Malaya for the reasons given above. A good desk soldier, etc.

Our Corps Commander Lt. General Heath was a real fighting soldier. Sadly the only battle he had any say about was the one that we were winning until Telok Anson, and I suspect that he wanted to stay and sit it out. I heard him address us, withered arm and all and was impressed. He had had a good record of success in Eritrea and Abyssinia. Pity that he never got his head. In overall command of the Far East was Alexander, whom I saw once steaming by in a staff car. He returned my salute but did not look a happy man. He must have known we were doomed, even as he was going into "the last round and the last man" routine.

My half section and I did our job to the best of our ability throughout the campaign. I received no criticism ever. I was proud of my team. Amongst my lot I had some rogues, I must admit—but they were the salt of the earth as far as I was concerned. I think that the kingpin was Scrafton; he must have been a poacher by trade. He rode beside the driver. His eyes swept the ground for anything living and edible; he would shout the driver to stop, leap out and return with the next day's dinner. Neville is a couple of years older than I and was with Jim Finlay and me in the 15 cwt, crossing the Causeway at the end and as far as I know is the only one out of my lot, left today (14/5/09).

At first, I was annoyed about my job, because the Div. Sigs. had a cable section of its own, but I soon realised the plusses of independence. I never saw my C.O., quite understandable, I never saw my O.C, incredible, pure cowardice or self-preservation to be kind and I only saw my ex-C.O. for whom I was working again, once before the surrender. I had for some reason to meet with him at a planter's bungalow; an air raid started, not terribly near. However he instantly fell flat and tried to insert his head in the drain under the front step. Even if he had taken off his tin hat, he still could not have made it—I found myself talking to his ample posterior as it waved about while he tried to force his head into the drain! Not too bad a bloke, but to be asked pointedly by the General at a Staff meeting, why it was that he could only be seen at Advanced Div at night when there were no Jap planes about! I would have been black affronted. He just smiled, I was told.

He was a competent peacetime soldier, but real live war was definitely not in the contract when he applied for a Commission. However, in his favour, he left me alone to get on with my work. Major Vickers, who had brought us out to Malaya, was completely different; I would have volunteered to serve under him anywhere. Many a good piece of advice he gave me; he would appear silently round a corner while we were sorting a fault, not to criticize but to help. A quiet man, fearless, knowledgeable and very competent, he was the very best type of regular officer. It was a real tragedy that he did not survive captivity. I never saw my O.C. after the Crazy Gang farce on the first day of the campaign, until the Surrender. Once I had been seconded to assist Div. Sigs, he washed his hands of me. I was too near the sharp end for his liking. He claimed that the administration of his company kept him at base, nice, comfortable and of course safe!

There was a busy crossroads in the lower half of Malaya, and the telephone pole was situated on top of a kind of raised island in the middle carrying lines four ways, leaving four little gushets.

The island formed a raised star and, unusually, was in open country. I found a cat's cradle of twisted wires and cables. It took some sorting out. Accordingly I sent the trucks back down the road to get under some trees. We set to, to sort out the faults; we had just got stuck in when, "Lo and Behold", one of these little spotters arrived and decided to have a go. You could hardly call it hide and seek, there was nowhere to hide. We did not take much seeking; he could see us only too plainly. What saved us was that he was slow and we could see the direction he was coming from, and he tried all of them. We could then scuttle round the vees and take shelter. It was a distinctly hairy quarter of an hour until he started to run out of fuel. I have no doubt that the pilot thought it very funny to see us scuttling around. We did not see the joke till much later. We sure wasted no time in sorting the faults and were pretty pleased to get back into the anonymity of the trees. With air supremacy these little spotter planes patrolled with impunity and at such low levels that, due to the canopy of trees, while you could hear them it was difficult to see them until they were upon you.

The Japs clearly thought that this pole had some strategic value and gave it a torrid time. We, therefore, spent time, every day, sorting out the tangle of wires. As it was very exposed, our trucks were kept hidden under trees, further away. The Jap spotter plane, unable to find the trucks, concentrated on us, who were heavily occupied in the open. Fortunately the spotter plane was pretty slow, so most days we had a game of musical chairs. We spent a fair bit of time jumping from gushet to gushet and getting a little work done in between times. Musical Chairs with a vengeance! This must have exasperated the Japs, because they started sending five planes at a time to do a sort of mini-pattern bombing. How none of us were wounded I do not understand, except that their pilots were poor. The wires and cables took a terrible pounding and we seemed to be living permanently at that crossroads.

I can only guess at the reason, but probably, because I had complained at the constant harassment, some real Mobile 3.7 A.A. arrived overnight. They were veterans of the London Blitz and knew their stuff. The five Japs came over as before, thinking their only opposition were the customary Bofors, their tracer pattern pretty but their range short and ineffective. The Japs got the shock of their lives. The London lot downed four before the fifth hightailed it for home. We cheered them to the echo; it was the first aerial success we had seen. These men were no amateurs. That was a wonderful sight and the only time I saw the Japs get hammered and knew that it was true, because I saw it with my own eyes. The sequel came the next day, when back they came *en masse* for their revenge and pattern bombed the site from a great height. To do this they came over, 27 in formation, and when over target, the leading pilot let off a burst from his machine guns and the whole lot let go everything. I took this to be a sign of a lack of training in their pilots. We were told, true or false, that the pilot of the leading plane was always a German veteran of the Blitz. The A.A. battery, of course, had moved; they were not called mobile for nothing. It did us so much good to see real professionals at work and we set to, to sort a tangle of twisted wires and cables in good heart. The 27 Japs had pattern bombed all around and left us a right mess to clear up. When I heard the noise and realised the number of planes, I pushed my lot a couple of miles down the road and got us all under cover until the Japs had shot their load and turned for home.

Life went on relentlessly 24/7 as they say nowadays. One night we were sorting a break in pitch black darkness, when a tropical storm lit up the sky and Wattie Blue, an ex-Glasgow Corporation electrician who was sorting the joint, levitated a couple of feet off the ground; the lightning must have struck the cable somewhere close. He did not seem to see the joke as funny as we did. First class craftsman, he survived and returned to Glasgow, but died a good few years ago. Another time, later, the same Wattie was up an iron pole in Singapore, (the termites were death on wood), ignorant of the fact that there was a 3.7 static A.A. gun a few feet over his head. A Jap plane came within range; the breech was slammed shut with an enormous clang as if a Giant's oven door was being slammed shut, followed closely by the gun firing. I never saw a man come down a pole so fast. We thought it screamingly funny; he did not. Life went on, too busy to think about anything but work; the closer we got to Singapore, the more intense the bombing, and the more work for us.

Our Corps Commander Lt. General Heath was a real fighting soldier. My half section did our job to the best of our ability throughout the campaign. I received no criticism ever. I was proud of my team. I had for transport in addition to my 15cwts, a Malay built Ford 5 tonner, which I daren't let off hard standing. Good for the men to keep their kit in and sleep in, in emergencies, otherwise useless.

By the way, according to the Intelligence Corps, we were not to worry because the Japs had no tanks and there was no need to guard against them. Tell that to the Argylls at Slim River. They had been withdrawn from the Grik Road, flanks too exposed by the retreat of the Divisions either side of them. In order to join the main body they were relaxing, waiting for orders, when the Jap tanks attacked. Effectively we had no defence against tanks. Of course, they did not exist!! Infantry battalions were equipped with the odd Pyat antitank rifle. This had to be fired with the soldier prone on the ground. It fired a .5 inch bullet and each round was reputed to result in the soldier being shifted a foot backward by the recoil. There were also a few primitive two-pounder antitank guns. The net result was no damage to the armour; the little shells just bounced off. By the Grace of God the tanks were through the Argylls before they tumbled to the onslaught. Otherwise there would have been mayhem. As it was, the battalion found themselves behind the Jap advance and had to scatter through the jungle; some finished up prisoners in K.L.; others had to find a way through the jungle and get round the Jap front line. Not happy bunnies were they. I have to agree with their opinion of the Intelligence Corps. Unreliable is the politest word to use. The name Intelligence was a misnomer, if I ever saw one.

A tremendous act of bravery then ensued, I was told. The Adjutant and Battery Sergeant Major of the 25-pounder battery, which was resting at the side of the road, unhitched the limber of one of their guns; the GunQuad, swung the gun round, opened fire over open sights and knocked out the lead tank; this stopped the column in its tracks (no joke intended) as the tanks dared not get off the road; the monsoon ditches were too deep and full of water. A lot of lives and possibly the whole Division were saved by this action. The tanks would have broken clean through and caused tremendous death and destruction. On this subject, I was told that an Argyll shot down a Jap spotter plane with his Pyat antitank rifle, broke his shoulder in so doing and was decorated with a Military Medal. Deservedly so. An incredible feat standing up to fire that monstrosity.

We had enough Generals to start a platoon. First Percival C-in C, a full General, two Corps Commanders, Lt. Generals, three Divisional Commanders, Major Generals, two Fortress Commanders, Brigadier Generals, the R.A. and six Brigades with Brigadiers and all the Aussies; probably many more that I did not know about, I could not count them all. They all required staff. As for the Quartermaster's stores, here we were back to Napoleonic standards. I was entitled to a Tommy gun and having seen them used in many American Gangster Films, lusted after mine. Could I get it issued? Not on your life. I finally got hold of one on my one day off by bearding the Singapore stores in person. I felt that I was back in the Napoleonic era. Not only did I have to wake up the store man, sign for it and for the ammunition as well, although at the time the Japs were less than 50 miles from the Causeway and advancing. I have to admit that I found the gun a bit of a let-down. It had more sharp edges than you would believe. Finding this out pretty quickly, I appointed a bodyguard, who was so pleased to have the honour of carrying it, that he discounted the inevitable bruises and abrasions. Tropical kit was thin and gave little protection.

The main threat came from the air. The Japs obliterated our antiquated fighter/bomber squadrons, the first day, by waiting for them to land and refuel and then pattern bombing the aerodromes. Their little spotter planes could fly anywhere unmolested, strafe any small groups of men and transport and suss out our positions for their bombers. Accordingly, I had to select my bases, near enough to the main cables, but far enough from the road and with good tree cover for concealment. Cooking fires had to be under a really big tree so that practically no smoke was visible. On one occasion this worked against us. A small Indian Army convoy was being shot up by one of these spotters; they abandoned their vehicles opposite our camp and dived smartly into our trees. This was annoying and I had to get my men further back and leave the unfortunate operator listening at his post. I was none too pleased either as I had been snatching a bit of kip after a busy night, when the fracas broke out. I can tell you that being strafed in your underpants is bad enough but not having your boots on is the very end. I really felt extremely vulnerable. Having moved my men to safety, I thought "to Hell with it, I'm going to die with my boots on at least", donned them and exiting from my tent started to have wild ideas about organizing my men to give the Jap a salvo or two. He was systematically flying low up and down the road, strafing the Indian's parked vehicles. I noticed that the rear vehicle had a Bren gun mounted and I raged around looking for the Havildar (sergeant), found him buried deep in a ditch and ordered him out to man the Bren with me. I fairly regretted not having paid attention at O.C.T.U. for I had no idea how to work the thing. He was glued to the bottom of the ditch and by the time I had drawn my revolver and told him that it was either the Bren or him, the Jap had completed three runs each way and gone back to refuel.

When my back was turned, trying to spot the plane, the Havildar had scuttled off with his men and I never saw him again. I then had a look at myself and saw that I was fully stripped for action, socks, boots, underpants and nothing else. I must have picked up my pistol before leaving my tent. The troops fairly enjoyed that and it took me a long time to live it down. My language was reported to be vintage. What was lucky was that the Jap had no bombs left. What was irritating was that we had been sussed; some of his mates would be back directly; we had to pack up, move and find another billet quickly.

As far as my men and I were concerned, we were hard at it all the time, day or night. The Japs had the aerodromes and the planes, could bomb and machine gun at will; one fault in the lines followed another; except generally at nights, when the Japs' lack of training in night flying gave us some chance to relax. Some Hurricanes arrived (I found out post-war that my aunt Rena in the U.S. had been part of an organisation raising money for fighters for the Battle of Britain and raised the money for a Hurricane, which was named after me. I never found out what happened to it); the Hurricanes did a fair bit of damage to the Japs, who put over their groups of 27 bombers, protected from above by an equal number of fighters.

The Hurricanes were unfortunately too few and arrived much

too late. Incredibly the most successful planes which we had were the Walruses or Stringbags, as we called them. I remember them as ancient biplanes with pusher propellers. They were so slow and flew so low that the Japs found them very hard to shoot down. We saw them occasionally, literally staggering through the air on a mission, like a boy's box kite trying to rise in a wind. As they wavered along you would think that a strong wind would halt them in their tracks. I take my hat off to the pilots. The planes were of the same vintage as the Argyll's armoured cars. Apart from the air, the main threat to my section was the danger of ambush on the deserted roads. If the lines were down, there was no time to wait for the protection of an armed convoy. Many times we would have no troops within ten miles of our little billet. With hindsight, I wonder if that, strangely enough, was an unexpected protection; we were close to the road but far enough from the action; the Jap patrols probably used the jungle tracks.

One long stretch of road near Gemas was reputed to be partially under Jap control and you can bet that we did not loiter, either when working or travelling on it. I believe a few convoys got shot up; they made the mistake of stopping to move an apparently fallen tree. It was an old trick and they should not have fallen for it. We stopped for nothing and no one. The main roads, except for the one bit from Tapah to Kampar, were bounded by jungle or mature rubber trees. In either case a few yards off the road and you were on your own. My drivers were not encouraged to dawdle; petrol was plentiful.

Life went on relentlessly. The Scots and Northern English seemed to gravitate to me. This suited me fine. I think I must have had a guardian angel, the same one who saw to it that the charges were not properly set on the first bridge after Jitra. If they had gone off first time I would have had to swim for it and my career could have ended rather suddenly. I had no time to ponder. The isolated life suited me and my section fine, very different from working in a Signal Office at Div HQ under the eyes of a C.O. and O.C. and no control over rations or accommodation. Working independently, I could always wangle better and more food for my men. As long as the lines were maintained, I was my own master and my methods were never questioned; they worked.

Life went on, we were too busy to think about anything but work; the closer we got to the Causeway, the more intense the bombing, resulting in us just snatching a bit of kip as and when. Adrenaline and mugs of hot sweet tea were largely the fuel that I ran on. A 2nd Lt was the bottom of the heap, but living and working so closely with the men, my thoughts were concentrated solely on keeping the lines working and my men safe and as well fed and housed as possible. I can put my hand on my heart and say that I never was afraid for myself; not that I did not dive for cover, when necessary. Just the men and the work came first. I found it interesting watching how men reacted under active service conditions. I lost my big sergeant early on; he was far too valuable back at Corps HQ. The substantive NCOs, good peacetime soldiers, were often found to be wanting when the chips were down and in some cases had to be busted. They had missed the fine print, when they enlisted, the bit about live ammunition travelling the wrong way. I soon found myself working with Acting Lance Sergeants and Corporals, often promoted in the field. I was very fortunate in my bunch, largely composed of rogues who could look after themselves extremely well. Fulton (strangely, he turned out to be the favourite uncle of the anaesthetist who presided over the repair to my broken leg years later) and Finlay, already recommended for promotion, were no rogues but luckily for me first class Post Office engineers and could handle the men, who respected them for their technical ability and leadership qualities. Both were always well turned out, clean and ready to go. The system worked pretty well. The men soon got the hang of it and faults were dealt with expeditiously. No chance of hustling them; they were proud of their tradesmanship; every job was done just right. Mostly it was all routine stuff. I had a really good team; our work was never criticised. When the lines were down we worked flat out regardless of time, day or night, or enemy action. Finlay I lost touch with twice post-war. Both times he found me in the phone book and rang me up; once he and his charming wife came to Winchester Drive, but we were both so engrossed, at the time, in our careers and raising a family that we did not meet again until after retirement, when we had a coffee, a bun and a chat once a month until he died. He was the one who told me that the men referred to me as "the Topper", not a reference to my school regalia, but a genuine compliment. I had no idea! I thought I knew everything that was going on in my section, but clearly did not.

Finlay had a most remarkable tale to tell. We got split up after the completion of the Railway and he was one of the unlucky ones, who were shipped in rust buckets to Japan. His ship was carrying copper ore, a dense cargo, which left room above in the hold for rough sleeping platforms to be erected for the POWs, who were packed in like sardines with only one ladder to the deck per hold; access very restricted. The rectangular portholes were crisscrossed with wooden battens to prevent escape. Once down in the hold, Finlay eyed the setup, realised that, in the event of being torpedoed, there would be such a scrum round the ladder that few, if any, would get out onto the deck and picked a bed-space against the hull near to the biggest hole in the wooden gratings covering the long porthole. He decided that his only chance, if torpedoed, was to force his way through the hole and swim for it before the undertow pulled him down. This in fact he did and came to, to find he was floating in a red sea of copper-ore soup. Seeing land at a distance he swam for it, was picked up and taken to Formosa in another rust bucket and spent the rest of the war as a gardener. It took a while for the skin to grow back on his shoulders and hips. A remarkable story from a remarkable man and a good friend, always intensely loyal.

When we got into Johore, things looked really bad; ambushes were the main problem; I did not need to tell my driver not to loiter. My policy was to stop for no one and no thing. Better to chance a puncture than end up dead. Quite hairy! A strange feeling it was, beetling along a straight road, lined with huge rubber trees either side, totally on our own.

I do not know if it was the C.S.O. before whom I had been paraded for tiffin in Singapore, but somebody high up had a thing about telephone exchanges, wee upright wooden contraptions with jacks and sockets and needing an operator to make the connection. Quite a few I had had to rescue on the way down Malaya. Where they ended up I have no idea. The last one sticks in my mind. It was in a village called Batu Pahat, which was bisected by a medium sized river. The road must have gone straight through on a water splash. The Japs were on the other side, mortaring any movement on our side. I decided to do the job between midnight and 2 a.m. The exchange was in a little concrete building on the right-hand side of the road. We crept down the road as silently as possible, moving only when the moon was obscured by clouds, sneaked off the road and put our vehicle behind the exchange, got out, opened the door, slipped in and shut it. Even that brief glimmer of light provoked a salvo from the Jap mortar; luckily well past us. There was one sentry inside, large, bucolic and English. While my men were wasting no time disconnecting everything in sight, the sentry's eyes were glued on the little .22 pistol on my belt which I had liberated from some police station, where I had been evacuating yet another exchange on the way down Malaya. It was nice and light. Pretty too, I quite fancied it. I handed it to him, warning him that there was not a round in the first chamber. The great gormless git took it, pulled the trigger twice and the live bullet from the second chamber did a wall of death, ricocheting off the walls of the shack. How many circuits, I do not remember. Seemed a lot to me. We all looked as white as sheets. Amazingly no one was wounded, but it was quite exciting and my men said that they had never heard me quite so fluent. I hustled the exchange and my men into the 15cwt. We sat there, with the engine ticking over, waiting for a decent sized cloud to blank out the moon, when we high-tailed it out and headed for the dump. That would be where I learned to leave my car always pointing outwards. Quick Getaway! The mortar cannot have had the range; we could hear the explosions behind us. It surely helped the driver to keep his right foot to the floor. Lucky!

My last job on the mainland was to provide and maintain the lines for the evacuation across the Causeway to the island of Singapore. The Argylls were to be the rearguard and I considered it a privilege to be working with them. All I had was a skeleton squad of a driver and a couple of linesmen. Looking back, I realise that the lines were the only communication across the Causeway and in one sense being given this job was a compliment, in another it proved that we were regarded as expendable. It was just another job as far as I was concerned, but it was quite a thought to see what was left of a complete Division passing through and across the Causeway. We soon got the lines run out and connected. Rearguard H.Q. was in a bungalow overlooking the Causeway and I got my men settled and just sat and waited for problems; none happened. Orders were that we should have packed up and crossed after sunset, but instead we spent the night on edge waiting for the missing Indian Brigade to appear, one of the two half trained jungly ones previously referred to. To this day I have no certain idea what happened to it, but suspect it went over to the I.J.A. The fact of no communication indicated that they were completely lost in the jungle somewhere and had vanished off the face of the map. They were just thrown away like the *Prince of Wales* and the *Repulse* as a sop to Australia and New Zealand, who had been paying us to provide their defence over many, many years. Poor devils, they were untrained, had learned as yet no Urdu, the common language in the Indian Army, were only weeks away from their little villages in India and were now lost in a jungle unlike anything they had previously experienced.

We passed a strange night in complete darkness, knowing there was nothing between us and the Jap army, and that if we were attacked, the causeway would be blown. I can still see Jim Finlay's face when he asked "What then?" and was told "Swim!" Jim wanted to know if sharks were about and if so, what size? We had to find somewhere to lie down. It was dry so we just lay down on the grass lawn and made the best of things. The Argylls must have fed us. I can't say that I slept much, just counted the stars. Strange, no Plough, just the Southern Cross. None of us slept much that night and at dawn we reeled in our cables and my 15 cwt took its place as the last 4-wheeled vehicle to cross the causeway, sandwiched between the rearguard company of Argylls and the stretcher bearers, who were pushing strange 2-wheeled contraptions, that reminded me of window cleaners at home hurling their ladder barras down the streets. In front of them went the little tin cans. I may say that we and our 15cwt were completely airbrushed out in the Argyll records, but I was there and tell the truth. Early breakfast and over we went, crossing in broad daylight; we had to slow down to marching pace, might aptly be called funereal, as mine was the only vehicle apart from the tin cans and we were reeling in the cable as we went. One company of Argylls brought up the rear and the evacuation of the Malay Peninsular was complete. We were worried that we would be bombed from the air. We need not have; I realised later that there was no danger from the air; the causeway was too valuable to the Japs for them to consider bombing it. I did not think that far then and felt very exposed. As it happened the Sappers made such a poor job of blowing the causeway that the Japs had it up and running in no time. I do not know the reason. Could be inefficiency, could be the belief that we would need it for a counter attack; whichever, the Japs found it no obstacle to landing on the island.

It was interesting to me that a friend in the Argylls sent me a Christmas card post war depicting the evacuation. My 15cwt had been airbrushed out. Same at the A&S Museum at Stirling Castle. We were there, I can assure you. Jim Finlay is dead, I have lost trace of the driver, (R. Langdon), but Neville Mitcham is still with us. We were only reminiscing about that episode on the phone last week. June 2009.

So that was us now on the impregnable island fortress of Singapore, where the big guns faced the wrong way, the Australian Division had virtually packed in; its General was organizing his flight, desertion I would call it, back to Australia; as far as I have been able to discover, his court-martial was fudged for political reasons. The Aussies had packed in (see above). The Japs wisely landed on the bit that the Aussies were supposed to be defending. How did they know? The Sikh battalion had made one very successful bayonet charge on the mainland and had then gone into a huddle and deserted en masse to the Japanese. The half squadron of Hurricanes had disappeared to the doubtful safety of Java, more likely a staging post for onward travel via Java to Australia. (Such a pity that they were so few. I do not think that they ever got more than two in the air at any one time). They were more than a match for the Jap Zeros, man to man. This is all with hindsight: my nose was too close to the ground to think about anything other than trying to keep communications going with the scratch

Brigade that was still fighting. Composed of the remains of the Argylls, the surviving Marines and what was left of the Gurkhas, each not much more than at company strength. There were three or four British Battalions somewhere about, but to be polite, I have to say they did not register on my radar. The Gunners kept going to the end, so my ears told me. Only two of the massive guns, which had so impressed me, could traverse round to fire at the advancing Japs. Not to mention that their only ammo was armour piercing, which meant that the shells went straight through anything in their way, and buried themselves 20 feet into the ground before they exploded. Not the best defence against attacking infantry. I shall never forget the noise as they passed overhead, like a subway train, only more so. First time I encountered it, I instinctively threw myself flat on the ground.

I wish I could say that my heart went out to the wretched natives; their homes were being pattern bombed and their whole lives turned upside down, but I was too busy, saving my own and my men's skins. On clocking in I found myself doing the same job as before, but now operating from HQ in an ever shrinking perimeter; my men on standard rations. No more Company Commander's powers for me now, living in an officers' mess, under the eye of my superiors whom I had never seen before. Not that I can remember Malin's presence at any time. He would have put himself as far as possible from the slightest chance of being exposed to enemy action.

I think the facts of life were at last beginning to sink in to the European civilians, who were starting to look a little jittery and telling their wives to get on a ship, any ship, A.S.A.P. Unfortunately, too many decided to stay with their husbands and suffered terribly in Internment. Particularly hard on the children. The military, however, had no idea and persisted in living the lives of a peacetime garrison. I felt that I had landed on another planet when encountering the Garrison mentality. Percival, good behind a desk but hopeless in a real fighting command, had a lot to answer for, much too weak to stand up to the real villain, Shenton Thomas. I was really angry to hear afterwards that Percival put the blame for the defeat on the lack of leadership of the junior officers; a classic case of ignoring the beam in one's own eye to criticise the mote in another's. The example always comes down from the top. A nice man, no doubt, but no wartime leader.

I never did get my spare specs which I had ordered on my one day off and lived to regret it. The Japs sacked the Alexandra Hospital, where they were waiting for me, in probably the worst atrocity of the war in the East, bayoneting doctors, nurses and patients indiscriminately, even a patient who was being operated on in theatre. It was only matched for sheer sadistic cruelty by them forcing the nurses, in their red cross marked uniforms, into the sea off Sumatra and machine gunning them, thus saving the effort needed to bury them.

You will understand why I hate them still. They were, in my experience, animals and I have no doubt, under the skin and their oily smiles, they still are.

The Oriental preference is to be on the winning side and so it was looking at the not too rosy outlook facing their previous masters. The only race we could depend on were the Chinese, who had good reason to hate and fear the Japs. They knew all about the Japanese atrocities in China. Here again the Governor was monumentally wrong. (See above.) Not only had he prevented proper defences being built anywhere in Malaya or on Singapore Island on the grounds that that would have frightened the native population, but also he had ruled out arming and training the Chinese because of the communist cell. That there was a strong Chinese communist cell at the time cannot be denied, but surely we had at that time a common enemy, and their armed support would have been of greatest assistance throughout the campaign. They were good soldiers and had ample motivation not to surrender. The Japs, after the Surrender, tied up with field cable any Chinese they could find, put them in open boats and threw them overboard to drown in full view of the civilian population as an example to the populace. Our infantry had been so cut up and demoralized by then, that only a scratch Brigade could be cobbled up from the remnants of the Argylls, Ghurkhas and the Marines ex the *Prince of Wales* and *Repulse*. The latter were well trained and well officered, with a couple of the best officers that I met in captivity. (See above and below.) The Australian Division had effectively packed in after failing to prevent the Japs from gaining a foothold on the island—"Oh what a surprise!" All that was left to hold up the advance was the scratch Brigade and no prizes for the name of the subaltern who was detailed to lay and maintain their lines back to H.Q.

18th Div had only just arrived and was far too late to be of any use; they were still not fully disembarked from their transports and were trying, in vain, to land their equipment and organize themselves.

As a last ditch attempt to hold back the Japs, a huge artillery bombardment was organised to prevent them getting too firm a foothold, or could it have been to exhaust as much ammo as possible before the Japs got their hands on it? The Aussies refused to cooperate on the grounds that they were autonomous and would only take orders from an Aussie General (he was winging it home as fast as he could); the Japs then in the Aussie sector were left alone and the whole thing was a complete washout. I have no doubt that this episode will be whitewashed, but I know my version is correct.

It was while I was on this line maintenance duty that I was picked for the escape party and my company commander claimed to be unable to find me. The truth was he was too big a coward to come out of the relative security of Corps H.Q. and risk getting too near to the action. We were all of seven miles away and in continuous contact at all times. I could have spent the rest of the war in comfort in Australia. That is what my substitute did and finished as a major; but, sadly, no promotion in a P.O.W. camp for me.

The confusion and chaos was so great that only two incidents stay in my mind. A wild goose chase looking for a small telephone exchange with a wrong map reference, when we found ourselves in some scrubland and stunted rubber trees. Suddenly I heard a burst of automatic fire. Aha! I thought, here is my chance to put my Tommy gun to good use. I positioned my men behind a rise facing where the noise had come from and told them to keep very quiet until I knew what was going on. I would not say that my men were wholly enthusiastic, but the only trouble I had was with an only child from Hillhead (the poor man died in captivity, the only man I lost in my lot), who started to bubble and make signs of legging it. In the best Gung Ho tradition, I drew my pistol and told him that if he made a move I would shoot him. Whether I would or not, I cannot say, but the threat was enough—nobody moved. After a fraught ten minutes and no more shooting we withdrew smartly to our truck and got off our marks in record time. We were all pretty relieved: the exchange, wherever it was, was left in peace. I reported that the map reference was wrong and heard no more.

In the other case, we were resting in the sun at Advanced Div HQ enjoying a very welcome hot meal. All round us were the remnants of the Ghurkhas doing the same before regrouping. Each man had been issued with a carton of Players Navy Cut cigarettes and was very determinedly smoking his way through it, lighting the next cigarette from the stub of its predecessor. That was real chain smoking and they were thoroughly enjoying it. They were also carefully and lovingly cleaning their weapons. In the background you could hear the engines of the staff cars, kept running, all set for a quick getaway, so typical of the staff mentality from start to finish. The Ghurkhas had noticed this and every now and then one of them would put one up the spout, point at the sky, say something in Ghurkali and pull the trigger. Out came the staff at the double, leaping into their cars, revving like mad. The Ghurkhas fell about with laughter; the staff slouched back to their vans looking pretty sheepish, until the next time. The Ghurkhas were the tops and we got on well with them. They thoroughly earned our respect.

Eventually our perimeter shrank and I even got a relief, by name Sutherland-Brown. Note the hyphen. What follows may explain my allergy to the hyphen in my baptismal name. We were supposed to do day about, but he did one shift, did not like it and said he was not going out again, it was too dangerous and he was not well. A poor story—the yellow streak down the middle of his back was obvious; he and Malins were a pair. Interestingly he went to pieces in captivity and a kindly M.O. put Premature Senile Decay on his death certificate. He died not long before we were finally released, as I remember. Why he was not court-martialled I have no idea.

Once again no prizes for guessing who went in his place. I had completed my 24 hours and was just sitting down to breakfast on my "day off" when I was told the main line was down again and that my oppo was not going to do his job. Actually the Japs were heavily plastering the city with pattern bombing, the Hurricanes had departed and it was probably a waste of time mending the line, but pride made me go through the motions.

I, of course, did not know then that it was the day of our Surrender. Boy, was I thick. Singapore was taking a terrible pounding; the pattern bombing was never ending during daytime, as one flight of 27 bombers left empty, another one arrived, bombed up. A fair imitation of the *Blitzcrieg*. The destruction was enormous. Amazing to see the roof of a tenement rise slowly in the air, seem to float for half a minute and then crash down in pieces. The only plus was that you could hear the bombers coming and the planes were flying so high, you could actually see the bombs falling, estimate where they would fall and take the appropriate action.

The streets were littered with the debris of shattered buildings, broken poles and twisted power and telephone cables. Driving became an obstacle race. The huge oil tanks had been set on fire and a stinking curtain of filthy black smoke made a greasy backcloth to my drive out to sort the cable fault. The roads were deserted and no wonder. Anyway off I set on a hopeless task. No sooner did you mend one break than the constant pattern bombing caused another. Taking men from the other man's section proved to be a big mistake. I did not think it was right to take mine out after they had been promised a day off, particularly when there was a fresh squad available. They were competent enough, but it became clear that they had not had the experience or training of my lot.

We sorted the fault and set off for base, knowing full well that by the time we got back, the line would be down again. I had posted a man in the back of the 15cwt to keep watch and warn me of any air attack from behind. I was so accustomed to implicit obedience from my own men that I did not check whether the idiot lookout was doing his job. However, when I heard the little spotter's engine, I shouted at the driver; he slammed on the brakes and swerved to the side. The pilot had not anticipated this so he overshot us and the anti-personnel bomb went off about 50 yards ahead of us, blowing the leg off a Tamil cyclist who happened to be in the wrong place at the wrong time. The driver and I were lucky enough to get off with the hair on our necks singed, tin hats protecting our head hair; the front of the 15cwt took a bit of a beating, but it was drivable. I turned round to give a roasting to the lookout only to find him slumped on the floor. We belted off to find an ambulance and came across one right away. We loaded the man and I told my driver to return to base and report, while I accompanied the wounded man to a C.C.S. We did not know whether he was dead or alive. The ambulance was one of those old high sided wooden things and we sped off, only to be hit amidships by a truck at a crossroads, and turned upside down and was left resting on its roof. It may sound trivial to you, but I got the acid from the accumulator down my back and my only pair of glasses smashed. I wrestled my way out, tore off my shirt and went round the back to find the wooden doors jammed and had to find a felling axe to break them open and get the man out.

Another ambulance appeared; they were pretty busy that day; we finally got him to a C.C.S., only to be told that the man was dead on arrival. Amazingly a bomb splinter had gone between the driver's head and mine, passed through the mesh grill that he had been looking through instead of watching out the back and directly into his heart. You could hardly see the entry wound. I suppose it was Poetic Justice. If he had been doing his job as instructed, he might still have been alive today. My men only had to be told once; they knew fine that I had a good reason for giving an order and trusted me just as I trusted them. All that was left for me now to do was collect his paybook and dog tags, and hitch a ride back to base. I was not full of joy, but utterly determined that I would only work with my own men in future.

Our mess/base was a large stone built villa, with its own grounds and sported a grass tennis court; it must have been like the house my parents qualified for, when my father became Number One in Bousteads on his last tour.

Having handed over the paybook and dog tags with ill grace,

I went out into the garden to simmer down; the Japs decided to make the house a target for their French 75s. You could hear them at quite a distance, a very distinctive rhythm, almost a drum beat. The beat was okay but the shells were really vicious at the wrong end. They zipped in and you felt that each shell was coming directly for you. The house, being stone built, suffered little damage except for one shell, which went in through a window and I was told that two men inside were severely wounded. There was a shallow dip round the tennis court, probably caused by subsidence after the drainage had been inserted and after the first shell hit the house. I lay as flat as I could in it and counted the rounds. Well, you have to think about something. However I found, on getting up, that a tiny splinter, no bigger than half a gramophone needle, had scored a thin red line across my back. I tried to keep it for a souvenir but lost it. I still bless the dip round the tennis court for the fragment was going at a fair speed and it could well have been curtains for me, if I had been an inch or two higher off the ground. Lucky again!

The villa had suffered from aerial bombardment in the past in addition to the attention of the Japanese /French 75s. In spite of the perilous state of the plumbing everywhere, we still had a working storage tank and on the arrival of the daily Sumatra, an interesting scenario was to be viewed.

The saving grace to the lack of piped water was the daily tropical downpour, even if it only lasted a few minutes. You could see the dark shape of the Sumatra racing across the sea towards you. Just before the first rain, naked bodies appeared from everywhere to great shouts of, "Send it down David!" Where this phrase came from I do not know but it was the signal for all to turn out and get rinsed off in clean water, better still if you could find a broken gutter and stand under the resulting water spout. Soap soon became a precious and scarce commodity, but even to get your body rinsed off in that sticky heat was a bonus. Someone had found a 15-inch shell casing and an old fashioned rocking pump operated by two men, probably some sort of old fire fighting device, similarly operated to the things you saw rocking along the rails in old Westerns; all three were connected up with chunks of fire hose in order to fill the holding tank. We took it in turns to man the pump, trying to fill the tank before the rain stopped, while the rest of us, equally naked, pranced about enjoying the cold rain rinsing off our sweaty bodies; it was hard work, but we did not complain. Clean water had become a luxury. It is not easy to describe these Sumatras as they were called, for they came from that direction and were like thunder plumps only more so; a child could drown in a monsoon drain minutes after one had started, and a man would have to move fast to get out. Our Mess was luckier than most to have this source, but water was still rationed. "Send it down David!" was like a joint prayer to a Greek rain god and I heard it many times and always relating to cleansing rain.

CHAPTER 14

THE SURRENDER

THE NEXT THING was to be told the unthinkable—that we were surrendering at 4 p.m. and must hand over all our arms and equipment intact. I did not think much of this and was not at all convinced it was a good thing to hand over my vehicles and valuable equipment to the enemy. The other Section Officer, Mason, was all for compliance but not averse to turning a blind eye, as long as I accepted responsibility. I told the men what had happened and what I proposed to do, and advised them to salvage anything they wanted to keep, including clothing and rations. We then loaded our vehicles and drove them down to the canal and onto some empty barges, put a few bullets into the petrol tanks and set fire to them. Complete destruction including all my virtually new Barathea Service Dress. A sore loss! In my silly way, I think I regretted most the loss of my Sam Browne belt; it was always well polished and I fair fancied myself in it. However I was determined that the Japs would not get anything of value that I had responsibility for. I was past feeling anything. I just could not believe it, still expecting the arrival of a relieving force any minute. I could not believe that Britain would leave us to such a fate. Wrong, Wrong, Wrong!

Our minds, of course, turned to thoughts of escape; a couple of my men had fallen in with a party of Scots, who had commandeered a sampan and offered Finlay and me a place in the boat. The plan was to slip out under the cover of darkness and make for Java. I had a look at the boat and returned to the mess to collect some kit and have a meal. I was challenged by a Major English, hitherto unknown to me; he seemed to have established some sort of command. When I said that it was my duty to escape and told him of my plans, he threatened that, if I went, he would personally see to it that I would be court-martialled for desertion when we got home. Idiot that I was, I still believed that rescue was just round the corner and took the threat seriously and did not go. Actually Finlay and the others were stopped by the Redcaps from boarding the sampan. If you read George Haddow's notes, you will see his opinion of the "boy major" as we dubbed English, a poor representation of 'a would be', but highly unqualified leader of men, bumptious, interfering and brainless. Looking back, it was a good thing I had had no dealings with him previously, otherwise there would have been real trouble, but I have to concede that he probably prolonged my life, if you can call the following three and a half years a life, by blackmailing me to stay. The Jap Navy, British trained, and efficient, was waiting outside; Jap planes were everywhere and we had no night time navigational expertise; anyway Java surrendered practically instantly making sailing, in daylight, suicide.

The next day was spent in limbo, waiting for instructions. We were in a state of total shock. Rumours, termed by us as boreholes, proliferated and continued to dominate our lives for the next three and a half years.

Looking back, this is how I see the campaign in retrospect, a "worm's eye view" as opposed to the official version. Take out the Argylls, Marines, Ghurkhas and the Artillery, we were a pretty unprofessional army, still living in a Colonial atmosphere, generally speaking, largely untrained and ill prepared. My men were the exception and I can say without fear of contradiction that they were a cracking lot. I never had a moment's problem. The Air Force, equipped with obsolete Aircraft apart from a few, far too few, Hurricanes were no protection and provided free ready-made aerodromes for the invaders. The Navy provided no protection either. After the *Prince of Wales* and *Repulse* were sunk by wave after wave of Kamikazes, revelling in the British lack of Air Cover for their Battlewagons, there was no R.N. to speak of.

The Argylls were the only Infantry regiment, apart from the Ghurkhas, properly trained for fighting both in and out of the jungle. Their C.O., 'Busty Stewart' was for real and saw to that; a hard man but "fair"; his troops worshipped him. The Far East was littered with his officer rejects doing R.T.O., A.P.O. and suchlike jobs. The A&S battalion did far more training days operating in the jungle than all the other British Battalions did in aggregate. Each Indian Army Division carried the odd British battalion per Brigade to stiffen it up. Don't make me laugh. This became very obvious in the campaign. I was past feeing anything, just numb with shock and utter disbelief that this could happen to the British.

Malins, on being instructed at the end of the campaign to make his recommendations for decorations for his company, put every officer's name down in alphabetical order, finishing every citation by claiming that he had no hesitation in making the recommendation as he was personally present at the time that the act of extreme bravery was performed, (hoping that at least he would collect a D.S.O. out of it, but fortunately in vain). He also headed the list with the names of the two Malay Post and Telegraph officers who had been seconded to his company as liaison officers. Accordingly they each got an M.C., in spite of never having left the safety of Div. H.Q.! They were two decent men, but it was a bit hard for the rest of us to take. A loathsome man, Malins—I cannot think of one redeeming feature. Indeed, part way up the Railway he confided to me that I had been chosen for the last escape ship, but he could not find me to give me my instructions. A likely story as I was never more than five miles from him at that time and in touch by field telephone at all times, but, of course, I was working with the fighting Brigade HQ, far too near to the Jap front line for him to risk his precious skin. I as near as dammit throttled him on the spot. I think I might have got off for extenuating circumstances. The man who went in my place spent the rest of the war in a cushy job in Australia and finished up a Major. But no promotion for me in the Prison Camp, except the automatic one to full lieutenant, 18 months after being commissioned.

Next morning the first Jap troops became visible. To our surprise, they were tall and not the little bandy legged men we were to meet over the next three and a half years. It seemed to be okay to walk about a bit. Not that we went far, but curiosity made some of us put our noses out. One came back and reported that he had watched a Jap trying to wrestle the wristwatch off one of his companions and reported it to a passing Jap officer, who drew his pistol and shot the Jap, leaving him dead in the gutter. We approved of this; however it slowly became clear that these were the elite Jap troops who had led the invasion. They could not believe their luck to have defeated vastly superior numbers in such a short time. They were quickly off to continue their victorious career through the Dutch East Indies, with their eyes firmly fixed on Australia and New Zealand, leaving us in the duplicitous hands of 2nd class Line of Communication troops, their Jackal Korean conscripts and the traitorous Free Indian Army, a most unsavoury prospect.

The Gunners had good modern guns, 25 pounders and 4.5 ins. Gun/How.s and they knew how to handle them. Unfortunately the jungle terrain did not often offer an open site for their O.P.s, observation posts, but even then they possibly accounted for more Japs than all the infantry put together. They were highly trained and truly professional.

No praise of mine would be too high for the Ghurkhas. Their loyalty was of an order to be wondered at; even in captivity it never wavered. The Japs could do nothing with them. I wish I could say the same about the Indian troops. Of those that turned, many were bigger sadists than the Japs. The Japs, I was told, even tried hanging a Ghurkha drummer boy out of a multi-storey top window by slamming the window onto his wrists. He did not turn. I met an ex- Ghurkha colonel in Spain many years ago, who discovered two miscreants who had turned and had to lock them up under a British guard as their own people, if they could have got at them, would have dismembered them slowly and painfully. As P.O.W.S, if they were on a working party outside and one of their officers passed by as part of another working party, they would down tools, stand to attention and give him their Huzzoor salute. The Japs would go spare and rush about bashing all and sundry, but it did not do them a damned bit of good.

Hearsay but reliable—a few unwary Japs strayed too near their lines at night and were never seen again. More than one Jap went involuntarily to sea inside a 40 gallon oil drum. I spoke with a man who was taken prisoner after the capitulation; his unit put in a stockade near a Chinese kampong outside our camp. One night as he sat beside a fire he became aware of eyes staring at him on the other side of the fire. The Ghurkha put his finger to his lips and in a whisper asked if my friend was British. On being reassured, he told him that he would see the heads of two guards on the gateposts the next morning. Sure enough two heads in the puggarees of the Free Indian Army were there to be seen as he went out to work the next morning. I just hope they were Sikhs. Some of the Indians, who turned, treated us badly enough, but the Sikhs were absolutely vicious. Sadists, they revelled in the power which they had over us. In many ways they were worse than the Koreans, who were bad enough; jackals to the Japs. The biggest insult you could give to a Ghurkha would be to say that he was Indian Army. He would soon put you right: he was a soldier in the British Army, and very proud so to be. I doubt that you would be pushed to find many Sikhs employed in Singapore, even today. 2010.

At this distance in time it must be very difficult for you to comprehend the problems that the different races and creeds posed for the Indian Army. Religion, as ever, was the main problem. The Hindus revered cattle, allowing them to stray anywhere they pleased and would not eat beef. Their caste system made it possible for a sepoy (private soldier) to be of a higher caste than a V.C.O., Viceroy Commissioned Officer. You may think that there is a class system in the UK, but it is insignificant compared to the Indian Caste system, which includes/excludes the Untouchables.

The Mohammedans, Muslims, abhorred the pig, smoked but did not drink alcohol. A likely story! Neither would eat food prepared in an alien kitchen. Even the water tankers had to be separate. Add to this the Jains, Sikhs, Jhats and the Lord only knows how many other sects and sub-sects. The Punjabi battalions had separate companies of each religion following the old 'Divide and Rule doctrine'. It made for huge administrative and logistical problems, not to mention considerable overmanning.

Life of a sort went on in a stunned atmosphere. None of us could conceive of any General surrendering his army so easily. We were informed that the Japs had seized control of the water supply to Singapore and threatened to cut it off. This blackmail was enough to force capitulation. Shenton Thomas again. The civilian population would have suffered severely, I admit, but it was worth a try. I think to this day that Churchill in spite of his vicious speech about the surrender of Singapore, and the War

Cabinet knew that Malaya was a lost cause and we were abandoned to our fate. We felt seriously let down by the High Command throughout the campaign, and were. I suppose his priority was to get the Americans into the war, hold on until that happened, preserve Egypt, the gateway to oil, and fight to control the Mediterranean by aircraft and submarines.

That night we were informed that the next day we were to march to the Changi Barracks area and were warned that it would be highly unlikely that we would ever see again anything left behind. From then on, every time we moved, we had to decide how much we could carry and discard the rest. Wheeled transport on this occasion was reserved for food, cooking utensils and the sick. Malins instantly went sick, RAT that he was.

Thus we spent the last night of any vestige of civilization for the next three and a half years, not that our present conditions were anything to write home about. It was a good thing I did not know the future or I might well have done something desperate. I just did not believe that Britain would leave us there to rot. I was sure that a large relieving force was already on the way. How stupid can you be?

CHAPTER 15

CHANGI

AS ORDERED, we paraded the next morning and marched to Changi Barracks (not Changi Jail), the peacetime barracks for a regular infantry battalion, (Gordon Highlanders), carrying everything we hoped to salvage; only the sick and heavy equipment was to ride on transport. Malins, having reported sick, rode on the transport leaving his wee nyaff of a batman to march carrying all his spare kit as well as his own. Typical!

A nightmare journey it was, through wrecked streets with a backdrop of oily black smoke from the blazing oil tanks. Bloated bodies lay stinking in the tropical heat everywhere. The windows of the native houses had suddenly blossomed with little flags of the rising sun of Japan, more succinctly termed by the troops as the flaming arseholes. I do not blame the natives, it would have been more than their lives were worth not to have flown the flags, but it did occur to me to wonder where all these flags had suddenly sprung from. It was a truly miserable march what with the heat, the dust, the stench of rotting dead bodies and the dawning realisation that we had lost and now were P.O.W.s, in the hands of an unknown quantity. We were stunned by what had happened and slogged along like zombies, just looking straight ahead with sightless eyes. A most unpleasant march: both sides of the road were decorated with these little Japanese flags and a Chinese head on every available spike. We put one foot in front of the other and, with eyes doggedly to the front, slogged along. The population watched with deadpan Oriental faces as their previous rulers marched sullenly into captivity. There was no singing, just a funereal silence, broken only by the noise of tramping boots. The last thing we wanted was to let the natives see our inward dejection.

Changi barracks, stone built and its environs became a P.O.W. camp; we were guarded by the traitorous Free Indian Army, a villainous looking crew; their actions matched their looks. I found myself billeted in coolie lines, a downhill row of little concrete shacks, each designed for a native family, but now we slept hugger mugger on the floor. Bedbugs entered our lives. They sucked our blood at night, made a foul stink when squashed and were ineradicable. We grew to loathe them as probably the worst of the many plagues which we were to encounter on the Railway. Being young and well fleshed at the time, I became an unwilling target. The wicker chairs made a desirable home for them and were therefore soon burned, but once introduced these parasites are permanent.

On arrival at Changi Barracks all seemed chaos and confusion, but with hindsight it was remarkable how quickly we were billeted and reorganized. It did prove that there were some competent organisers on the staff. It was such a pity that they were all in Singapore during the campaign and not active in the field. Possibly better at billeting than fighting.

Still impatiently awaiting the arrival of a rescue force, I found myself allocated a bed space in these coolie lines, sharing a small room with three others. My billet was at the lower end of a long row of one up, one down concrete houses. This was fortunate as an army of bedbugs was massed at the top end and attacked a new house every week. How they transported themselves, I don't know.

We were an army, in a communal daze, crushed by the ignominy of defeat, an army, amongst whose members were many who, once the brain had cleared, increasingly felt that they had been sold down the river; the Argylls with vivid memories of the botch up at Slim River were on the brink of insubordination, trusting no one and for a short time insisted on drawing their rations individually; little cooking fires were to be seen all around, until they ran out of fuel. The Indian Army officers, trying to adjust to the removal of their troops, had the hardest adjustment to make and suffered throughout captivity more than we did. I at least had my lot of ruffians to worry about. We lived hugger mugger in an unknown environment, slowly becoming aware that the Japs changed the rules as and when it suited them, and did not accept the Geneva Convention, unless it suited.

The men could have dropped me into real trouble in the knowledge that the Japs would have rewarded them with food for doing so; but not so; time and again they covered up for me. I know that having a common enemy creates a bond, but they went over and above that and I shall never forget it. I reciprocated for them too, whenever I could, but the first few weeks were hairy to put it mildly. Fortunately strong discipline had been re-established before there were problems with the rations. It was hard enough adjusting to our world collapsing, but suddenly to find that we had to change from a European diet based on meat, bread, tea, milk and sugar to broken rice, green tea and what we could scrounge was hard to take.

The first thing to learn was how to cook rice in bulk. The U.K. was not invaded by Curry houses and Chinese restaurants until quarter of a century later. Rice pudding and jam, as a treat, now and then had been okay, but plain salted rice ad nauseam was a different matter, and not just a plateful but an alleged pound a day. A pound of rice bulks up considerably, when cooked. While it fills the stomach, it is only temporary. 20 minutes later you urinate and are starving again. I should explain that our alleged pound of rice was not composed of the pristine white grains we see today on the Supermarket shelves. It had passed through the hands of the Jap QMs, who were not that much different from ours, only more so. We lived off the end product of the rice mills including the sweepings of the floors. Broken and dirty it was; the weevils etc. came as fat passengers.

To be fair to our staff, they had made quite a good fist of finding space for all of us in such a short time. We were a beaten army; we felt it; we looked it. Anything could have happened. Luckily, discipline held, but it must have been a close run thing. The Japs only provided Korean or "Free Indian Army" guards and rations largely of rice in the various camps, and took very good care, themselves, to live outside, leaving the administration to the P.O.W.s. This suited us in the sense that we could maintain some sort of army discipline, occasionally by fairly crude methods. It did however show up the differing systems and standards of control in the different camps and nationalities. By far the highest standard that I came across was the Tasmanian Battalion, where everything was shared equally regardless of rank. They had the most remarkable esprit de corps as a result.

One camp, through which we passed on the way back down the Railway, did admit to having had problems. The cure, they found, was to hand the miscreant over to a pair of tough sergeants who took him into the jungle and gave him a good hammering. Not very civilised I agree, rather tending to copy the Japs, but in the absence of any viable alternative, it did prove effective. There was really no other way. We certainly did not want to hand them over to the Japs and admit that our troops could descend to that kind of behaviour or that they were out of our control. Also a few weaklings had to be firmly handled. Some might have turned traitor and handed over damaging information to the Japs in return for a bit of extra food. They were of the type that had to be made more frightened of us than of the Japs.

Common sense, pride and a growing fierce hatred of the Japs gradually stiffened backbones. We were absolutely determined not to show them our true feelings of betrayal by Percival and all the Bone Headed, red-tabbed Staff round him. It was essential to maintain our discipline and never to admit to the Japs that we could not control our own men. It was essential for our own self-respect that our own criminals should be dealt with outside the ken of the Japs. I cannot deny that some on our side were tempted to and indeed did let us down. The threat of punishment in the long term, under Army Law, largely maintained an uneasy control of 99% plus of our people, who were intensely loyal and acted in a civilized, law abiding sense with regard to our own affairs, but from time to time the worst elements would emerge. Desperate men do desperate things, of which even they must have been thoroughly ashamed later. A warped morality could persuade a vicious character that to steal the blanket and possessions of a dying man in order to buy food for himself did not matter to the victim, who was already unconscious, as he would be dead in an hour or so. This did happen in front of me in one of the camps that we stayed in overnight, during the ten-day march. I reported it, but fear that nothing was done. When men were dying like flies, the priorities of the individual Allied camp commander set the rules. Some of my men may have been rogues as far as liberation of certain consumable items were concerned, but my section was exemplary in its conduct.

The Japs tried in every way to belittle us officers in the eyes of our troops. They were so stupid that, with few exceptions, it made the men show more loyalty, and indeed on the Railway, time and again they saved my bacon. Some were much worse off. The Argylls in particular took defeat badly, no wonder, and in the absence of Busty wavered on the edge of mutiny. They trusted no one. I do not blame them. However there we were, locked away until the end of the war or rescue, whichever came first. It took a long time to adapt, both mentally and physically. For quite a few weeks we waited anxiously for the arrival of the relieving force and as hope slowly faded, we began to face facts. We had all read about the treatment of officers under the Geneva Convention and confidently awaited boredom, Red Cross parcels and letters. Disillusion set in, as it slowly became clear that the Japs made their own rules and changed them to suit themselves as dictated by Tokyo. As a 2nd Lt. and gaffer cum tea boy on the Railway, I found myself responsible for any faults in my team's allocated work and was the first to be beaten up; much handicapped by the loss of my glasses; my men always safeguarded me to the best of their ability there, knowing that I would always stand up for them.

Our tinned rations, even being used sparingly to help with the wershness of the rice were, diminishing rapidly and our silhouettes changed. A skeletal frame now supported a rice belly, so that we soon represented the same look as I see in the papers of the Darfur and Eritrean refugees as I type this today (2010).

The medics scratched their heads and came up with the idea that we should stew alleged lemon grass and Hibiscus leaves to provide some vitamins. Our M.O.s were wonderful. I cannot praise them enough, though we did not much approve of some of their suggestions. I spent many a day on the island of Singapore scratching for alleged lemon grass, probably the Eastern version of our couch grass. Boiled and boiled and boiled, it produced a noxious green/yellow liquid, which was alleged to provide some of the vitamins we were lacking. Worse was gathering the leaves of the Hibiscus shrubs which grew in profusion everywhere; they were so bitter that some preferred to take a chance with Beriberi.

The next plague was that the morning visit to the latrines was a total failure. Some of my friends could go a fortnight between visits. I gave the matter a lot of thought and decided to keep up my routine visits, even if nothing happened, in the belief that things would improve and at least my system was not experiencing a routine change. Please don't blame me for labouring the subject, but it was dawning on me that I was in this for the long haul and it was important to hold on to anything that linked me with real life as I remembered it. I managed to have a smoke after the evening rice every night, bar one. On the Railway someone hid my pipe as a practical joke. I had words with him. He never tried again. Perhaps he was envious, because I was careful always to have a pipeful ready for the next night. It cannot have been pleasant, dying for a smoke to watch me puffing contentedly, if only momentarily. After I had finished with him no one ever tried it again. I managed my nightly smoke only by ruthless rationing and a great degree of selfishness. Desperate pleas from tobacco addicts met with a stone wall. I was prepared to share anything with my immediate mates (Kongsi) except my nightly ritual. It gave me a few very, very precious moments to reminisce; most important to me, I felt Bette was with me, a sort of personal victory; it gave me a few moments to ponder a previous civilised existence. One poor addict, whose catchphrase after he had conned a smoke from someone was "Ah Nicotine you Winsome Bitch", was so desperate for a smoke that having none left and having infuriated everyone by his constant cadging, threw himself over the banisters onto a stone floor, (preferring death to a life without nicotine). That was that. I never fathomed him. He claimed to be a real tough guy, a racing motorcyclist and ice hockey player. I often wondered whether he really preferred boys to girls. He was very good looking and much concerned about his hair and appearance.

A Kongsi (my attempt at Chinese) consisted of a group of 4-6 like-minded men, not necessarily bosom pals, who looked after each other. If you had Malaria and could not collect your rations, they were soon swallowed up by the leggie queue, lost and gone for ever. Members of your Kongsi drew them and tried to force some down your throat, in the knowledge that you would do the same for them. The lone wolf did not survive.

Sometimes I smoked some very odd things in my pipe. Flowering Cherry leaves, so foul that no flowering cherry tree has ever been seen in my garden; dog ends, preferably off cheroots—I was not too proud. I tried drying the leaves of the tobacco farm we were briefly in and curing them. Nothing made it smokeable; it would blow your head off. I kept the end of a plug for my uncle, who smoked like a chimney. Even he had to give it best. Perhaps that is why I was largely cut out of his will. I was not worried about the content; the ritual was the important thing. I even made pipes out of bamboo; I felt that, for a few moments, I was with Bette and in tune with civilisation. I know that it was very selfish of me; the ritual itself was a great help to stiffen my determination to survive.

Another camp on the Railway was situated beside a duck farm. Great long sheds had been built at the top of the riverbank and I remember watching the big heavy doors creaking open as we went on parade in the morning and this regiment of ducks quacking pell-mell down to the river from each shed and thinking about the eggs. Often, too, as we stood for the nightly tenko, we could see the last stragglers being herded in before the big doors creaked shut.

Not only had the Japs convinced themselves that we were non-persons (see above) and deserved only enough rations for minimal survival, but also they could see that once the stores in Singapore were exhausted, they would be strapped for food. Our lot tumbled to this too; all tinned food under our control was promptly reserved for the hospital; rice became our staple diet. Not the lovely long grained white rice, nor the red health food unpolished grains that you see in the supermarkets today, but the sweepings and dirty broken grains lifted off the floor, after the raw rice had been processed in the mills, weevils and all. It must have been faintly nourishing, if unappetizing, judging from the girth of the weevils. It provided starch only but no vitamins, which resided in the husks; the Japs then milled (see above) these husks into powder and sold the result to those of us who had any money left, as rice polishings, an alleged source of, in particular, Vitamin B12; thus they foisted rubbish onto us as rations and made a profit out of the milling by-products as vital vitamins. They won all over. I hardly need to point out that the rations were issued through Jap Q.M.s, who could have given lessons to ours on skimming. The change from European rations to a mainly rice diet was traumatic physically and mentally and the cemetery began to fill. Shades of Cargilfield's "Debtors"! A sluggish system is bad enough but an unused one was a recipe for big trouble later, so I thought to myself. It was amazing how, after a few short weeks, we looked greedily at stuff at which we had turned up our noses in the recent past. After a fortnight's rice diet, a tin of Pilchards in tomato sauce, previously rejected as inedible, was priceless. One spoonful could fairly help a mess tin of rice go down. We went through a really bad time; the MOs got very worried. The first hint of Beriberi and Diphtheria manifested itself; deaths started; malnutrition hindered recuperation. The first to go were some solitary planters, who had been living on a bottle or two of whisky and a couple of tins of condensed milk a day (true) together with some men who had lived unhealthy lives.

The Japs in their usual "charming" way offered us as balance to the sweepings of the vitamin-less "polished" rice, the ground up husks left from the "polishing"; this allegedly contained the vitamins and were for sale, in the knowledge that we had to buy them for the malnourished hospital patients. Scratching about

.

for the alleged lemon grass became a daily chore. When boiled it and produced a urine-like, foul tasting liquid which most of us dutifully gulped down. The stewed Hibiscus leaves tasted so bitter that I baulked at eating them from time to time. If truth be told, if one is hungry enough, one can eat the most revolting food. Through time I ran the whole gamut from elephant dung beetles to some very odd clams and bony, muddy tasting fish. If we reminisced about our wives and mothers, the talk rested not on their comeliness or other virtues, but on their culinary skills and on magnificent meals enjoyed in restaurants with them. Believe me, Marylin Monroe, pushing a trolley of porridge, could have walked naked and unscathed through our hut on the Railway; the battle would have been for the porridge. Healthy hunger is good, but real starvation is so awful that its pangs are difficult to describe. The loathsome green tea, milkless and unsugared, we got used to and would anticipate its arrival for a "Smokeo" during work on the Railway with some slight enthusiasm. Occasionally on the Railway we would be issued with dried green alleged vegetables in huge baskets; these had to be soaked in the river for at least 24 hours before they could be cooked. Foul also, but by then we were so hungry that it just became fodder. Permanent gnawing hunger is in a class of its own. You may think that I am besotted by food, but it is the most essential basic after water, needed for survival. The change of diet affected our systems. It did not help that the Jap Army's attitude to the sick was the complete opposite of ours. The sick could not work, therefore, in their extraordinary philosophy, they were removed from the ration strength. We on the contrary believed that the sick needed extra rations to build them back up to health. Acting on our principles, the sick got the best possible. This in turn reduced the rations for the rest of us. A race of militaristic savages, the Japs.

According to their Bushido tradition, we, by surrendering and not committing Hara Kiri, (suicide by disembowelment), had made ourselves non-persons and were accordingly treated like dirt. How much of this was a convenient manipulation of their traditions, on being faced with an unexpectedly easy and swift victory and the sudden arrival of an enormous number of mouths to feed; how much true, I do not know, but I strongly suspect the former. They were a totally militaristic nation which had been completely brainwashed; and so much so, that they were convinced that Japan was destined to share leadership of the world with Germany. I suppose nobody had told Hitler!

In Changi was our first encounter with bedbugs. They were to be with us for the rest of our captivity. There seemed to be no way to eradicate them. They were bloodsucking insects with a heat-seeking device that tuned into body warmth and plagued us as we tried to sleep. They were easily killed by squashing, when they popped like bubble gum and the resultant stink was indescribably foul. They lived and bred in cracks in the building, in the furniture, particularly in cane chairs. They were the worst of the plagues because they killed any decent sleep and were far ahead of the competition; there was plenty of that; they clearly preferred younger bodies to feast on. Perhaps the skin was tenderer to penetrate. I seemed to be a prime target and there was no escape once they became co-lodgers. My first billet was at the end of the coolie lines and we could trace the progression of these insects from the other end, roughly taking over a new shack every week. It was a helpless feeling. We never did get rid of them. How they travelled from camp to camp in virgin jungle I do not know, but they did. There are always dirty folk who care not for their fellows. Old sweats told us that Egypt was the worst barracks for them. They were impervious to blowlamps or saucers full of paraffin.

As our health deteriorated, we began to suffer the other plagues of deprivation, which began to flourish; the Japs neglected all the highly successful British anti-malarial works and both types of malaria reappeared on Singapore Island and were with us to the end. We were sitting ducks. Diphtheria too reared its ugly head. Largely unknown today it was a killer then. Our M.O.s were beyond praise and I was told constructed an apparatus that produced an anti-Diphtheria serum. Dysentery, both types, was always with us; however I was lucky there. Enteritis was all that I suffered from and that was bad enough. For about 18 months, I spent half of the night trying to sleep and the other half crouched over the open latrines. Vitamin deficiencies took their toll. Beriberi soon marked out those poor sods whose bodies could not store Vitamin B; it was a slow killer as the victim's heart eventually drowned in his own liquid; some went blind. The victims, if they were lucky enough to get some, could keep the worst effects at bay by swallowing the aforementioned rice polishings, which cost money and tasted of straw. I always felt that to give us the sweepings of broken rice for our staple ration at the rate of an alleged pound per day per worker and then make us buy the polishings of that rice to keep alive and to deny us that, when the money ran out was one of the worst of their many crimes against humanity, not that the Japs could spell that word.

We were moved about a bit in Changi. I cannot remember why. I do recall the basement of one large stone building, early on, where we slept as if in a giant hospital ward. It was there that the lack of vitamins and the deterioration of our normal resistance left us wide open to many skin complaints. 'Singapore Foot' was particularly unpleasant; it made any attempt at walking difficult and painful. Very contagious and well nourished by the high humidity and our close confinement, the fungus spread like wildfire. The whole instep blew up like a huge blister full of nauseating stinking pus. I only had one go and that was plenty. 'Happy Feet' went side by side with it. All the little bones in the feet became painful and in bed your feet would jerk about uncontrollably; mine still do occasionally. The most disgusting, I think, was 'Changi Balls'. The skin of the scrotum started to weep, turned scarlet and sticky, and walking became extremely unpleasant. It. was very difficult to get rid of and indeed some poor sods never did shake it off, until they got some decent food after liberation. I got it off and on, but was lucky enough to escape the killer, Beriberi. Lack of a decent continuous water supply made personal hygiene very difficult. Ringworm, another horror, started to appear. Unlike at home, it stopped when it reached the hairline; highly contagious, it would start with a spot and spread and spread, creeping outwards, until the whole of the back was covered in great whorls, moving inexorably until they reached the hairline and died. At full stretch a man's back looked like some sort of surrealist tattoo or mosaic. In that heat, often sweaty, the leading edge stung and made sleep nearly impossible. Lice started to appear and became permanent residents. Pretty degrading it was to be assaulted by scabies, as I once was, but a liberal application of a sulphur shower cleared that up. How we rigged up the shower, I don't remember. The smell of sulphur lingered for days telling all and sundry that you had "crabs". Embarrassing to put it mildly. Talk about the seven plagues of the O.T.—we had more than our fair share of them. Small Pox, we avoided. As time slowly passed, it became attractive to many to succumb to the temptation of that peace promised by the cemetery. Along with the majority, I adopted the policy of survival, come what may, combined with the determination to win any possible encounter with the Japs by any means in my power that did not threaten my survival. The smallest and most insignificant victory and we had quite a few of them, was an enormous boost to our morale.

In that same building, we watched the Jap Battle Fleet pass by. Very impressive and highly intimidating, they towered over us.

We must have been near sea level. We saw them again next day, but in reverse, just as intimidating. No wireless then, no source of news. We had no idea what was happening and learned later that they had gone to bomb Colombo. The Yanks seized the opportunity and sent their carriers to bomb Japan, which sacrilege caused the Japs to recall their fleet and instead, ordered them to frighten the daylights out of the Aussie population by threatening to bomb Australia from the sea, without much success.

Also there we received Red Cross parcels. There had been a changeover of Japanese and British Diplomats. The ship carrying the Japanese back from Capetown called at Singapore to collect the local lot of British and American (?) Diplomats.

Somebody in Capetown with brains had made a collection for us and forwarded it on to us under the aegis of the Red Cross. Somebody, also intelligent, saw to it that it was delivered into our hands before the Japs stole it, as they did all the Red Cross parcels sent to us during the whole of our captivity. We each received the equivalent of a 6th of a monthly parcel as received in other POW camps. That was my lot over 3½ years of captivity. The Japs stole everything.

The natural resilience and inventiveness of the British began to surface and various ploys were started. An open air theatre was constructed in Changi; the footlights were coconut oil lamps with reflectors made out of four gallon tins; some remarkable shows were put on; so many of us being in the bag, there was always someone with expert experience in every field; sure enough an ex-London West End impresario and some friends were able to reconstruct the scripts of some well-known shows. Female impersonators and the ability to make costumes, both male and female out of improbable scraps of material, gave a touch of the real thing in the dim lighting.

To us, these shows seemed quite professional. Musical instruments were fashioned out of the most unlikely materials and quite a fair jazz band was formed. Not exactly the *Quintette du Hot Club de Paris* that I remembered from the good old days with Bette at the Cosmo Picture House, but a fair imitation. I particularly remember a square double bass, made largely out of tea chests. This was played with great abandon by a real enthusiast. It was the first time I had seen one spinning like a top during a hot run; very impressive; we were not a very critical audience, but it was wonderful to lose oneself in the fantasy and forget for an hour or two the Hellishness of our daily life. Some Dutch P.O.W.s had started to arrive from Java, mostly coloured. Some of the best female impersonators came from them. One show in particular consisted of a demonstration of Balinese type dancing with an explanation of the meanings of the different gestures. The hand and arm movements were especially significant. A most interesting show. Quite genuine, I was assured. One of the dancers had been an instructor to the dancing girls' troupe of some Rajah; he told us that they start off as small children and it is a great and totally unrefusable honour for a family to have a girl chosen as a palace dancer; feudalism still existed. A ribald Dutch comic gave his impression of a tightly corseted society lady undressing; it was the first time I had seen that act and along with the others I thought it hilarious. The jazz band also formed the nucleus of a concert orchestra and the performances were generally good enough to attract the Jap officers. This made it essential that any anti-Jap allusions were so skilfully written that they did not twig. This made the joke all the sweeter.

Books were available and went the rounds so that generally each one of us had a book at any one time. Finished, it was swapped for the next one on your list. Many, out of boredom, perforce read books which normally they would never have opened. I was introduced, amongst others, to *Cold Comfort Farm*, *The Sun is my Undoing* and a remarkable translation of a Chinese book, a sort of cross between the Decameron, the Kama Sutra and the Arabian Nights. Nowadays it would come under the heading of medium porn; there was a long waiting list for that one. I doubt if it is freely available in this country. The name was Chinese, something like *Ching Ping Mei*, but my memory is vague. Believe me, the Chinese had fertile imaginations. The outstanding tale was about a Chinese Emperor who amused himself during siesta time by hanging one of his concubines naked and upside down by her feet, legs well apart, in a doorway and trying to hole out in one with ripe plums as he reclined on his bed. Male chauvinist pigs had not been invented then, but it made us whistle. Some of the other stories were not far behind and you had to be a quick reader as there was always an impatient queue waiting their turn to read them. The Japs had one of their rushes of blood to the head later on, on the Railway, and decided they would censor all our books. As soon as the first was returned duly marked with their "chop", we had a copy "chop" made, which was immediately applied to any dodgy literature we did not want them to see. We could always beat them intellectually.

Then in Changi there came the bright idea of forming a University. There was enough talent available to staff one and I believe it was highly successful. I decided this was my chance to learn Gaelic and duly enrolled. Unfortunately I only attended two lectures. The Japs had also made a decision and that was that they were going to use us as slave labour to build a Railway connecting Bangkok to Rangoon. So all I learned of "the language that was spoken in the Garden of Eden," was its antiquity and its hyper intricate and convoluted grammar. We were told that it was the most difficult language of all to learn unless at home in the family. I believe it.

I think I had a lot to thank Fettes for, regular hours, plenty of sleep with wide open windows and unlimited amounts of plain wholesome food. Not that I completely escaped the effects of the deprivations, but I suffered less than the majority and a great deal less than the unfortunate ones who could not store the vital vitamins, or those who were hopelessly hooked on nicotine.

Hunger of a type, which I hope you will never have to endure, changed our standards of what was appetising and what was not. It was soon brought home to us how circumstances alter cases. As I said, within days of being forced onto a rice diet, a tin of pilchards in tomato sauce, an army ration which we had previously unanimously spurned as foul, became a prize worth risking a beating, to steal. (See above.) There were always some brave spirits prepared to take the risk and trade with any Chinese who could be contacted. It was a bigger risk for them, but their inborn instinct for trade could not be suppressed. Money soon ran out and much barter went on; a lot of clothing disappeared. Working parties were demanded by the Japs and it did no harm to have a contact in the working party on the docks. How men, who had practically no clothing, were able to smuggle the odd tin back to camp was not looked into too deeply. It helped to have an Aussie hat. I hope that no reader of this ever knows what real hunger is. It blots out everything. For three and a half years I never knew when or if I would ever get anything to eat again; moments after each meal I was starving again. On the Railway we were issued with a pound of rice a day. That is a pound of rice before cooking and indeed for a few weeks we got a pound and a half until the Japs discovered their mistake. Of course even that contained so little nutrition that we were permanently hungry and developed rice-potbellies. At the worst part of the Railway, when I had constant enteritis and recurrent malaria, I would not have weighed more than six stone.

Luckily I seemed to be able to eat and digest almost

anything and could store vitamins as well as anyone. I have a lot to thank my parents and grandparents for passing on genes so suitable for survival on starvation rations, a high pain threshold, fast healing and a dogged determination to survive, come what may.

The non-smoker was *a rara avis* in those days. Smoking was not, then, considered anti-social but quite normal for both sexes. I wonder how long the war would have lasted without tobacco. In fact, I can remember my father instructing me never to trust a Teetotaller, Non Smoker, and I found it pretty sound advice. It was discovered that the extra fine paper in Bibles and Prayer Books was ideal for the purpose of roll ups; thus they acquired a new value more on the side of Mammon than of God. One just had to assume that the Padres did not smoke cigarettes. They must have been strong silent pipe smokers.

Before the move came The "Selarang Incident". The Japs had had one of their rushes of blood to the head and ordered everyone to sign parole forms. This would give them a clear-cut excuse to execute, without trial, anyone attempting to escape (all contrary to the Geneva Convention). Naturally we refused and were then ordered to go with our belongings to Selarang Barracks, the peacetime home to a battalion of Gordon Highlanders. Thus about 16000 men, encumbered by as much of their belongings as they could carry, including cooking utensils, were crammed into an area of eight acres!! See photos overleaf.

These are but copies of copies, taken I was told, with a box Brownie, the film then buried in a sealed tin and hidden in a grave in the cemetery until after Liberation – so they are genuine and reflect the situation at Selarang (The Gordon Barracks) at the time. No wonder the copies are a bit fuzzy.

Selarang Barracks and Square during those days of September 1942   when 15,019 men, four goats and a pig were incarcerated

230

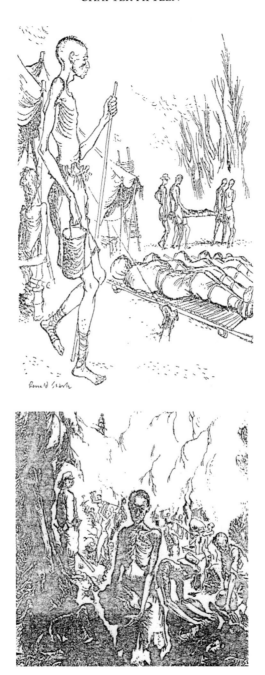

This act of defiance perked the troops up no end. We set to, to make a new home as best we could. We were late comers— surprise, surprise! The buildings round the Square seethed with humanity; even the flat roofs were covered. Have you ever tried to erect tents on thick tarmac? What the "died in the wool" Gordons thought about latrines being dug in their precious Square, I leave to your imagination. Apoplexy? Add to the above a couple of trigger-happy Japs, with machine guns, covering the perimeter angles. I only saw one water tap with a never ending queue tailing off it. There must have been others, but I saw but one. We all recognised that this was a turning point and buckled down, carrying on as if this way of living was common practice. This lasted a few days, until the Japs delivered the killer blow, threatening to bring in the patients from the hospital. I should point out that the Japs had waited until our top brass, who might have caused such a stink that the Japs would have had second thoughts, had been shipped to Formosa, before perpetrating this atrocity and excepting the 18th Div, which was still in state of shock; we were largely stuck with a gaggle of unsuitable for promotion Majors, but now due to the war Lt. Cols.

Fortunately the Medics went to our senior officer and said that there was already the beginnings of a serious epidemic of Diphtheria, which would be greatly exacerbated if the hospital was brought in. Half a dozen cases had already been reported. Diphtheria was a killer in those days; this was not news to the Japs and perturbed them not a bit. It was sign or else! Such charming people, the Japs are! You can understand my undying hatred of them.

We were then instructed by our hierarchy to sign but to understand that a signature given under duress had no validity, not that that would have presented a problem to the Japs from swiftly executing any escapees. So we signed some very odd names. There were a lot of Lt. Joe Soaps, Donald Ducks and so on, causing quite a bit of hilarity. I think a few claimed to be in the Horse Marines. We then went back to our lines to find that the "Free Indian Army" had systematically looted anything of the slightest value. I suppose that having carried out Tokyo's instructions, the local Japs filed away the papers without looking at them and were satisfied. Escape being very much in their minds, they then demanded a return of all tattoos and other unusual distinguishing physical features. I wondered what the chap with the hunt tattooed on his back admitted to. The Japs would have been very impressed.

At least the hospital had been left in reasonable peace. I suppose this affair was a Japanese version of the Black Hole of Calcutta. It was a most unpleasant experience and a foretaste of the ruthlessness of the Japs in enforcing their will upon us, regardless of the Geneva Convention or any humanitarian feelings. They had none. We were non-persons and thus expendable; an obvious War Crime in my book. The real difficulty about escaping, apart from the distances involved in reaching our own people, was not only our colour but our noses. Where we had obvious noses the natives had only nostrils. You could dress in native clothes and dye your skin, but a hooter was something you could not disguise. The fact that the Japs had in the early days publicly and clumsily executed some escapees, added to the foregoing, was a powerful deterrent. Digging your own grave before being bayoneted into it was no game with these animals. Again the Geneva Convention stated that provided an escaping POW surrendered and had not killed anyone during his breakout, he could not be executed. This meant nothing to the Japs. A bayonet was cheaper and they were rotten shots anyway.

The nearest thing to a real escape was a story that did the rounds about a man from the last lot to come up country from

Singapore. They were brought up by train, as far as the track and rails had been laid, unlike us, who had marched all the way from Bampong. They were heading into Burma. The train stopped; he was taken short, bolted into the jungle to relieve himself and on reappearing, found the train had gone. New to the jungle, completely lost and not knowing what to do, he stumbled about, until he arrived at a Burmese village. Being Buddhists, they agreed to take him in, on condition that he lived in a cave at a distance from the village so that, if the Japs found him they could claim to know nothing about him. They also agreed to feed him if he did his share of the work in the fields along with the women. (Men did not demean themselves with such work.) At a whiff of a Jap patrol he was stuffed back into his cave and its mouth camouflaged. They told him that there was a British post, probably Chindits, a couple of hundred miles to the north. They refused point blank to take him there, however much money he offered them. Their attitude was that they did not like any foreigners, British or Japs, running their country, but for humanitarian reasons they would not hand him over to the Japs. Understandably they did not want to get involved in a war not of their choosing.

It did not take him long to realise that without a native guide he had no chance of reaching the post and stayed with them for several months, until unending bouts of malaria wore him so far down that he realised that, without medical treatment, he would die. The villagers, who must have developed immunity to Malaria, agreed to lead him to a bit of the railway where there was a British working party. He hid just off the trace and contacted a man who had come into the jungle to relieve himself. Word went back to the officer, doing his ganger, and in the dark they fooled the roll call and smuggled him into their camp. This was not too easy as by this time he had a long beard and hair down to his backside. The darkness was a big help. In the camp the difficulty was how to square the numbers. Fortunately for him, two men had died that day. The two corpses were so emaciated that they could be sewn into one blanket and buried in the one grave. He took the identity of one of the dead and was smuggled into the hospital hut, generally cleaned up and survived the captivity. Could possibly be true; certainly it was a very strong rumour, but I hae me doots.

Eventually we moved, buoyed up by promises of Red X camps with running water and electricity. After innumerable countings and re-countings, off we set for Singapore Railway Station with all sorts of promises about our new Red Cross Camps ringing in our ears. There was a fair amount of scepticism about, but the general feeling, mistaken as it turned out to be, was that anything would be better than Changi. Our train was, to say the least, lacking in priority. We quite enjoyed, however, sitting on our kit on the platform. The army had accustomed us to long waits during transportation and we could see reasonably normal life going on around us for the first time since our captivity.

Eventually we were packed into steel rice wagons at 30 plus per wagon. These were to be our home for the next five days as we crawled up the Malayan Peninsular, giving way to all other traffic. Twice a day the train stopped for us to be fed rice and hot water. That was our opportunity to relieve ourselves. Quite a sight it must have been to see us all squatting at the side of the track, the more desperate ones only managing onto the track itself. No segregation between officers and men then. Poor Dennis, suffering a horrendous and perpetual case of Changi Balls, proved a source of great hilarity to the Japanese guards who in their accustomed "humane" way started shying flints from the ballast at the scarlet target offered. I suppose that, in our cowardly way, we were quite relieved that this distracted them from using us as a target.

Constructed of steel, the wagons were scalding hot by day and perishing cold at night; too many bodies, too much kit; there was not enough room to lie down. We sat on our kit and took it in turns during the day to sit beside the open door and get a little fresh air. By night the doors were shut and the fug, condensation and overcrowding made sleep impossible except in brief spells. There was naturally no opportunity for washing and you can imagine the foetid atmosphere. We trundled along so slowly that it was possible to see the Jungle sliding by in detail. A huge monitor lizard crossing a river bank, to our eyes, was only a meal missed. It was so big that, at first, we thought it was a crocodile. Few other animals were to be seen, just the odd monkey or so, but the rain forest itself was very impressive. It seemed never ending, hot, dank and vast.

Water was provided from the water tanks, normally used for topping up the engine boilers. That was the first time I had seen the great elephant's trunk thing being swung round and water gushing out as if from a fireman's hose as the giant pump handle was slowly cranked. Fires were lit to boil the water and cook the rice. No shortage of fuel; our introduction to the first of the many beneficial properties of bamboo that we were to encounter.

We went so slowly that we could read a book and anyone taken short could stick his bottom out of the open door while two others held his arms to prevent him falling out. That would have been suicide. There were armed guards at each end of the train watching both sides; they would have dearly enjoyed a bit of target practice. The whole thing was a bit like a Western film set. The same method was used for urinating but it was not recommended to put your head out until you had made sure that no one was performing further up the train. Talk about "*Gardez Loo!*" At night of course there was no chance and we had to hold on until the breakfast stop. We had in our truck one poor soul with enteritis; all we could do was give him a bucket in the corner and put up with the stink; he should never have been sent up to Siam. Slopping out in jail at home would have been a piece of cake for us.

We quickly learned that, if a native offered to shake hands with you, possible because we went so slowly that there was ample time as we rumbled along, it was not brotherly love that inspired him. It was your wristwatch he was after. It only happened once. After that there was no further interest in fraternisation. Some of us still had watches, but not for much longer.

Eventually, we crawled into Bampong in Siam, not even knowing when we had crossed the border, the jungle being the same on both sides. Bampong was to be the junction for the spur railway line from the main North South line to the new East West Siam-Burma Railway. So there we were in that camp, all inhabitants having started as equals in material matters. All except one private of Levantine extraction, circumcised no doubt, who had early on established himself as a trader, bribed the guards, and was doing a roaring trade in army surplus shirts, blankets and so on. It had finally sunk in that, from now on, a man could only take what he could carry. The spiv had taken care to avoid being sent on drafts going to the working camps. Perhaps more than the Japs were getting backhanders! Don't be so naïve as to believe that no British colonel was susceptible to the odd sweetener. This spiv had so much loot, mostly cigarettes, which were the favoured currency, just like in our gaols today, stashed under his bed that he was able to employ four security guards to protect his possessions and his person round the clock. Unsurprisingly, they also, somehow, avoided being sent up to work on the Railway. It was thus forcibly brought home to me that, while my duty lay with my men's welfare, number one had also to be looked after. I do not know what eventually happened to that spiv, but it was an object lesson to me that a bunch of men can start off all equal but, very soon, some will have a lot, some but a little and a few nothing. We moved soon, thank God.

Relieved to be quit of the filth of Bampong, (the drainage of which left much to be desired—it was like living in a swamp of faeces) we encountered for the first time the Kwai Noi river, along the north bank of which the Railway was to run as much as was practicable and beside which we were going to live for the best part of the next three years. We were, to the best of my memory, ferried across in the little Siamese boats, which we christened PomPomPoms from the sound of their little inboard single cylinder engines. They plied up and down the river supplying the little hamlets on the river banks. In the silence of the jungle you could hear them coming from miles away. Often crewed by one man, his wife and children; it was their home even to having a bamboo box built out over the bow to provide a latrine to be used in privacy. They knew every nook and cranny of the river banks, just as the old puffer skippers knew every bay, sandbank and current on the west coast of Scotland. The river here was about as wide as the Clyde off Dumbarton Rock, varying according to the monsoons. There was a bullock track up the North side of the river, but it was only suitable for small loads; during the monsoon seasons, parts of it were impassable to anything on wheels, however big.

Having crossed to the north bank, we started to march up this track carrying all our worldly possessions. This was not the first, nor the only time that I saw Malins walking unencumbered while his wretched batman staggered along carrying two kits and wearing three of everything, one of his own and two of his master's. Malins complained that as a Field Officer he should have had transport for his kit. The lack of his customary large intake of alcohol had so shrunk his frame that the little batman had had to turn himself into a tailor, so that the extra shirts etc. fitted him better. Once Malins had sussed out the "Red Cross Camps" and the prospective future on the Railway, it was not long before he got himself transferred as far back as he could. I never saw him again, so he must have got back to Singapore or died.

The slimy wet mud made walking, let alone, marching, difficult; two abreast was as much as the track allowed. We were still reasonably fresh and so pleased to get away from the filth of Bampong, that initially we made quite good progress, but were exhausted by the time we reached Chungkai, where we received our baptism into the top end of the accommodation which we were to encounter in Siam. Downhill all the way thereafter. We realised slowly that all the talk about Red Cross Camps was a Con and my opinion of the Red Cross has never recovered. Whoever was representing it was a hopeless failure and never checked what was happening in reality.

The huts at Chungkai were of the same type as those at Sungei Patani but of much inferior construction. Ronald Searle's book gives some idea of the huts. As each new camp was constructed, the Speedo got worse and the hut construction became more and more inferior. We were allotted 2 ft bed width each, giving five men to a bay. A female bamboo, cut to length, joints cleared out and suitably slit at the joints was rolled out, made topping for beds. Unfortunately the bedbugs found the split bamboo an ideal environment for breeding and concealment during the day, only coming out at night for their midnight feast, homing in to the heat of our bodies. They bred at an unbelievable rate, destroyed sleep and were ineradicable. Outside the monsoon period, we would sometimes be permitted to strip these bed slats and lay them on the ground between the huts before we went to work and on lifting them on our return, the ground would be covered with shrivelled carcases, thousands of them. This method, used regularly, did keep them slightly under control. Unfortunately the heat did not kill off the eggs, so there was always another contingent to deal with. Of course during the two monsoons there was no sun and the bedbugs prospered unchecked. My main problem was that my bedmate on my right, George Bristowe, was 20 years older than I and had spent many years in the Malayan Posts and Telegraphs Department. The bedbugs were not slow to differentiate between a succulent young body and an older leathery one.

In addition he had salvaged his Officer's valise. Mine had gone up in flames with all my other kit. I was too quick off the mark that time. The bedbugs multiplied in the seams of his valise and migrated every night to feast on me. When I remonstrated with him, he could not understand what I was complaining about as they never touched him. Eventually I persuaded him to lay his valise out in the sun and he was very astonished at the number of corpses, which he found on returning from work. Otherwise he was a good mate and companion, always good natured and easy going apart from a short bout of jaundice when he became a bad tempered curmudgeon, a Jekyll and Hyde transformation. Soon however, he recovered himself.

The first shock for me, however, on our arrival in Chungkai, was to be handed a parang, a broad bladed jungle knife, and told to make my own bed. The officers were to have their own hut (good idea) and it was decided that we should have individual beds. That did not last. I had never made anything in my life since I had managed to lose my set of tools at Cargilfield, where I had laboriously constructed a lopsided box with the aid of a saw, hammer and chisel and landed all and sundry, relatives or not, with crude fretsaw jigsaw puzzles as Christmas presents. The tools were not there when I returned from holiday for the next term; I got the blame and was sternly told that, if I could not look after them I would get no more. Behind my indignation, I was probably quite relieved, as I had realised by then, that I would never become any sort of a tradesman. It was however an object lesson on keeping a firm eye on my belongings when in close proximity to my fellow men, a very valuable lesson during my time in the ranks in the army and later as a P.O.W. Needs must, however, so I had a look at what my neighbours were doing and laboriously constructed a bed frame out of bamboo. Not perfect and with a distinct list to port, I was nevertheless very proud of my handiwork, and was sad when we were moved shortly afterwards into a traditional officers' hut with platform beds.

The climate at Chungkai was very different to that of Singapore. There was a dry season before, during and after Christmas. Nature therefore in her clever way had adapted the flora in order to protect them from herbivores. All the bamboos and scrub in the dry zone were armed with vicious thorns, a marked contrast to the lush soft greenery of the monsoon country. A single blanket was little protection against the cold at night. This affected us worst at the full moon in a clear sky. There was plenty of wood about and easily collected. We made braziers out of 4-gallon tins and kept them going overnight. Looking back I cannot understand how we did not burn the camp down. Apart from the thorns and mosquitoes it was a much healthier environment than the one which we suffered later up country.

At that early stage Chungkai comprised of a few atap huts, as above, for us, and a parade ground of bare earth for the innumerable Tenkos. There was also an armed guard, complete with guardhouse, sentry box and adjoining "no-good house" (an underground bamboo cage, so designed that it was impossible to lie down or sit up), also a flagpole. There was an extraordinary ceremony beside the Guardhouse every morning, when the Japs and Koreans were raggedly lined up in their scruffy uniforms with a lot of bowing and chanting, each line ending in a bow and a loud "OOOSH". This was some sort of oath of allegiance to their Emperor. Addressed to the rising sun, of which he was the God; it looked more like a cartoon comedy to us. The guards, Koreans, lived outside the camp along with the Jap officers and N.C.O.s.

The Koreans were generally worse than the Japs. They were like jackals to lions copying and outdoing their masters. They were pig ignorant paddy-walloppers. One in particular could not even count in Japanese and would walk up and down the ranks singing some sort of rhyming Korean counting song, similar to the way that we as children used to do: "one potato, two potatoes". He was so stupid that, in spite of the length of time he kept us standing while he tried to make his figures make sense, we preferred him as we could easily fox him over the numbers. Especially in the dark for the last roll call, when we could switch a man from the back of one squad to another to cover for someone, who was otherwise occupied. (The Griff dissemination system demanded bodies flitting about in the darkness. See under.)

He was the one who really brought my heart into my mouth. I was in a hut one day, very early on in Chungkai, helping to build a wireless set. This was before we had been forced to go out to work. Tom Douglas (ex-BBC Engineer), who had been in my squad at O.C.T.U., designed and built the sets, as I remember. We had only got as far as cutting the chassis out of a flattened 4-gallon tin and were starting to do a bit of soldering, when this turnip face appeared in the doorway. I thought, "This is it!" He was so stupid, however, that, by the Grace of God, he had no idea what we were doing, just grunted and moved off. After that we took good care to post a sentry when we were working on a set. It was no laughing matter. We heard later that the Japs had found a pukka set in another camp, arrested 12 suspects and handed them over to the Kempetai (Jap S.S.). The Jap's system of detection was simple: arrest a goodly number of possible suspects, preferably sharing a name and then systematically beat them up in no particular order until they extracted a confession from the culprit. On this occasion they beat the first two to death and threw their bodies into a latrine. I was told that, after the war, when the remains were recovered, there was not a piece of bone to be found bigger than your pinkie. They half killed the next four and then got bored and let the other six go. They never did establish the true operator, but amongst the victims was Eric Lomax, whom they suspected was heavily involved; a bit of a railway buff, he had innocently made some sort of railway map, which was found on him and he was shipped down to Singapore for the rest of his captivity in Syme Road Jail, operated by the dreaded Kempetai. It was a jail where torture was commonplace. I am glad to say that in spite of them breaking both of his arms, he was still alive when I first wrote this and in spite of the legacy of ill health did a great deal of good work for our Association. He did not talk about it much, but I do have a great respect for him. Our lot in the above camp had found a civilian wireless set, powered by an accumulator battery; they were also using a 15 cwt. truck for their work and by swapping the batteries were able to power the set. This was all too clumsy and blatant to avoid eventual detection. Even the stupidest Korean would instantly recognise a civilian wireless set.

In those days wireless sets still needed valves and condensers. Each Signals officer on his journey up to Siam carried a piece of a wireless set in his pack. Wisely, it was judged that a search might turn up a single piece, but the average Jap would not recognise what it was by itself. Not that we could be certain of that. I carried two condensers, hidden inside a pair of socks. Once it was realised how important total concealment was, Tom Douglas, I think it was, devised a very cunning plan. I think that Tom constructed the set and the Webber brothers operated it, but being only on the periphery, I took good care not to know the true facts and thus, if tortured could not reveal what I did not know. The M.O.'s army issue water-bottle had twice the capacity of the standard P.B.I one. Tom melted the solder on the bottom of one, removed it and built a wireless set onto it, to fit inside the water bottle and then finished the job by building a false bottom near the top of the bottle. This was kept topped up with water in case any Jap got too curious. A second M.O.'s water bottle was similarly treated, but filled with dry torch cells. The two water bottles were then hung innocently above a bedspace. The Japs never tumbled to it, not even the Kempetai, the Japanese Gestapo, who carried out many snap searches, and who had a good idea that there had to be a wireless somewhere. I took care not to know anything about this, so that, under torture, I could not reveal what I did not know.

Hogmanay that year was slightly alleviated by sharing a bottle of the local hootch with a fellow Scot. Called Arrack, it was distilled from liquid tapped from palm trees and definitely lethal. The head took a long time to clear the next morning! It was very strange drinking this foul stuff, thinking back to other Hogmanays and wondering if I would ever get back to Scotland to celebrate it properly with my love. The news (Griff, see under) was still uniformly bad: the Yanks chased out of the Philippines, the Japs knocking on the door to India, the 8th Army in and out of Tobruk like yoyos and Europe, Britain excepted, firmly controlled by Fascist and anti-Semitic brutality.

Sanitation, Japanese style in all the camps, was primitive. No more cosy boreholes, where the maggots, carefully kept in darkness, could not evolve into bluebottles. I would have called them greenbottles—they looked green to me and I sure saw plenty of them. Indeed, if a man was too sick to go out on the Railway, he had to sit up in his bedspace and kill 100 twice a day: not too difficult as they descended on us in hordes. For a latrine, a narrow trench was dug, with never enough time allowed to dig it deep enough. A few strips of bamboos for footholds and there we squatted. No screens, no privacy. The maggots did their best to keep the trenches from overflowing, but not always too successfully during monsoons. Squatting cheek to cheek alongside enteritis and dysentery sufferers in the pitch black of night, and sometimes up to ten times a night with the maggots swarming half an inch away from your private parts was not pleasant. I was lucky only to suffer enteritis and that for not more than eighteen months.

As a sanitation system, it left a lot to be desired, practical maybe under the conditions, but neither hygienic nor aesthetic. It took some time for us to accept that jungle green leaves had to take the place of lavatory paper; great care had to be exercised in the choice of leaves, particularly at night; some had spikes, which could cause pain and irritation. You learned the hard way. Later on the Dutch showed us some gymnastic exercises using a bottle of water; far cleaner and more aesthetic. Fortunately coconut oil glass bottles were plentiful.

For urination, in camp, ingenious contraptions named by us "Pissaphones" were made out of 4-gallon tins. The designer must have spent some time in Paris pre-war! There was a distinct flavour of the "Pissoirs" about the design, the aura too! Funnels four at a time, expanding in diameter until wide enough to act as individual urinals led into a large funnel sunk into the ground. These were very efficient and a tribute to British engineering. It was no surprise to us that the jungle covered our camps so quickly after being deserted. No wonder; the abandoned camps were instantly covered in a welter of lush green and disappeared. The ground was well fertilised. But the smell lingered on. You could get wind of a camp half a mile away even a year after it had closed down and was obliterated by greenery.

One advantage, which we had in the early days in Chungkai, was that we passed through a small Siamese open air market, going to and coming back from our work, and were at that time allowed to buy a few things, such as tobacco, coconut oil, duck eggs, Gula Malacca and chillies to give a bit of flavour and variety to the endless diet of plain rice. Among the market traders was one Lulu, who for ten cents would make a fast omelette with a duck egg and some coconut oil. Very welcome too. After a bath she might have been quite presentable. She had a notable cleavage, which did not hinder her from getting more customers than her competitors for her omelettes. The Japs had had another rush of blood to their heads and printed some worthless Siamese Bahts to make it seem that they were paying us for our labour. What we got after deductions for the sick and the hospital did not go very far.

The tobacco was something else. It came in rectangular pillows, henna coloured and shredded for cigarettes. It was not really suitable for a pipe, but better than cherry leaves. It was so dry that after filling my pipe and applying a bit of burning bamboo, flames would appear and I was lucky to get more than three or four puffs before it burned out and died on me; more red than brown, it rejoiced in the name of Sikh's Beard or Hag's Bush for scatological reasons. In each camp hung, permanently smouldering, a thick length of old rope to provide a light for cigarettes.

The Japs never lost an opportunity to rub in to us how inferior we were compared to "the master race" and greatly enjoyed lecturing us on our failings. The day after our arrival at Chungkai, we were paraded in order to receive a lecture from the Jap colonel in command of 2 Group of which we were now a part. Formed into a hollow square, we stood patiently; he, not much taller than his sword and with huge white gauntlets, spurs and fractured English, was not really equipped to mount a soap box on his own. Completely ineffective as an overall commander, he took good care not to see what he knew fine was going on, so that he could deny any knowledge of it later. We then got the first of many lectures to the effect that we were very lucky to have the privilege of working for the I.J.A. on the construction of this historic Railway and that as long as we worked hard, we would be well treated but if not, we would be severely punished. He enjoyed it much more than we.

We suffered another indignity from the idiot colonel, who I am glad to say, in spite of claiming to have known nothing of the atrocious treatment we had received, was to the best of my knowledge hanged after Liberation. He decided that for Christmas there would be a ceremony to honour the dead on both sides of the Malaya Campaign. The only good thing was that we did not go out to work that day. A ghastly wreath about ten feet high and made out of jungle branches and leaves was erected. We were fallen in on four sides while he gave a hypocritical tribute to the dead in his fractured English. We were utterly disgusted; what made it worse was that he had persuaded some idiot on our side to do the Rupert Brooke thing. When he got to the bit about some corner of a foreign field being forever England, no mention of Scotland of course, I was nearly physically sick.

One of the first tasks, quickly learned, on starting a new camp was to construct a vegetable garden; in that climate, growth was so fast that something edible such as sweet potato tops and spring onions could be cropped within six weeks. Tomatoes and ground nuts, not long after and even papaya trees grew and fruited within twelve months. All depended on how long we were in a camp. We planted with optimism, however.

Pearl Harbour, although it seemed at the time to be a disastrous defeat for the US, proved instead to be a wake-up call to that young country, unburdened by the mind-set and bureaucracy of a Colonial Power; it quickly tumbled to the fact that the future for naval warfare lay in Aircraft Carriers and not with the Battleships of W.W.1 and quickly got down to work building them and their naval aircraft to a band playing. The day of the "Battlewagon" was over. Nobody knew as much about mass-production as they did; the idea of Naval Task Forces then took root and changed their war strategy.

The Jap forces had met so little resistance that they must have thought that the British and Dutch Colonial powers were so effete that their Colonies were like ripe plums ready for picking. Their advance careered on regardless of any thought of consolidating their lines of communication, which became over-stretched, particularly so in Burma. There the leadership of General Bill Slim was the opposite to that of Percival. The retreat of the 14th or "Forgotten" Army was controlled and bridges were properly blown, etc., slowing the Japs down. This gave our troops time to regroup on the Assam border and provide more resolute resistance at Imphal and Kohima. The boot was on the other foot now. The Allies had the advantage of land based modern aircraft and short lines of communication. The battles at Imphal and Kohima were so fierce, almost hand to hand, that I was told that the Q.A.I.M.N.S. were issued with pistols to use on themselves rather than fall into the hands of the Japs. Eyeing them on board with us on the way home, I felt that they and particularly their matron/colonel would have taken quite a few Japs with them. A formidable lady, not nicknamed "the Atom Bum" for nothing. They were the real heroines.

The Japs had been, for some time, hammering at the gateway to India, where they confidently expected the population to rise *en masse* in their favour. The "Free Indian Army" eagerly awaited, but was too frightened to show face prematurely. The I.J.A. was now stuck in the Arakan, one of the most inhospitable and fever ridden regions in the world for an army to be stuck in. How now could these troops in the Arakan be supplied? This greatly exercised Tokyo. They had not reckoned with the very real threat from Allied submarines. This was soon brought home to them, when, after losing a few merchant ships, they discovered that their shipyards could not build replacements quickly enough to maintain their Navy, let alone their merchant fleet. Their yards were too few and far more valuable to them for naval construction.

Some other method had to be found. What ships that had survived would be better employed on a very much shorter and safer trip, hugging the coast to Bangkok, where land based aircraft could give protection and whose shallow waters Allied submarines found inhospitable; a quick turn round and then transport the looted iron ore, tin and rubber, brought in by rail from Malaya, etc., back to Japan. Supply by aircraft was still just a glimmer in some boffin's eye. The deep Indian Ocean was far too submarine-infested. Thus their shipping was reduced to hugging the shallow waters of the coastline on their long voyage from Japan through the China seas to Bankok in the Gulf of Siam, where their cargoes for Arakan could be unloaded and looted supplies for Japan loaded for the return voyage. The long trip round the Malay Peninsular and up the west coast of Malaya and Burma, in order to service their troops in the Arakan, was too slow and dangerous. A good system for supplies returning home, but not for supplying their troops in the Arakan. All deep water was patrolled by Allied submarines. Much too slow and cumbersome a solution for their supply problems for Tokyo.

A road from Siam to Burma was judged impractical: two monsoons (close coupled annually), and the consequent mud and shortage of fuel killed that plan. A Railway connecting Bangkok to Rangoon, while desirable, had twice been surveyed between the wars and twice condemned by the International Consortia concerned as impossible to construct because of the terrain and health problems for the large workforce needed. The Japs had in their hands a vast number of P.O.W.s who by meekly surrendering, had become non-persons and so, according to their peculiar doctrine, expendable and were at that moment in Singapore, idle and eating their heads off. The fact that so many

International experts had ruled out such a railway as uneconomic if not wholly impracticable or that the Geneva Convention prohibited the use of P.O.W.s for military purposes deterred the Japs not one bit. Necessity drove them and the more their troops were first stalled and then slowly driven back from the Indian border, the more grew the urgency for a safe supply line to their troops in the Arakan, which had become a deadly battleground for them. Well at the top of any list of highly endemic Malarial environments, it was one of the most inhospitable areas in the world in which to ask an army to live/and fight.

Siam and Indo China produced rice in abundance. Track and rolling stock could be looted from China, Java and Indo China. Wood burning locomotives would find no shortage of indigenous fuel. Put all these together and Hey Presto! Problem solved. A Railway was the only answer. We unfortunate P.O.W.s became the slave/manpower required to build the Railway. To put it bluntly, we were no more than modern-day slaves. It took quite a time for this to sink in. Many myths died. We involuntarily disproved the one that Europeans could not do physical work under the tropical sun, another that white skins could not bear that tropical sun, although my skin has never recovered from the constant exposure to the tropical sun and is so sensitive that to this day I cannot use any shower gel or soap and need prescription unguents; otherwise I would tear my skin to pieces. That Europeans would get instant sunstroke without a pith helmet was another myth.

Neither in Bampong, nor in any Camp on the Railway, were we surrounded by barbed wire as would have been the case of a European P.O.W. camp. The boundaries were sometimes marked by some sort of bamboo fencing, but generally, it was no problem to slip out of camp in the dark. Escaping from the camps was easy, but as I have explained, avoiding recapture was impossible.

I do not know of any confirmed successful escapes. Undetected trading with the Siamese villagers was a different matter. That was how the spiv became so prosperous. Bribery ensured that he would never get caught and brought to trial. One of our troops however was not so lucky. In the early days in Chungkai, he saw a good chance of laying a woman. Clearly a better or fitter man than I, he decided to take a leaf out of the spiv's book and disappeared one night, with an army blanket under his arm. He had no problem explaining the trade he desired and the lady was willing. However, a Jap patrol came upon the couple as our man was going hard at it. Following the Japanese peculiar moral code the sentry indicated to our man that he could finish what he was doing while he spectated, complete with cigarette plastered to his lip, fixed bayonet and holding the torch for illumination. The job completed, he arrested our man, took him back to camp for punishment, but did not forget to take the blanket as well for evidence. The lady protested but to no avail. I forgot to add that, before lifting the blanket, the Jap gave our man his gun etc. to hold while he enjoyed the lady as well!! I may not have been present, but I heard the tale from many and believe it to be true. Typical of the Japs' fixation about sex as you will realise as you read on; they seemed to have nothing else to talk about, once they had acquired your valuables by *force majeur*. Opening conversation ran as follows: "You watcho, peno" or anything else he coveted? He would then offer a ridiculously low price for what he was after. Straightforward theft was a punishable crime for them, but if they had paid, that was different. You then were faced with either accepting the low price or future regular beatings on trumped up charges, when his version was always believed over yours. Transaction completed, conversation then went, "You wifeo?" If the answer was yes, the moon face lit up with an evil lascivious grin. JigaJig No one? Yeough! A repulsive race in every way.

Construction of the Railway began soon after our arrival at Chungkai. A typical day for us for the next two-plus years started with breakfast in the dark, half a mess tin of watery plain rice, called Pap, followed by tenko on the parade ground; squads of men were allocated to individual Jap engineers, issued with tools and marched/shambled off to their tasks; these largely consisted of digging cuttings or building embankments; tools consisted of Eastern type heart-shaped spades and chunkles (sort of hoes cum pick axes); both made of very inferior metal, which kept the Jap blacksmith busy trying to keep them serviceable. We also built culverts and bridges as required and in one case in my experience drilled holes for blasting a cutting on a cliff ledge, of which more later; the day was broken by an a.m. and p.m. "Smokeo", green tea (no milk, no sugar) and lunch of plain rice and green tea again. Task completed, tools checked, we were marched back to camp. Lastly, interminable counting and re-counting before we could finally get our evening meal, eaten in the dark, always hoping that there might be something to go with the rice to give it some sort of flavour, whatever the cooks could rustle up, plus anything grown by ourselves, but sometimes only those ghastly dried green vegetables which had to be soaked in the river for at least 24 hours. Then lying down, anxiously awaiting the arrival of the Griff, which gave us a slight idea of what was happening in the real world, although I now realise that it, probably, was not as up to date as we thought, in case someone inadvertently mentioned in a Jap's hearing something that gave away that we had a source of news. All so monotonous, so exhausting, so many medical problems, so little food, so many savage beatings; as pressure from Tokyo increased and the ferocity of the Speedo took effect, mostly for no apparent reason, it was not surprising that many just gave up and died. After a few months it was forbidden to play the Last Post at funerals. It had become a daily event and too depressing.

Washing had to be done out of working hours and in the river. When it was in spate, during the five months of the two monsoons, one did not so much get clean as move the dirt around. Soap was at best, scarce, expensive and coarse. During the monsoons we were wet for months on end anyway. Nothing could keep out the wet.

Cooking was done by the fortunate few, under a leaky atap roof, in "Qualis", shallow hemispheres of cast iron, about two to three foot in diameter, like huge woks. These were set into mud brick (we learned like the Israelites how to make bricks without straw) structures, four at a time, like a honeycomb; a fire burning bamboo under each led to a common vent. The food was no better than at Changi, except that the rice ration was usually bigger when we were working. We could consume a pound of rice a day per man, nae bother; that is a pound before cooking and was a lot of rice. Indeed we would gobble it down fast, so as to be at the front of the queue for seconds, if any, called the *Legge* (a Malay word) queue. I never qualified as a cook; that required influence. Cooks in the army always feed much better than their customers. That is a fact of life; nowhere was it better demonstrated than in the P.O.W. camps. They did not have to go out to work on the Railway, but it paid to keep in with them. I swallowed my pride, as far as possible. They had had to learn quickly how to cook rice in quantity. A measured amount of rice with some salt, if available, was covered with water. The fire lit and the whole brought to the boil; the fire was then drawn and the rice left to steam, while the cook stirred it vigorously with a paddle, similar to a canoe paddle. The rice was then put into 4-gallon tins. The volume of them was well known; the number of scoops per tin was equally well known and woe or something worse betide the cook whose number of scoops did not work out. Sticking to the metal of the Quali was a skin of half burned rice. A kind of ersatz toast, this was highly prized. Unfortunately the cooks and their fortunate friends usually got it. Only occasionally was I lucky. I, if in camp, was not too proud to hang around the kitchen at the crucial times.

Razor blades were hideously expensive. Fortunately some genius had discovered that stropping a razor blade on the wet inside of a bottle could extend its working life to a year and more. Hacking away with a bluntish razor, in cold water, was hardly a pleasant pastime but needs must. Hair cutting required the compliance of the Jap engineer in charge of the squad as did visits to the jungle for bowel movements. *Benjo* in Japanese. This pattern ruled our lives throughout the construction of the Railway; work went on during all the hours of daylight in an atmosphere ever more hectic as the "Speedo" was inflicted on us ever more violently; finally, if the Jap schedule got too far behind, even the sick were stretchered out to the trace to break up stones for ballast as they lay in their stretchers in the mud; the shouts of "Speedotana, Dammmeda and Buggero" resounded, followed by the bashing of all and sundry within range. We were driven on in a growing frenzy of shouts and indiscriminate bashings. Little did the Japs realise that the whole thing could have been accomplished far more quickly by using some forward planning and issuing decent food and humane treatment for the labour force. We quickly learned that we were expendable slaves in the hands of ignorant barbarians.

All this was carried out against a background of plagues of lice, bedbugs, ringworm, repeated B.T. Malaria and constant Enteritis. A civilised regime knows that a sick man needs rest and extra nourishment in order to bring him back to health and strength. Not so the Japs, who deducted the numbers of sick (designated as non-workers and therefore deserving no food) from the ration strength. We of course took the opposite view. The extra rations, which we provided for the sick, reduced what was available for the workers. This slowly dawned on me. The horse doctor, who from the Japanese point of view was in overall charge of our health, worked sufficient miracle cures daily (Jesus was no competition) to declare enough sick men fit in order to fill the engineers' demands. Why did we do it? A naked P.O.W., barefoot, clad only in a G-String, faced with a ranting Jap holding a rifle and fixed bayonet has little option. We were slaves pure and simple. You obeyed or were bashed into submission. If they had had enough sense to break us in gradually and used a little common sense, the Railway would have been built quicker and our lives would have been easier. We, who had been conned by the promise of Red Cross camps, equipped with electric light and running water instead became the unpaid and eminently dispensable slave labour force to build a Railway through virgin jungle right across Siam into Burma.

What saved us from even worse, strangely enough, was the climate. We soon learned that the first thing to do in a new camp, after building the huts and seeing to the sanitation, was to find somewhere to plant a garden. (See above.) In that heat and humidity everything grew like it was in a greenhouse. If we stayed long enough, not that we always did, we could have sweet potato tops and shallots in six weeks and tomatoes not too long after that. In the main camps, papayas could be had within a year of planting. Ground nuts, as we learned to call peanuts after the war, could give a good crop in a few weeks provided that you beat the ants to it. They were excessively fond of them. An extraordinary plant, one peanut planted would produce a small bush. The lateral branches then sent thin black shoots down into the earth and the peanuts formed underground. I would not have believed it if I had not seen it. These along with the bananas and duck eggs, if you had some Bahts, (newly printed paper money) offered a little variety. Killers quick like cholera and cerebral malaria, slower like Beriberi caused by the vitaminless diet, promised a slow and unpleasant death. They were the biggest problem for the medics. It was pathetic to see a man slowly deteriorate, first his legs swelling up like bolsters with oedema until he could hardly walk, then his trunk bloated. Some even went blind or their lungs drowned in the excess liquid; they died a horrible slow death, fighting for breath. The doctors, who were beyond praise and unremitting in their determination to save life, set us to fermenting any fruit or pumpkin skins with Gula Malaca, which seemed to be the skimmings off the sugar vats, so as to make a kind of alcohol. This contained enough vitamin B12 to have a startling effect on a bad case. Given a dose of this stuff a man would lurch off to the Pissaphone and stand there for what seemed a quarter of an hour; you could see his legs and torso slowly reverting to their previous shape while the liquid poured out of him. If it had not been so serious, it would have passed as a clever conjuring trick. The sad thing was that for the unfortunates, who could not store up vitamin B12, it was only a matter of days before the oedema reappeared, and the process had to be repeated, but was only effective as long as the supply of alcohol could be maintained.

These killers had not taken long to make their presence felt; Diphtheria was not far behind. There our doctors showed their mettle; they were absolutely magnificent right through the captivity and I could not adequately praise them enough. They had nothing except what they could carry up to Siam and what Nai Boon Pong (see under) could smuggle. They were masters of improvisation and must have saved thousands of lives. They would have saved many more, if the means of convalescence, or a supply of drugs had been available; so many deaths were registered as caused by a disease name followed by "and despair", meaning that the poor sods would have lived if they could have been given any hope and to have hope to live, they needed to have hope of nourishment.

The epidemic of Diphtheria caused the doctors to take

decisive action or the death rate in those early days would have been catastrophic. We had so little resistance. However they set to and using primitive Heath Robinson equipment, produced from a standing start a vaccine and brought the epidemic under control. They worked under a further enormous handicap, in that overseeing them was the Japanese alleged doctor. He was, to the best of my belief, a horse doctor, not even having veterinary qualifications. He did not possess a stethoscope and, on being gifted one as a peace offering (bribe) by one of our doctors, he hung it over his ears as he must have seen doctors do in films. He was never known to put the ear-pieces in his ears. It was just a status symbol. On one notable occasion on a sick parade, which he was supervising, our M.O. tried to explain to him that the soldier in question had a floating kidney. When the gist of this sank in, the bold lad told the soldier to jump up and down and, if he could hear the kidney rattling through his stethoscope, which he persisted in hanging round, but not in, his ears, he would excuse the man from work. After a minute or two he claimed that he could clearly hear the kidney jumping about through his unconnected stethoscope and the man was dismissed to hospital!

No wonder, none of the Japs or Koreans, if they were ill, would go near him. They invariably bribed our doctors to treat them. This gave our doctors a chance of some discrete blackmail to acquire the necessary medical supplies. The Japs and Koreans were the greatest hypochondriacs that I have ever known, terrified of illness at the best of times; the thought that they might fall into his hands petrified them. Having seen him at work I cannot blame them. Once I was passing the hospital tent while a Jap or Korean was having his appendix out; no anaesthetic available, four Japs held him down by his arms and legs while the alleged surgeon carved him open—all by the light of a homemade oil lamp. It was like a scene from the Napoleonic wars. You could hear the patient scream from miles away. This mountebank was officially in charge of the health of 2 Group, numbering several thousands.

I was known to claim that he worked more miracle cures than Jesus Christ ever did. You could be dying, but if he ruled that you were fit, you were fit and had to go out to work even if you had to be stretchered there. We learned very quickly how to handle him. Unless you were in the middle of a rigor or bright purple, it was no use going sick with malaria when he was supervising Sick Parade. So the thing to do was just before the parade to drink some very hot "coffee" (I shall explain later how we made "coffee") and wrap yourself up in a couple of blankets so that you arrived on sick parade, sweating like a pig and highly coloured. Mind you, I have never seen a pig sweat. Then, if you were lucky, he might just authorise some Quinine and pass you as sick. Much depended on your timing; the flush could wear off if he was late; also the number of miracle cures which he carried out referred more to the demands of the Jap engineers than to the patients' health.

The Japs controlled virtually all the world's stock of Quinine, which was an initial advantage. Quinine, however, although a good treatment for B.T. Malaria, is not a prophylactic. Allied researchers finally invented Atebrine (see under), a synthetic substitute for Quinine, which effectively killed off the Malaria, where Quinine merely treated each bout individually. Mepacrine, a further advance from Atebrine, could be used as a prophylactic as well. As long as the prescribed dose was taken daily, a man had a very good chance of avoiding falling victim to Malaria. He would go a fairly strong shade of greenish yellow but could still function as a fighting soldier.

CHAPTER 16

THE SURRENDER

"Once I built a railroad, made it run,
Made it race against time.
Once I built a railroad. Now it's done
Buddy can you spare a dime?"

STRANGE THAT THE ABOVE HIT SONG from the Depression years in the U.S. made such an impression on me at the time. The haunting lyrics gave a clear picture of how badly ex-servicemen in the U.S. were treated in the inter-war years. It was no better in this country. I can well remember the pathetic little quartet of ex-service officers, in their British Warms, sporting their medal ribbons, shuffling a little portable piano, (similar to the ones seen on Clyde cruises pre-W.W.2), down the gutters of Renfield Street playing old wartime songs and begging for pennies. Kipling, as usual, was so right. When peacetime arrived, the nation was only too quick to forget those whom they had hailed as heroes a few short months before. A lesson I too had to learn. *Plus ça change, plus c'est le même chose.* We built a railroad and yet, as I write this, our government steadfastly refuses to support our rightful claim to compensation from the Japs and with an election looming Blair bought us off with a miserable ex-gratia payment for the disgraceful and inhumane treatment which we received; this paid for by the taxpayer at that, not by the Japs. 66 years on, no change.

The Railway was constructed from both ends; we were to meet the Burma contingent just over the border. Our side ran North and West from Bampong. The P.O.W. labour force was divided into four main groups plus rail laying and signalling sections. I was in 2 Group, based in Chungkai, a camp which was quite small when we arrived, but developed into a huge base cum hospital camp. As the Railway progressed, we were moved in batches to a series of smaller camps, finally finishing up at Krian Krai, just short of the Siam/Burma border and the final camp for 2 Group's second tranche.

The Railway did not do them a lot of good, I am glad to say; completed it was, if you can call the end result completion, but too late to give any effective help to their troops in the Arakan, except to evacuate some of their sick and wounded. (See under.) It was shockingly badly built; we certainly did our best to help that along; the Allied planes gave the bridges and rolling stock a hard time; progress was slow due to the peculiar thinking of the Jap High Command; all that mattered to them was that the time table be kept to. An order had to be carried out to the letter, however stupid or impractical it might be. Otherwise a senior officer would be made to lose face, something quite inconceivable to them, but an enormous cost in deaths of our men.

Each new camp had to be hacked out of the jungle and built at breakneck speed from scratch; thus they were ramshackle affairs and quickly swallowed up by the jungle after being abandoned. The workforce constructed the basic track up to what one might laughingly call rail laying standard in both directions from each camp to meet up with the workers from the neighbouring camps. I think that George Haddow's diary is an accurate account. I cannot remember the names of all the camps we worked in but it must have been well over half a dozen. Depressingly repetitive. Each Group had a specific length to build both ways to meet its neighbours. When that was finished the Group leapfrogged the other groups (see ten-day march below) and repeated the process further up the railway. Included here is a Dutch map, which lists all the camps. I shall try to mark those that ring a bell.

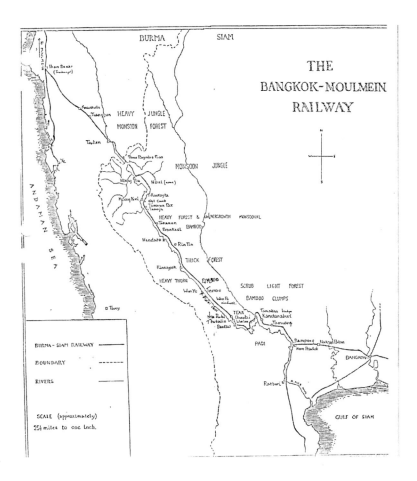

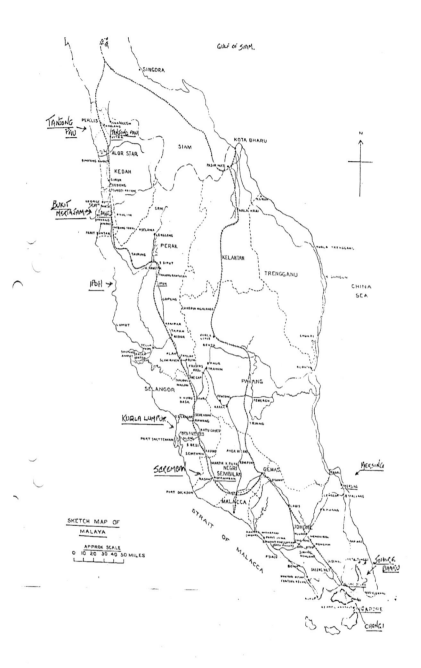

Pet animals did not figure much in our lives on the Railway. Mongrel dogs materialized, attracted by the smells of our cookhouses and were trapped and eaten by the Japs and Koreans, not us. Cats, kink tailed, appeared from time to time and became as near pets as cats allow. We were regularly deeved by reminiscences from our local know-all of his two Siamese cats, who met him off the commuter train every evening. Our local cat decided to have her kittens under the bed-space in our hut. This led to more pontificating from our feline expert. Crowds came from other huts to view the scene of domesticity and listen to his pontifications. The cat did not care for the excitement and decided to move. We watched in awe as she picked each kitten up by the scruff of its neck and carted it off to the other end of the hut; appalled, we were to see one kitten left behind and volunteered as one man to cart the abandoned one to join its siblings as instructed by our F.E. Mother cat reappeared later and tossed the kitten out. We tried again, she tossed it out; eventually someone timidly suggested that we put the kitten back, only to be shouted down by F.E.; in his absence, kit was put back; mother appeared, picked her kit up and carried it to her new nest; harmony was restored and F.E. ceased pontification.

One small camp included a couple of goats. Billy was dead nuts on his conjugal rights. Nanny, either not so, or desirous of more privacy, managed to frustrate Billy by charging recklessly about the parade ground and camp. Evening Tenkos became even more chaotic than usual with Nanny, hotly pursued by Billy, charging headlong in and out through the ranks as the Koreans tried fruitlessly to count us. This suited us fine; it greatly helped the organization of procurement and distribution of the Griff. We soon found that the goats were excessively hooked on tobacco and would stand blissfully, wagging their stumpy little tails, if you blew smoke into their nostrils; bleating for more. One of my Kongsi stupidly left a split newly purchased pillow of "Sikh's beard" on his bed-space when he went out to work, only to find on his return no pillow but two comatose very happy goats.

The Railway was completed at an enormous cost in human lives. It is no exaggeration to say that a man died or, not to put too fine a point on it, was murdered by the Japanese for every sleeper on the Railway. The numbers of workers dropped so much that the Japs had to bring up hordes of wretched coolies (and their wives probably—I cannot remember, but I think so) from the plantations in Malaya. What they contributed to the Railway I do not know, but it cannot have been much. Our death rate was bad enough, but theirs was unbelievable. When cholera struck they were all but wiped out. Tens of thousands of them died. They, poor souls, had no idea about hygiene, nor did they have any medical back up and died like flies. It was not unusual to see them drawing drinking and cooking water from a pond in which they were also doing their laundry, bathing, urinating and defecating. Their skeletons could be found scattered in the jungle alongside the trace. An elephant would suddenly shy away at a sharp trot and sure enough there was a skeleton stretched out on the ground, with the skull resting on an ornamental china pillow; the only flesh visible was the soles of the feet. A lifetime of walking barefoot had turned the soles of their feet into the equivalent of the leather sole of a boot, fully half an inch thick; even the maggots found it impossible to masticate them.

The trace for the Railway was cut by a special squad of Jap engineers working ahead of us. Thus we would find nearby, on arrival at a new camp site, a strip cut in the jungle about 70 yards wide where the trees, heavy scrub and bamboo clumps had been roughly felled and bamboo markers for the camber etc. of the embankment set out. This was to be our workplace. Our job was to construct the track up to a standard suitable for rail laying, either by digging cuttings or building up embankments as the contours of the ground dictated. Our first job was to excavate the tree roots—a formidable task. We were dealing with jungle giants, bastard teak, etc. Bridges and culverts were included in our remit. When possible, we would try to fill in over the tree roots before the Jap engineer realised, in the hope that they would rot away and cause enough subsidence to capsize an engine. Sometimes this was successful; it also meant less earth to be excavated and carried. We did not often get away with it, but it was most satisfying when we did. Any cliffs had to be tackled by blasting out cuttings broad enough for the single track railway. Any rivers and streams had to be bridged which cheesed the Japs off considerably.

Our first task on the Railway was to howk out a large cutting, but very soon the Japs found all these men in a lump impossible to handle and realising that a disciplined organisation was there in front of their eyes, decreed that the officers should start supervisory work on the Railway—strictly against the Geneva Convention; we refused initially, but the arrival of an ex-British 15 cwt. truck with a machine gun manned and facing out of the back gave us reason to think seriously. The doctors and the senior officers were paraded; we were then informed that they would be the first to be shot; we would be next, unless we agreed to go to work.

Remembering their ruthlessness in the Selarang incident, a face saving compromise was reached whereby officers would only accompany their men every second day out to the Railway and act as supervisors. This was the thin end of the wedge, but a machine gun aimed over the back of a 15cwt at one's colleagues and the threat that we would be next, unless we agreed, is a pretty powerful argument. Our duty according to our rank was allocated as ganger or supervisor, mine (a mere 2nd Lt. graduated from ganger to ganger cum teaboy) as the Speedo rose to a crescendo, but always in inverse proportion to the numbers fit and available to work, was originally to take out a squad every second day, allocate jobs to the men individually, accept responsibility for the completion of the day's task by your squad and get bashed for any mistakes. Here, I must put it on record that my men shielded me from many a bashing. Lack of glasses was a considerable handicap.

The Indian Army officers and some Volunteer officers, who had virtually no troops, still stayed in camp, the rest of us slaved out on the trace; this cheesed off the Japs considerably. Hence *The Bridge over the River Kwai* book and film, which entertained millions without telling anything like the true story. I was later told that the French author had never set foot in Siam. As I understood it, the true story was that the Indian Army officers had no troops with them in Siam and the Malay Volunteer Officers had but few (see above). Thus the ratio of officers to men was disproportionate. To find, as the pressure of the Speedo increased relentlessly, these surplus officers sitting in their huts, while everyone else was being hounded out to the trace, infuriated the Japs, and a war of words ensued until a compromise was reached. The spare officers offered to build this particular bridge without Japanese supervision, claiming that they contained in their ranks sufficient qualified experts; this would ensure the finest ever end product. They doubtless would have done so eventually, but they suffered from the same problem as I had experienced in the O.C.T.U. squad at Prestatyn. Too many experts, leading to arguments over procedure, meant that the work progressed at a snail's-pace, until the Japs, as we knew they would, lost patience, took charge and gave the officers' squad a really torrid time from then on: once again too many chiefs.

Going out to work every second day for the officers had

started contrary to the Geneva Convention. We had also reluctantly reached an agreement with the Jap Camp Commander that a cubic yard (a ton) per man was a fair day's task and that every week one cubic yard per day multiplied by the number of men in a squad would form the target for that week and if the squad finished it within six days, the seventh, aimed for a Sunday, would be a rest or "Yasume" day as the Japs called it. The measurements initially were done by our own C.O. and things ran fairly smoothly for a few weeks. The men felt that the extra effort was worthwhile so as to have Sunday off, when they could attend to their own chores in daylight. The Jap Camp Commander had apparently previously run a chemist's shop. This qualified him as a railway engineer in the I.J.A.!! Named by us "Teeth and Trousers", he was the stereotypical Jap with glistening teeth spattered with gold, set in a moon face, baggy shirt ballooning over baggy trousers spilling over his jackboots and a trailing sword which caused him continual trouble by threatening to trip him up. He was fat and rolled from side to side as he walked about, fairly revelling in his self-importance; not much between the ears though. He had been carefully watching our C.O. doing the measuring and pretending to check the measurements and the arithmetic. Whether he thought that the C.O. was slipping one over him or that he was losing face by letting the inferior P.O.W.s make the decisions, I know not.

Whatever it was, he decided to reverse the procedure. He would do the measuring and the calculations and our C.O. would agree the figures. Unfortunately, while it was quickly clear that he was unqualified to do the job, he was equally unable to concede that he had made a mistake. That meant losing face, something impossible for a Jap Officer. He was thick, even for a Jap, and arithmetically inept.

Progress was therefore very slow on his first task, but the Jap either would not or could not admit his fault and instead decided that we should work day and night, with two hours to get a hot meal round about midnight, until the task was completed. We worked by the light of the moon, stars and jungle torches of leaves soaked in some sort of resin. It was an eerie sight, like the illustration of a sweat shop in a Victorian novel, hundreds of barefoot men, mostly clad only in G-strings in the middle of the jungle slaving away with primitive tools by moonlight and flaring torches. The work rate naturally dropped in spite of alleged Jap engineers making a show of dashing about, shouting abuse and lashing out indiscriminately. There was no incentive to progress; this did not cheer them up a lot. They were none too happy either about working double shifts. They knew fine whose fault it was, but dared not open their mouths.

After a week of little apparent progress, even our chemist realised he had made a monumental boob; not that he would ever admit it. He therefore suddenly appeared about midnight in order to give us his version of the old tune that we were lazy; Japanese soldiers would have had the job completed long ago. He finished his tirade by shouting out that the first slacker he saw he would strike with his sword like this. Suiting his action to his words, he thereupon drew his sword, for him quite an operation in itself, and slashed at a bamboo beside him. He had clearly never, in his life, cut a large, growing female bamboo. It is essential to cut at an angle and follow through. Otherwise the bamboo closes on the blade like a vice. There he stood, frothing at the mouth, his baggy shirt and trousers flapping with the unaccustomed exertion, vainly wrestling with his sword, trying to free it. We fell about and even his own men, aghast, had to turn their backs to hide their faces. The more he struggled the more firmly the sword stuck; this was bad enough, but one of the Geordies next to us, who had gone into the jungle to relieve himself, shouted out: "Cock A Doodle Doo!" I hoped that Teeth and Trousers was going to have Apoplexy. The symptoms were there; his face was red and covered in spittle; however no such luck. One of his sergeants extricated the sword, which he wrestled clumsily back into its scabbard. By this time he did not need to work himself into a frenzy. He was hopping mad and ordered the miscreant to come forward. No one moved. He then announced that until the man appeared we would work non-stop without food or water until the job was finished. The joker then had no option but to give himself up and after a hefty beating was ordered to strip off his G-string and stand to attention for the rest of the night beside a flaming torch. The mosquitoes had a delicious banquet of parts not normally available to them. The bold warrior did not enjoy the mosquitoes much either—the torches attracted them; he sweated freely but always had to be in the spotlight. (Not a good combination); and after a short interval had elapsed to make sure that he was not coming back, the victim was smuggled back into camp for some very necessary medical attention. He may have been a temporary hero, but was not fit for much for quite a while. 'Teeth and trousers' did in his dim way realise that he had made a fool of himself over his measurements and paid a bit more attention to our C.O.'s figures from then on.

As a postscript to that episode: when the first 4-engined Liberator bombers flew over Chungkai, the same courageous warrior drew the same sword and charged about the camp waving it and shouting threats at them. I gathered that he was challenging them to come down and fight him like a man. A real head case and not by any means unique among the Jap hierarchy. That of course happened after the railway was finished and we had returned to Chungkai.

My oppo, also Signals, but a red headed Geordie, was damned if he was going to work for the Japs. He had a tiny ulcer on the little toe of his right foot, went sick and was excused duty. I accordingly found myself going out every day while he sat in the hut reading. He and his mate, whose name I can remember as Bakewell, were voracious readers, literary types from Oxbridge, they wanted us to think. More likely Red Brick. Then the most extraordinary thing happened. He developed Diphtheria in this ulcer, was carted into hospital and died of Diphtheria. Absolutely true! I, accompanied by about a thousand expectant bluebottles, followed his corpse to the grave. The whole affair was astounding and an object lesson to me; there and then I decided I would never try to dodge an unpleasant task, nor would I volunteer for anything. Not much fun working for the Japs, but a lot better than having the Last Post blown over your corpse.

Split into teams of two men, one digging with the chunkle, the other filling rattan baskets or makeshift stretchers, for a team of carriers to remove and deposit the earth elsewhere; the stretchers consisted of a couple of rice sacks and two bamboo poles. Each squad had to remove a cubic yard of earth, per man per day (see above). All this in blazing sun or monsoon rain. Our previous amusement, watching Tamil coolies working with these heart shaped shovels, one man pushing the shovel into the earth and the other lifting the loaded shovel with a cord tied to the blade turned to envy as we were hounded on with curses and blows. "Speedo ta na!" was the constant shout usually accompanied by "Kurra, Dammeda!" or "Buggero!" and an indiscriminate bashing of some poor soul.

It was very odd to be slaves to these ignorant paddy-walloppers, who did everything back to front; their augers had to be twisted anticlockwise, their saws had to be pulled instead of pushed and so on; the list is endless; we knew that the Railway would never work for any length of time. Jerry-built would be a compliment; we were not inclined to put them right; indeed, if it was possible to avoid detection, we sabotaged it in any way we could. Inserting termites under bridges and culverts probably did no good except to our morale. Under an oppressor, the slightest moral victory was a huge boost to the necessarily concealed knowledge of our superiority.

The embankment and cutting at Chungkai eventually completed as far as we were concerned, off we set on our first move; this was to our next camp a few miles upriver, rejoicing in the name of Wan Lung. The monsoon had set in and we marched in lashing rain, carrying everything; anything left behind was lost and gone for ever. Included in our loads were our tents such as they were and our cooking utensils. We were learning that anything inessential had to be jettisoned; that was the way it was and the way it would be in the future as we progressed from camp to camp. That march from Chungkai to Wan Lung was a foretaste of things to come. The mud and the rain made it a two-steps-forward and one-back affair. I was carrying in addition to my kit, a 4-gallon tin loaded with kitchen equipment, which gave me a considerable list to starboard; outside Chungkai we had to cross the skeleton of a bridge, still under construction. Walking along a wet slippery baulk, 12 inches wide with a fair drop beneath, was an experience I could well have done without. There was no way round and the torrent below was impassable. I decided that if the others could do it, so could I and only looked down once. That was enough. One man fell, I was told. The Japs just left him and I do not know whether he survived or not. Thankfully he was not one of mine, so my conscience was clear along with my cowardice. Once arrived at Wan Lung, we found that the camp had been built in the middle of a Siamese tobacco plantation. The temptation was too much for us; try as we may, we had little success in curing the leaves. We dried them on the hut roofs when we went out to work, provided it was not raining. We rolled them into long sausages, whipped them with twine and hung them up in the sun in the hope they would be cured. Some even soaked them in Gula Malacca. No matter what we did, it still was foul to smoke. A few puffs of my pipe nearly blew my head off. Even when mixed with the native Sikh's Beard it was practically unsmokeable. I kept some for the Hell of it and presented it, when I got home, to my uncle, who regularly went through a pound of Waverley mixture every week and still lived into his eighties. Even he gave up.

The Japs gave us little time to establish a proper camp. The Speedo had started in earnest and life became progressively more unpleasant from week to week and month to month, until our section of the Railway was completed. Lashing rain, mud, flies, mosquitoes and malnourishment began to affect our health. We were still stuck with our miracle worker, the Jap horse doctor, whose diagnoses of fitness matched directly the demand for labour from the Jap engineers. The next eighteen months, as we dragged ourselves up the track from camp to camp, were sheer Hell. The same loads had to be carried; the same harsh work; the same beatings; but there were less men at each stage, as they died or were lucky enough to be sent down on barges to Hospital at Chungkai. We too were progressively weaker, due to severe malnutrition. (See above the cantrips of the Jap Q.M.s.)

After a week or two at Wan Lung, we began to hear tigers roaring away at night—fortunately on the other side of the river. I suspect the noise of our working frightened them from turning on us. The roaring, like the Speedo, got worse. One day as we were building a straight low embankment alongside the river, suddenly there was a lot of shouting and confusion. We looked up to see which poor sod was getting beaten up this time and were stunned to see a herd of some hundreds of wild pig massed on the opposite bank, starting to swim across the river straight at us. A complete herd was escaping from a tiger. Where we were working that day, the low river bank must have tempted them as an easy crossing place. Luckily the tuskers led the charge and along with the big sows had gone through us, heading, panic-stricken, for the jungle and safety. Believe me, we did not stand in their way. Then we tumbled to the fact that fresh meat was passing before our eyes. All work stopped and grabbing our tools we laid into the pigs with gusto. There were hundreds of them. Men rushed about hitting the younger ones with anything that came to hand. Fortunately we managed to stop the guards firing their rifles. They were such hopeless shots that they would have missed the pigs and killed some of us. Their rifle barrels wavered like tall grass in a breeze. It must have been the best part of half an hour before the last piglet reached our bank. It was an unforgettable sight; they were swimming across pell-mell, like a cattle stampede in a Western film, in rows, anything up to ten across, at a time. Some Siamese, who had materialised out of nowhere, were out in a canoe drowning them and pulling them into their boat; not a lot more work was done that day; we accounted for a little over a hundred of them; we fed well for the next two days. The meat was white and very tasty, resembling a gamey chicken, young and tender, but went off very quickly in that heat and humidity. Six were captured alive and put in pens, but did not survive. The stragglers and the main body vanished. It was all over seemingly in minutes; it happened so fast. I never knew pigs could swim. They sure can. How many were killed? I do know that just over a hundred went to our cookhouse; about half a dozen were captured alive and put into a pen, hastily constructed. They did not survive, as I said. How many the Japs and Siamese took, I have no idea. Our palates were unsophisticated, but I enjoyed it. The scene sticks in my mind, reminiscent of the stampedes in old Westerns, but of pigs, not cows.

As best I remember, after Wan Lung and before the long march there were at least two camps, Bankao and Tarkalin, as the railway trace crawled North West; sometimes digging cuttings; mostly building embankments. Being a natural coward as far as labour was concerned or to put it more politely, never one to lead off on some new physical enterprise, I would usually be found at the back of the queue, eyes peeled. I had so much to learn. All my army life up till then I had given the order, someone else carried it out. My education started in Chungkai, a simple job of carrying a sack of rice down a slope, across a burn and up a wee hill to the dump. Rain had been falling for weeks and the track was extremely slippery. As I watched the other brave souls fight through, I said to myself, "No way Jose." I suddenly found myself alone with a sack of rice on my shoulders and all my mates watching from the other side. Pride—or was it fear?—took over and I suddenly found myself over okay. Before I leave that dump, a remarkable act of prestedigitalisation took place. It was pure magic. Beside the dump was a small atap hut; in that hut were cases of ex-British Army tinned food which the Japs had stolen. A slim member of our team lifted up an atap tile, slipped inside; next thing a case of Bully poked through the atap, followed by Slim Jim to muted applause. Our Jap was having a smokeo with his back to us, a bit too near for comfort. How the case was broken up and buried and each one of us transported a tin back to camp I am pretty vague. Most of us were only wearing G-strings. I did say it was magic. I was learning fast. Lesson 2 was tougher; it was crossing the above sopping skeleton of a half-built bridge on an 18-inch wide slippery baulk, my possessions on my back and kitchen implements in my hand.

Loss of face by a Jap Officer was an insurmountable obstacle. I never saw one admit he was wrong even if it was staring him in the face. On top of all this was the fact that their word was absolutely valueless; the goalposts varied according to their mood or the hours of the day. A superior could arrive and countermand any agreement made by a junior and it was a grave mistake to argue the point however much you were in the right. One flagrant case had just happened in a camp, which we were passing through on the long march on our way up country to our second *tranche*. (See under.) The working party, in this case, had completed their agreed task, collected their tools and were marching back to camp, when a particularly poisonous Jap Engineer officer appeared and ordered them back to work. Our officer tried to explain that his men had completed their task and were correct in returning to camp. The Jap flew into a rage, not unusual, marched the squad back to the parade ground, formed the men into a hollow square, ordered the officer to kneel in the middle, drew his sword and announced that he was going to behead the officer. He then proceeded to make the sword whistle round our officer's head, while he tried to work himself up into a big enough frenzy to carry out his threat by a lot of blood curdling bawling and shouting. This went on for about twenty minutes until the Jap lost his bottle, cut off the head of his pet monkey instead and stormed off still raving and making bloodcurdling threats. I am glad to say he was one of the first to be tried and executed. The amount of evidence against him was enormous. I was not present at this display, but was staying the night in the camp during our ten day march and spoke with some of the men involved.

That was an extreme example, but we learned early on to recognise the storm signals. The Japs must have had some peculiar internal conscience because, if they were going to go beyond the normal slap and thump, they had to work themselves up into a frenzy, literally frothing at the mouth. The spittle flew in all directions. Most unpleasant it was, to have to stand there and get it spattered all over your face. In some ways it was worse than the beating which inevitably followed. There was a school of thought that, if you saw the signs, the worst thing to do was to be passive; it was much better to shout back at them. Then they would get so mad that they could not time their blows accurately and you might get off more lightly than you would if they were fully in control of themselves. If it was clearly inevitable, it was thought better to get the thing over and done with.

That is how I lost the hearing in my left ear. It could well have been worse if the Jap had not gone berserk. Early on, one of my men had been the innocent and random victim of a vicious little Jap engineer, who had been the real cause of the cock-up, but who, to save face, put the blame on my man and gave him a bad bashing. I went straight to the Jap Camp Commander to lay a complaint. He did not listen past the first few words, but went into a typical Jap tantrum. He picked up a thickish bamboo and tried to beat me about the head with it. Finding he was too short to reach up, he made me stand in a hole where a tree root had been excavated. Being beaten up was nothing special, but I found being made to stand in a hole rather ignominious and harder to take. The rat who started the whole thing, having won, became even more difficult to handle.

We did have one or two traitors, who would inform the Japs in return for special treatment, even for a tin of Tuna fish. I am not too sure that they lived, I did not enquire. The troops knew fine that there was a wireless set somewhere. I confined myself to saying very occasionally to my own men "The Griff is good", but no details, and only when I was telling the truth. It was a big help to their morale; they knew that they could trust me to be honest with them.

The boost to my morale, which the nightly dose of Griff gave me, cannot be exaggerated. It was an highly organised operation; after Tom had so cleverly made the sets, the two Webber brothers took over; after listening to the news from Delhi, they reported the Headlines to our O.C., who relayed them to the C.O.s of the different Nationalities in the Camp, who decided whom to trust; I think that the Yanks and the Brits only allowed the Headlines to be entrusted to their Officers, resulting in a shadow plumping down in each bay, as we lay down in the dark and relaying the Headlines and finishing up with, "Forget it." It was a highly organised affair and I took good care not to know anything except the above.

Firstly it gave the lie to all the Japanese propaganda with which we were saturated. Secondly I knew after Alamein, (the first time that the Germans had been beaten fair and square) that we were going to win the war however long it took and, from where I stood, it certainly looked like being a very long time. Our news, of course, always antedated that of our guards by a good two or three weeks. Probably it was post-dated for us also, for security reasons. It was very strange to look at one of them and think to yourself, "He does not know that we thrashed Roemmel at Alamein, or about the U.S. victories in the Pacific or D-Day or later even more importantly V.E. day." The knowledge that the war would end in our favour gave many of us the will to live in some pretty desperate situations. We could see clearly that, if the Japs won, we would be slaves until we died. Those two Webber brothers really earned their decorations, which they received from the king himself. I can remember so clearly, on hearing about Alamein, rolling myself in my threadbare blanket and saying to myself, "We are going to win this bloody war! I must make damned good sure that I survive to see my love again." Much against the odds, I did.

The Japs were not so stupid as not to have a strong suspicion that we had access to news and that in the jungle it must emanate from a wireless. They searched frequently without warning, but never looked in the right place. We had a warning system, which operated at the first sign of a search. So many possessions were forbidden; we all had our own hiding places. It was getting the stuff covered up in time that was the difficulty.

Failure on your part led to yet another hammering at best or sometimes worse, a stay in the "No Good House" as it was called. You could only sit in a hunched position, a most uncomfortable way of relaxing and food, if any, was plain rice and water.

The Japs treated their own men roughly in the same barbaric way as they did us. I passed, one day, as we went out to work, what would be their equivalent of one of our orderly rooms. The accused, i.e. "guilty" man was holding on with both hands to the lower branch of a jungle tree while a sergeant gave him a real hammering. Rough Justice indeed! Being picked on by the Kempetai was another thing altogether. That meant a trip to a purpose-built jail in Sime Road Singapore, where all kinds of interrogation and torture were regularly practised. That was why I was a bit worried about my name. If the Kernpetai had a suspect in mind, they would assemble everyone with the same name and interrogate them, i.e. systematically beat them up, until satisfied of guilt or innocence. Brown was rather too common a name for my peace of mind and I lived on tenterhooks in case some other Brown got into trouble. The received wisdom was, if interrogated, "do not open your mouth except to give your name, rank and number, whatever they do to you." Once you spoke, it opened the floodgates and you could not stop yourself. I am very glad that I was never put to the test.

I think we all went a bit round the bend at one time or another, very understandable under the circumstances. About four men did not recover and had to be segregated. You could hear them howling like wolves at night (especially if there was a full moon). (It could well have been a con to avoid working on the Railway.) Others, not so seriously affected, stayed with us. The Japs, in their primitive, superstitious way, treated them as special, thinking that they were possessed by spirits; they were then excused from going out to work. Some were not so mad as they pretended to be; it was one way of avoiding the working parties. Later in the first officers' camp, we had one; we made him do light work; the Jap officer got hold of him one day when he was doing a water fatigue and started to question him about the wireless set. We held our breath not knowing what he might let out. Obviously he had been cut out of the Griff network for some time, but had previous knowledge. However, he played the simple idiot to perfection and we were able to relax. The interesting thing is that as he came away from the interview he said out of the corner of his mouth, "You see, I am not so daft as you think I am." In that same camp, as two Jocks humping a half of a 40-gallon barrel full of water hanging from a bamboo pole, passed, I heard one say in a Glasgow accent, "Individually they're no sae bad but collectively they're a shower o' bastards!" Talking about the English without a doubt! The key link in the wireless saga was a very brave Siamese, Nai Boon Pong, by name. He was a river trader with a little PomPomPom; by supplying the Japs with special goods he was allowed to bring badly needed food and medicines for our sick in hospital. He also cashed cheques (possibly I.O.U.s) for our H.Q. so that we could pay for these supplies. This was remarkable because he was not to know that he would ever be able to turn the cheques into cash. He even cashed my treasured ten shilling postal order from Bellahouston Parish Church, which I had carefully hidden from the Japs. It helped me to buy some duck eggs when I was having a hard time with Enteritis and Malaria. I was glad to hear later that every cheque was honoured by the British Government. Most importantly he kept the Webbers supplied with dry torch batteries, following us up and down the river from camp to camp. A remarkable man, I was told he received a richly deserved decoration from our King after the war. He risked his life every time he came up river. The Japs never tumbled.

The Siamese really hated the Japs. They unlike their neighbours had never been colonised throughout their history and were very proud of that. Faced with the military might of the Japs there was little they could do. I was told that they were guaranteed safety in a narrow corridor round the Jap communications system, but not outside it, and that any Jap stupid enough to ignore this did not survive.

Japs and Koreans were very fond of dogs, preferably in a curry sauce. Inevitably, a camp would, through time, attract from nearby kampongs a number of stray dogs, which would hang around the cook house and the soft headed British would let them clean up any scraps, not that there were that many. Sooner or later, the Japs would set out traps at night and enjoy a feast of dog meat. I suppose that we could understand their desire for a change of diet, but, starving though we were, we had no great wish to join them in this particular item of menu. What really sickened me about the Jap attitude to dogs happened, early on in Chungkai. One afternoon, I was walking along in front of the huts, when a mongrel pup saw me and started in my direction wagging its tail hopefully. As it crossed the parade ground a Korean sentry waited to see if I responded, so that he could have an excuse to bash me and failing this bayonetted it, tossed it ten feet in the air and left it lying on the ground squealing as hurt puppies do. I could see by the evil gleam in the Korean's eye that he was still trying to tempt me to go to its aid so that he could enjoy bashing me. When he saw that I was not going to fall for his plan, he stalked off leaving the pup to die, kicking its legs and screaming. He thought that the best joke for years. Not I.

Embankments and simple cuttings occupied us, until we arrived at Wampoh South when the Japs began to turn the screw in earnest. Cuttings of rock cliffs were a very different story. Here I met the compressor, ancient and battered. Like the mother-in-law joke, it came too and haunted me right to the end. Here, we encountered elephants for the first time and were involved with a couple. A long cutting had to be carved along a cliff face with trestles at either end to keep the track level We worked on the cutting, which initially was only about two feet wide; we worked in pairs; as I remember it, each pair had to drill three holes in the cliff face ten inches deep, twice a day and we took it in turns to hold the jumper, a sharp-edged steel chisel, not named jumper for nothing, while the other man swung the hammer. After each stroke the chisel was rotated through 45 degrees. Swinging the hammer was the harder work but holding the chisel was more dangerous; a miss-hit could break your wrist; you had to trust your mate. The repeated blows would start to splinter the head of the chisel; small white and very hot sparks of steel erupted from it with each blow of the hammer and burned the hair on the holder's wrist; quite painful. A primitive wire, looped at one end, was used to hook out the dust from the hole. At the end of each shift, if the holes had been drilled deep enough to satisfy the Jap Engineer, the charges were fitted and we retired to safety, at the bottom end of the cutting, while they were blown. The Siamese riders, clad in our army issue, (the Levantine clearly was prospering in Bampong) then guided their charges onto this narrow ledge to deal with the big rocks. A fascinating sight, it was, to see them delicately pick the biggest boulder, cant it up to the point of balance, steady it with its forehead and one foreleg and finally kicking it like a football over the side with the other, peer over and watch it bouncing 20 odd feet down the cliff and splash into the river below. Nothing would persuade it to tackle the next rock until it was satisfied that the first had landed correctly. All this with its great head cocked to one side, ears flapping and a wicked gleam in its little piggy eyes. The Siamese riders put paid to all my preconceived romantic ideas of the rapport between elephant and mahout, such as I had gathered from my schoolboy readings of Kipling, where the mahout treated his mount as one of the family. Here was no loving address on the lines of "Oh Pearl of

the Orient deign to raise your precious foot" and so on. The
Siamese Elephant School Curriculum clearly had never heard
of Kipling. Their idea of control was to scream a word of
command and then batter the beast's forehead on the saucer
shaped indents above the eyes with the back of his parang, until
the order was carried out. You could see the blood running into
the beast's eyes. Possibly the skin is thinner there. I found it hard
to understand why the beast did not turn on its rider. An angry
elephant is a fearsome sight; its roar could eclipse a tiger's. The
jungle resounded to their trumpeting screams mingled with the
rider's curses.

The oddest thing about the whole affair was that batter it as
he might, nothing would make an elephant do what it did not
want to do, or to go any faster. They could have taught our
Trades Unions a thing or two about working to rule. I sometimes
wondered whether all the cursing and battering was put on to
impress the Japs. There is no doubt that elephants were very
valuable assets in the jungle, capable of fetching and carrying
where no other beast or vehicle could. They were so wise, as the
following demonstrates. At the other end of the cutting was the
battered old compressor operated by a pair of Japs driving a
couple of ancient pneumatic drills. One day, as we worked at
the drilling, a young elephant appeared, bearing on its back a
kind of wooden seat cum saddle, *Howdah* according to Kipling.
In it lolled a portly and self-important Siamese gripping between
his teeth a fat cheroot, giving a fair representation of a Glasgow
Bailie going home after a good, wet, free, lunch. All went well
until they neared the noisy compressor going full bat; the
elephant shied like a horse, lay down, summarily ejected its rider
and headed back at full pelt. Without a word as far as I could
see, our two elephants stepped out and sandwiched the youngster
until "fattie" sweated back to remount and try again. This
happened three times before one of our Japs persuaded the two

on the compressor to shut the thing down until the youngster and its cargo had disappeared out of earshot. Remarkable!

We learned the hard way that in future the bare minimum as we progressed from camp to camp was one pair of boots for marching, one pair of shorts, a couple of shirts, if you were lucky enough to have two, easier worn than carried; they soon became tattered and torn in the permanent wet and sweat as time went by; a couple of G-Strings or Jap-Happies, as we called them, what was left of your mosquito net, a blanket which slowly rotted into holes with malarial sweats, and any remaining socks. Fortunately I had two pairs of hand-knitted socks. I had said goodbye to my old faithfuls, more holes than cloth. The communications squad had passed through our camp; Bette had knitted a long scarf for me and naturally I treasured it; I put two and two together and decided to try my hand at knitting a pair of socks. I found some offcuts left by the Communications Section, not Copper but Galvanised Iron wire, roughly the same length, cut them and sharpened the ends by using two grindstones. After unravelling some wool from the scarf, I found out by trial and error how to do purl and plain, changed stitch every two rows and ended up with a spiral tube instead of a properly turned heel. I used them as *erzart* socks and avoided chafed skin on the long march; gave me the last laugh over my scoffers, who had treated my efforts at knitting with considerable ribaldry. Also, if available, I carried some sort of headgear, eating utensils, tobacco, a pipe, a book, a pair of trompers and any private things which the Japs had not yet stolen . Trompers were fashioned in imitation of the native footwear in general use throughout the Far East. A small log of a medium sized branch, cut slightly longer than my foot, split down the middle, provided a flat surface for the feet; a rudimentary sole and heel were carved on the other side; a strip of material, preferably a slice of an inner tube, fixed over the toe end; this allowed you to hook your toes under it; and there were a primitive pair of clogs, excellent for keeping your feet out of the not too thick mud in camp. Strangely, although the two trompers looked identical and came off the same branch, they gave off different notes as you scuffed along. On a hard road the sound was reminiscent of the accompaniment to a Chinese Opera. We must have looked a really weird bunch as we clopped along on makeshift clogs.

Eating utensils devolved, as time went on, to half a mess tin, a dessert spoon and a mug made out of bamboo or glass; knives quickly broke and spoons became multi-purpose. The leading edge according to whether you were right or left handed was honed on your glass mug to a razor edge and doubled as knife or spoon. Not that there was much to cut, but what meat there was, was too much for an ordinary set of teeth to deal with. I never knew before, how many tubes existed in cattle—no wonder their entrails were referred to as organs. Great care had to be exercised to present the correct edge of the spoon to your mouth if you did not want a nasty cut.

After the cutting was finished, timbers were needed for the trestles at each end of the cutting: I was dispatched with a felling squad up the hill above the trace. The men worked in teams of three, each team equipped with a two-handed crosscut saw, a felling axe and a parang. Their task was to fell and trim to a stipulated length, three suitable trees per shift. This was not as simple as it may seem in such thick jungle. It was all very well standing clear and shouting "TIMBER!" as they listened to the tree crashing down. Each tree, in order to be counted, had to be clean felled, trimmed, lie flat on the ground and be easily available for the elephants to extricate. Until the teams learned a little wood craft, some cut trees were left propped up by neighbours and that team had to start all over again.

I was again gaffer cum tea boy; one of the better jobs. It was dry. There was no Jap standing over me; he only appeared from time to time to check progress and mark the correct length on each tree. We were on our own and far enough away to hear him coming. By this time we had learned the hard way and spun out the work to fill the day. If we had thoughtlessly exceeded our quota, the Japs would have upped it the next day. As long as I had the tea boiling at the right time and the men were seen to be working steadily, we were on to a good thing, so much better than all the shouting, cursing and bashing of the "Speedo".

Once the trees had been felled, topped and tailed, the elephants took over and hauled them out in a harness of chains. This took place 50 feet or so up above the track, and reminded me of the Velvet Pad in Innellan. The elephants hauled each log to the top of the slope and then down to the bullock cart track by the river. After the double monsoon rains it was not long before a greasy track of slimy wet mud had been gouged out into a near vertical slide and I, whose third job was to see the elephant deposit each tree trunk in the dump, had a grandstand view of the beasts sitting on their ample rumps, their four feet braced out in front of them, trunks curling upwards and squealing blue murder as they tobogganed down at some rate of knots, convinced that this bloody great tree trunk, scooshing behind them, was threatening to ram itself up their backsides. The whole jungle resounded to the roars. The tree trunk never did catch up, but there was no convincing the elephants of that. How the rider stayed on board was nothing short of a miracle. All this with their great heads cocked to one side, ears flapping, trunks waving from side to side and a wicked gleam in their little piggy eyes.

Once on the bullock track the elephant would haul the log to its destination under the strictest trades union rules, about 150 yards at a time, punctuated by two minutes standing time, while its food processing machinery went into full production; the odd banana tree and any greenery snatched from the side of the track was stuffed into its mouth. Its stomach rumbled away and the end products issued with monotonous regularity. Take my word for it, never stand too close behind an elephant; the least worst fate would be to be gassed. *Verb sap.* During all this, it ignored the blows and expletives of its rider, who sometimes looked on the verge of a seizure. Quite unperturbed, it would stand still until union rules had been satisfied and then lumber off on another 150-yard stint, repeating the process until it reached its destination, when it would toss the log onto the heap of timbers, higgledy-piggeldy. This was a surprise to me as Kipling had taught me that elephants could sort out the different lengths. The Japs and Siamese never bothered.

Each morning, my job was, as usual, to detail their task to each squad, get a good fire going, have the water at the boil for the tea at the morning smokeo and await the arrival of the bleary eyed Siamese rider, who would put his forefingers at the sides of his head (meant elephant and which way did I think it had gone?); usually not too difficult to discern. Elephants need not follow a track in the jungle; it appears behind them; fresh broken herbage was the clue. They were cheap to keep. After its evening bath, which it adored, its rider would shackle the beast's hind legs and turn it loose to graze wherever it chose. It could crash through a clump of bamboo the size of a tennis court, nae bother. Thorns and all.

One morning an elephant-rider appeared when I had a good fire going to make the tea. Squeaking emanated from the pockets of his British army shorts. Extricating handfuls of beetles, he threw them onto the fire, where they popped like chestnuts. Having poked them out of the fire with a stick, he discarded the shells and started to have a good feed, smacking his lips. On seeing the hungry look on my face, he handed me one. It tasted like crab and was quite delicious, until I discovered later that these were the beetles that Nature had invented to deal with elephant dung; although permanently starving, I probably, after that information, was not all that hungry; not that he seemed prepared to offer me another one anyway.

Elephants, bar the river boats, were the only means of transport available to us or the Japs, and thus were very valuable. I never found out whether the mahouts were drivers or owner drivers; possibly the latter—doubtful. The Japs let the riders off with a lot more than us. They would have been in real trouble if the riders had disappeared into the jungle with their beasts, unlike us, whose only way out was through the cemetery. We were told of the sight of 100 of them in single file, each trunk holding the tail of the one in front. It must have been quite something. I have always enjoyed circuses, as I feel I am watching for real, but since the above I have not enjoyed elephants being used as clowns; it demeans them. They are far too intelligent to be treated like that. Gentle beasts in my experience, I only heard of one incident when a cow with one tusk was alleged to have driven it through a man's face, in one cheek and out the other. Pity it wasn't a Jap, but one of ours.

They adored their nightly bath. After work, their riders would take them down to the river. It was like a toddler bathing without toys. They would lie on their side while they were scrubbed with big stones taken from the river bed. They loved it, drawing up gallons of water in their trunks and spouting in all directions; there again their wicked sense of humour showed; any passing human had to be prepared to get off his marks fast or get a good soaking. The sense of humour evaporated one evening when, after their bath, a wee mongrel yapped at their heels; the elephant has a remarkable turn of speed and that mongrel moved a great deal faster than it had ever done in its little life. An angry elephant at full gallop, roaring with rage, its tail streaming out as far as an elephant's tail can, its huge ears flapping and its trunk at the high port is an awesome sight. I doubt if that pup ever barked at an elephant again.

287

In the non-Cholera season, we relished a wash in the river, even in spate as it often was, and all one really managed was to move the mud around. For what are now coyly referred to as bodily functions, at work, it was necessary for me to get permission from the Jap engineer for him; the man then disappeared into the jungle at the side of the trace, but not too far. That was dangerous, not from wild animals which were too frightened by the noise of the work to come near, but from getting lost. If you turned round or were distracted, ten yards into the jungle, you were a goner. You could not see ten feet in any direction because the jungle was so thick in these wet conditions. Neither could you hear the sound of the work; I got lost myself once but found my way by stumbling on a tiny streamlet and following it, knowing that it would lead me towards the river and would cross the trace eventually. I used the same method twice on Lochfield. Working on a sheep in a thick mist and then standing up, I would have no idea which way I was facing.

If we had a half reasonable Jap engineer and provided that the daily task was going to be accomplished, he would allow a barber to operate in the jungle as long as he was screened from any superior officer and that he would also trim the engineer's hair. Not much trimming needed for them, all bullet heads.

There were quite a few camps between Wan Lung and Krian Krai, some worse than others but the general daily routine was much the same. Pap, watery rice eaten in the dark for breakfast, parade around daybreak for counting and re-counting, before being taken over by Jap engineers, walk out in the mud, carrying our primitive tools, to start work, where we had left off the night before, still in the half dark. Boring, heavy, relentless work with no protection from rain or sun. Half an hour for lunch, if you could call it that, in the middle of the day, plain rice and green tea; the temperature of the rice proportional to the distance from the camp; if you were lucky and the work was going well and the Jap engineer in a good mood, two short smokoes, one before and one after lunch. Just before sunset a quick count, a check of the tools and a slog through the mud back to camp, followed in the non-Cholera season by a wash in the river; all one really managed was to move the mud around. Lastly, interminable counting and re-counting before we could get our evening meal, always hoping that there might be something to go with the rice to give it some sort of flavour; one item, which the cooks could lay their thieving hands on, was coconut oil; it smelt foul, tasted even worse; but someone had found out that if brought to the boil and a green leaf thrown in, all smell and flavour was neutralised. No one has yet explained this to me. Aided by this the cooks devised "doofors", a sort of rice rissole mixed with onion tops or whatever the cooks could lay their hands on; it would then be deep fried and helped the plain rice down. Hence the cry could be heard as we lined up for our evening rice: "Doofors the night?" We followed this by lying down and anxiously awaiting the arrival of the Griff, which gave us a slight idea of what was happening in the real world; although I now realise that it probably was not as up to date as we thought, in case someone inadvertently mentioned in a Jap's hearing something that gave away that we had a source of news. All so monotonous, so exhausting, so little food, so much fever, so many savage beatings, that it was not surprising that so many just gave up and died. After the Diphtheria epidemic had been controlled by the excellent work of our doctors, Malaria became public enemy number one. Nearly all of the hundreds of thousands of bamboos cut down for hut building etc. during our time on the Railway were female and hollow except for the joints. These clumps grew up to 40 feet in diameter. The male bamboo is almost solid and much too hard to work with generally, but the female could be put to countless uses.

Necessarily cut between the joints, a clump of bamboo yielded a forest of upturned cups. These soon filled with rainwater and a perfect man-made breeding ground for mosquitoes appeared. You could see with your naked eye, the larvae swimming about in them. Even if we had had time and permission, it would have been a Herculean task to treat all these tiny reservoirs. We did try to cook the shoots to enliven our diet, but they turned out to be tasteless and stringy. Obviously the shoots served up in Chinese restaurants came from a different sub-species. Wild bananas were a great disappointment too, no flesh, just slimy seeds, like pomegranates.

Bridge building, of which I had my full share, perhaps showed up the Jap mentality most clearly. It was to be our next ploy. I just wish I was better able to describe a tale of a zanier than most Crazy Gang sketches, the humourless I.J.A.'s adherence to orders, however stupid, and a Greek Chorus of P.O.W.s in attendance, doing their best to thwart the Jap Engineer's plans, undetected.

You may be wondering what happened to all those tree trunks, which the elephants and I had shepherded to the dump. I had been taught that elephants were so clever that they could sort tree trunks into separate piles according to their length without instruction from their riders. True probably. But eyeing the higgledy-piggledy bing of tree trunks, I realised that either the Japs had not so been taught, or were once again demonstrating their total lack of any forward planning. I prefer the latter.

First take a river to be spanned, preferably not in a monsoon. Probably Ronald Searle sketched it better than my pen can. Erect a Heath Robinson bamboo rickety structure, supporting a sort of crow's nest, on which stood an ever more irascible Jap engineer, a grooved wheel and a heavy weight, known as a monkey attached by pulleys and two heavy ropes, one for each side of the river, then fanning out to tails, like a cat o' nine tails.

The idea was that, if a man was attached to each tail and all pulled together, the monkey would rise sufficiently so that if all the tails were released simultaneously, a sufficiently heavy blow was dealt to what it had previously been resting on, in our case, the head of a pile, and inch it down into the ground. The bridges were supported by trestles in the shape of a truncated A, made up of five piles fashioned out of newly hewed local tree trunks, which were driven into the ground and topped off to fit a squared crosspiece. All was held together by dovetailing and dog spikes, which were made back at camp by the blacksmith. (The only real Jap tradesman I ever encountered.) He worked full time; the metal for the shovels, and the chunkles were made of such poor material that he spent most of his time repairing them.

Timbers for locking the top of the trestles and the bearers for the sleepers were also newly hewn tree trunks roughly squared off by two men, using a very long two-handed cross-cut saw, one in a pit and the blacksmith on a platform above ground level. The finishing touches were put on by the barefoot, bearded Jap blacksmith, wielding an adze, cutting towards his bare toes. It looked madness to me; I shuddered to see how close to his toes he cut, but it worked and he still had all his toes the last time I saw him. He then chiselled slots to dovetail each baulk, so that it fitted snugly onto the tops of the piles and held tight the A-frame and so the bridge. To an observer from outer space it must have looked like a scene from Dante's Inferno. In the middle of one of the densest and most remote jungles in Asia and lashing rain, there was this Heath Robinson contraption of bamboo, pulleys and ropes, weird chanting, irregular thumps of the monkey hitting the piles, and 20 odd scarecrows, skin and bone, dressed in rags, rocking back and forth like some chorus from a Calvinist Hell. All the time Japs rushed about in all directions screaming abuse, lashing out indiscriminately and usually shouting incomprehensible and contrary instructions in their high pitched voices. The only constant was the rain, pelting down.

The "heid bummer" in the crow's nest seemed to be in overall control. It would go like this—the first scream would be "Pileo!" All Hell would break loose while we and the Jap engineers scurried about trying to find the next prospective pile (tree trunk). We would all help by pointing in different directions and shouting, "Pileo!" Eventually the pile was hauled up to the pulley, found to be the wrong length and off we and they went again tearing about looking for one the right size. The two outside piles were longer, having to be driven in at an angle; if we could add to the confusion without being belted, we did; nobody had of course thought of pointing the end of the pile in advance. More screaming of "Axeo!" leading to complete panic while we and they ferreted about for the axe, which they had earlier thrown down among the remaining tree trunks after pointing the previous pile. If we could do it, undetected, we buried it deeper. On the surface we were appearing to do everything in our power to assist while actually doing the opposite. We had to rush about or run the risk of being knocked over by a diminutive Jap engineer running about blindly with a felling axe in his hand. Finally pointed, the pile was hoisted up under the monkey, whose operator by that time was having paroxysms of rage at the slow progress. He knew we were behind schedule and that he would carry the can. Every Jap screaming, formed a background to our mournful chant as the pile was slowly driven in to the correct height, not depth. Screams of "Sawotana!" then erupted; we all joined in the pandemonium until the well-hidden saw was unearthed and used to square off the top of the pile. No fancy nonsense about theodolites. The top having finally been trimmed, the whole process was repeated again and again. They never learned. Shouts of "Kurrah!" and "Buggero!" were interspersed with the odd beatings. To the doleful chorus of "Ichi, Nee, Nosayo" (one, two, three) keeping rhythm as they hauled and let go the tails; to the bored and hungry POWs, each holding a tail and maintaining the expression of dying to help, if only someone told him what to do: add an assortment of Jap engineers dashing about trying to look busy. So it went on day after day depending on the length of the bridge. One day, the H.B. got so fed up at the slowness of progress that he shouted out "one for Tojo", (the overall villain of the piece and the Jap P.M.).The monkey hardly moved, adding to his choler and embarrassment. That was nothing compared to his reaction when one of us shouted out, "One for Churchill!"—whereupon the monkey went so high that it nearly knocked the H.B. off his crow's nest. He then tried "One for Hirohito!" but the monkey hardly moved and when our man replied with "One for King George!" the HB had to hold on to the front of his crow's nest to avoid being thrown off. Childish maybe, but we enjoyed it. The Crazy Gang would have made a wonderful sketch of it. The whole thing could have been finished in less than half the time with a little forward planning and simple organisation. The Crazy Gang doing their famous painter sketch were mere amateurs at creating organised chaos compared to that lot.

We of course thoroughly enjoyed pretending to be helpful, while doing all we could, to obstruct the process, never making it too obvious. It was amazing how the felling axe and the saw could become hidden from sight. Our shouts chorusing the Japs' commands as we rushed about in all directions did much to add to the general confusion. Some bold spirits tried to introduce termites into the base of the trestles. I have my doubts of the efficacy of this, but the idea did do our morale a power of good. The Jap on the trestle was failing miserably to create order out of chaos. They never learned; we enjoyed that!

They tried their damnedest to make us learn Japanese but finished up having to learn English, if they wanted to communicate with us. We were not so stupid as not to learn the odd Japanese word which was essential, such as *Yasume* meaning a rest period, counting and *Benjo* for a quick rush into the jungle or the latrines but no more than that. It was a matter of pride and a big morale booster to frustrate them in any way we could. It also united officers and men in a common cause. We could always beat them hands down in every way except physically. We hated them and despised them so fiercely that it burned inside us like a naked flame. The blacksmith never ceased his endless job of repairing the tools and making up anything not to hand, plus the dog spikes, etc. I never saw a nail or a tin of paint all the time I was a P.O.W.

They were so disorganised that one had to remind oneself that they were second-rate L. of C. troops. We, certainly, were not about to disabuse them, although by our demeanour, and superficial keenness to help, they were led to believe the opposite. There would be no respite until the Railway was finished. It was a vicious circle. The harder we were driven, the more grew the numbers of sick and dying and the consequent diminution in the rations, the fewer were the available workers, who in their turn were driven harder and so on. We were expendable; they made that very clear.

The Japs are the most unpredictable race that I have ever met. Just as brutal with their own lot, but not allowing any one else to touch their own unless it happened to be someone of a higher rank, when they would instantly become dumb and not lift a finger. Contrariwise, they would not assist their own countrymen in trouble but laugh at them as they struggled. One day, early on, at midday rice we were squatting, having a smokeo, when a scene out of the Napoleonic Wars appeared. A squad of about half a dozen Jap soldiers hove in sight, hauling a small old infantry gun on iron wheels through the thick mud. The original ropes had rotted away and they were using creepers instead. Chanting away incomprehensibly, they bent their backs and hauled away. They must have started from Chungkai and this gun was destined for some unit in the Arakan, hundreds of miles further on. If I had not seen it, I would not have believed it. We were scared that we would be dragooned into hauling the thing, but no, our Japs decided it was no concern of theirs and poked fun at them in front of us. It seemed to be what is mine is mine and I dare anyone to touch them without my permission. Such strange people, we had nothing in common.

Hundreds of our men developed tropical ulcers from scratches by the thorns, incurred while working at clearing the trace. They had so little resistance that the most horrific tropical ulcers developed even to the extent of exposing the bone. You could have put your fist all the way into a bad one. There was no treatment available from the Japs except creosote, which was very painful and quite useless. Creosote, liquid and in tablets, and Quinine were the only medicaments that they supplied; Quinine for fevers and creosote in liquid form for ringworm, external cuts and ulcers and in pills for stomach disorders. They stole all our Red Cross parcels, including medicines; the worst ulcer cases were sent down river to Chungkai, where they had to go down daily with a spoon, sit in the river and scrape out the pus and matter. Probably their only spoon used also for eating. We could hear the poor wretches screaming with the pain caused by scraping against the exposed bones of their legs and arms. There was no cure. Later successful experiments using maggots, which painlessly cleaned out the wounds, were carried out; amputation, in many cases, eventually became the only answer; usually without anaesthetic (unavailable). It was kept for intricate operations. Many died during the operation or from the after-shock. When we finished the Railway and were brought back down to Chungkai, we found a complete hut full of amputees, many double and a few treble. They were the "lucky" survivors.

In their extraordinary way the Japs had discovered that there was a Pasteur Institute in Bankok and had conned the Siamese and presumably, the Red Cross into allowing them to make use of it. This, to their hypocritical minds, allowed them to claim that they were keenly looking after our health. Looking back it is clear that their intentions were more like Hitler's, i.e. experimentation with humans. Fortunately for us, they were not as far advanced in Siam as the Germans were in Europe, although some unspeakable things were done to P.O.W.s on mainland China and Japan. From time to time we got jabs with blunt needles, I know not what for. There certainly was no discernible beneficial result. One obscene example happened one morning when during the tenko or roll call before going to work we were ordered to maintain double spacing between the ranks; then ordered to drop our G-strings and bend over. The next thing we knew was to have a glass rod shoved up our anuses. We were relatively lucky—I heard that in some camps bamboo, not glass rods, were used, more painful. No warning was given and I can tell you enough force was used to make it extremely painful. We were told afterwards that we were being tested for cholera, but as all the rods were later stacked into one bucket with no names attached, I do not know what they could have learned about any individual. It would go down in the records somewhere and be produced later, if need be, to show how carefully they looked after our health. After that experience I find it difficult to understand what enjoyment homosexuals can derive from their rumoured, peculiar practices.

It was probably a few camps later that we were allowed to send home a sort of Field Post Card. It was pre-printed on the lines of "I am well—I am not well" and so on. The idea was that you scored out the lines which were not applicable to you. We were allowed to print a short message at the bottom, no more than 25 words, and I was able to refer obliquely to the film which we had seen on our honeymoon in Oban "The Road to Singapore", so that Bette was able to confirm that I had been taken prisoner there and was still alive at the time of writing.

I offered to help any of my men, if they wished, to complete their cards and ensure that nothing in them would upset the Japs and cause the card to be destroyed, and came across a young chap, not from my unit, who was having a desperate time, his face screwed up in deep concentration. I asked him if I could help. He replied that he could not think of anyone to put in the last phrase; (remember me to-); there was literally no one except his mother in the whole world, who cared a damn about him or he cared a damn about. This was so sad. Eventually his face lit up and he wrote the immortal words—"to my motorbike". Later on, well up the railway, we were given a plain Post Card and allowed to write 24 words on it; censored of course. It was quite a challenge to compose a message in so few words, wanting to convey so much. They were the only two communications which Bette received from me during the three and a half years that I was a P.O.W.; she hated the whole P.O.W. thing so much that she destroyed them after I came home.

How did we convert coconut oil bottles into mugs? A thread soaked in coconut oil, tied tight round and just below the neck of the bottle and lit; the moment the flame dies, a sharp tap is immediately applied; if lucky, this yields a bottle top in one hand and a glass cup in the other; scrap wire from the same source as yielded my knitting needles soon makes a cradle and handle. Needs must applies even to the most handless, i.e. me. Through time I had to say goodbye to some special friends as the Jap searches multiplied. At this length of time it is difficult for me to be certain, but Cholera struck at Takenun, as I remember, and immediately the Japs and Koreans moved well away from the camp leaving only an unhappy sentry on the gate. At the same time all burials ceased and cremation, instead, became the order of the day. Cholera is carried by bluebottles and in water, where it passes through the ground by natural drainage, so a cholera corpse buried meant contamination. In the monsoon, the ground was waterlogged, so Cremation was the only answer. A Cremation Officer was needed. Not a very attractive job, so guess who was landed with it? You win another watch. For some inexplicable reason, I was appointed—never sussed that one out. It was hardly a job anyone would volunteer for. It did have, however, certain distinct advantages to balance my natural distaste for burning my fellow men even although they were very, very dead. Most importantly it removed me from the Speedo, which was under the direction of a most unpleasant Jap officer, the same one who destroyed the hearing in my left ear. I now avoided the beatings and the back breaking work on the Railway, rather the reverse. As I walked about the camp, the Jap equivalent of the "Press Gang" prowled everywhere, looking for skivers, and would pounce on me with great shouts and threats, all set to give me a hammering. All I had to do was to make the sign of the Cross, imitate striking a match; immediately, they would shout "Dammeda, Kurrah, Buggero!" and disappear at the speed of light. They were absolutely terrified of disease, not a surprise, having seen their idea of a Doctor. A separate Cholera Hospital was set up. By this time the Last Post had been banned from funerals; it had become so frequent, it was too depressing. I cannot say that I was too popular with my own folk. My bedfellows were pretty restrained, but clearly had misgivings about me sleeping on the same platform bed as they.

So crude and so different were my efforts compared to the Buddhist cremation, carried out by shaven headed yellow cloaked Bonzes, which I watched in a village where we stopped for midday rice one day. They must have used some sort of scented wood and poured sweet smelling oil on the pyre. It was an impressive and picturesque ceremony involving splitting coconuts, pouring the milk over the corpse, and chanting monks in their yellow cloaks circling the pyre. Incidentally, in the same village square, another day, a kind of fresh-air schooling was going on. The children appeared to be learning their counting, all chanting in unison and following the teacher. Adults were standing around, watching. Beside me was a woman suckling her baby quite openly, an amazing sight to us at that time. Beside her was a child of about six, standing and smoking a cigarette. Having finished, he threw down the dog end and latched on to the vacant nipple for a drink or a snack. The mother stood through all this, impassively smoking. A shock to us Westerners, but just run of the mill to them.

I was issued with four half-sick men (walking wounded) and the drill went something like this: after breakfast pap, I collected my detail and led them out to some open ground not too far away, marked a rectangle roughly about 8 foot long by 5 foot wide and said "Dig a pit about two foot deep"; an inset funnel, carved at the narrow end allowed me to thrust down a burning chunk of bamboo and set the whole thing burning fiercely and quickly. I then took a man with me to gather enough bamboo and wood (any amount lying about) to fill up the hole and create a funeral pyre. Once sufficient wood had been collected to build the pyre a foot or so above ground level, I would go off to the gate into the Cholera Hospital and shout out: "How many today?" Note, I did not enter, but stood well off. The answer would be a number and so many possible. The corpses had to be burned A.S.A.P. After making sure the pyre was big enough, I would go back to camp to choose a suitable blazing bamboo from one of the fires in the cookhouse; the cooks promptly evacuated and stood well up wind of me. Then it was back to the pyre, keeping the firebrand burning. Seeing me go by, a couple of orderlies would bring out the corpses each on a rice bag stretcher, with two bamboo carrying poles and lay them down. Two across the pit and two lengthwise on top and so on until there were no more bodies. My squad also stood well upwind. I then thrust the burning bamboo down the funnel, saw the whole thing burning well and took my squad back to camp for midday rice.

Then came the unpleasant part; I had to go back and see that everything was burning well. It was amazing the contortions that the corpses demonstrated. Some would sit up and point accusingly at me, their innards bubbling, others would thrash about as their innards seemed to boil. After seeing everything was going to plan, back to camp and make miniature vases out of female bamboos and fit lids to them out of wider ones from further down the stalk; I had already collected the men's dog tags and labelled the vases. The next morning, while my men were digging a fresh pit, I filled the vases with ashes from yesterday's pit and handed them and the dog tags into our H.Q., so that the caskets could be buried in a communal grave. How I was expected to define which bit of ash belonged to whom, no-one explained.

I know this sounds heartless, but it was a job that had to be done in order to save even more lives in the long run and I had seen, during the campaign and since captivity so many dead and dying, that I had become somewhat hardened, callous perhaps. What was left of our mess was sleeping head to head in two rows on a bamboo platform under a tropical tent outer sheet. Between George Haddow and me, slept Hallam, the heavy drinker and heavier snorer from O.C.T.U. days. George and I carried him, on a stretcher, to the gate of the Cholera Hospital and I cremated him two days later. Obviously my job did not increase my popularity with some, but I can put my hand on my heart and say no one paid more scrupulous attention to hygiene than I.

Bluebottles also were blamed for spreading Cholera, so at meal times as well as a 4-gallon tin of rice and one of tea, we now had an extra one of boiling water, into which we first plunged our mess tins before getting our rations. The next step was to cover the mess tin with one hand while we scuttled off and gobbled down the contents, before the Bluebottles could settle on them and the same with the tea. Definitely no unboiled liquid consumed and no bathing in the river, until the M.O.s gave the all clear. I avoided for a short time the Speedo on the Railway, which was growing fiercer by the day. The numbers available for work dropped dramatically due to deaths and sickness caused by the Japs' criminal policy towards the sick, which did its best to ensure that the cured could not convalesce.

Death certificates were terse and in most cases ran thus: "Dysentery", "Malaria", or "Malnutrition", concluding with the words "and Despair". To have hope, you need nourishment. I had decided to persevere through anything thrown at me; my hopes never rose above actually getting my next meal, often thanks to my Kongsi. It was a very rough time. I lived in a kind of limbo and wondered if I would manage to survive long enough. I had little doubt, after the news of Alamein, that we would win the war, but was not wholly convinced I would live to see it.

Then the Japs demanded an advance party to start up the next camp upriver; it was to be commanded by the Jap who beat me up in the early days and did my ear in. A regular, promoted to Captain as T.M.O. was put in command. He decided he was not going under that Jap Commandant and went to the Cholera Hospital, filched a sample stool and submitted it as his own (Incredible, but True), and was instantly admitted. I cremated him two days later. How stupid can you get?

It was being realised by the high ups that the job of Cremation Officer had hitherto unforeseen advantages, and it was suddenly decided that I should be taken off that job on the specious grounds that I was too young to be subjected to the trauma of burning my fellow men, and appointed one of their cronies to replace me. Guess who was appointed to go with the Jap Sadist and start the new camp? You have won yet another watch. Sticking to my principle of never volunteering for, or refusing a job, I took the squad, all prepared to march to the new location; we were directed instead down to the river to find a PomPomPom, with the famous compressor on board, (see above) and 40 bags of rice. We chugged slowly upriver (beats marching any day) and reached the spot where the compressor was to be unloaded. Typical of the Japs, the 40 bags of rice, destined for the new camp a mile upriver, had been loaded in front of the compressor. No argument. I was told to get the rice off, and up the river bank. I stupidly tried to explain to them that it was better to chug up to the new campsite, unload the rice and then coast back down and drive off the compressor. No chance. Their orders were to unload the compressor there first and that was all there was to it. Unloaded was the rice and carried up to the top of the river bank. The compressor wrestled to the bows and hauled up the bank. Then the Japs set to, to chug back upriver. I protested that it was wrong to leave the 40 bags of rice unprotected in the middle of the jungle; if stolen, damaged by rain or whatever, then no rations, and no food, no work. Even the Japs understood that and produced the inner fly of a tropical tent, erected it over the rice and again were ready to set off again, when I suggested to them that 40 bags of rice with no guard was not a good idea in the wilds of the Siamese jungle. They were getting very tired of me by then; I was risking a horrendous bashing, but this rice was to be my men's rations and I was prepared to take the risk. Hastily I pointed out that it was lunacy to leave the rations unprotected, in a tent on the river bank in thick jungle. As the only officer on the boat party and thus, in their eyes, the most useless (from the point of the "Speedo") person present, I was appointed guard. I cannot say that I was flattered, but it was a lot better than working on the Railway. Anything was better than that, with that particular Jap officer. I was detailed to sleep in the tent and guard the rice.

That would teach me to protest. I was glad to be out of the Sadist's sight. What I was supposed to do to protect the rice if attacked by Jungly Siamese was not explained to me. They were obviously, shaggy and jungly; definitely not the sort of men I would invite in for a cup of tea.

I felt very alone but have to admit they never came near; they must have known I was all alone, but would realise that I carried no valuables and if they fancied the rice, they would have the I.J.A. on their top. Doesn't stop you feeling vulnerable. Fortunately none of them seemed interested although I saw them from time to time passing by on the river paddling their canoes. They knew no law and certainly looked wild enough with long straggly hair and not much in the way of clothing. They were quite unlike the normal villagers, with whom I had previously come into contact, who were friendly enough; particularly so, if you had the odd Siamese Baht to spend. I just waved to them as they passed and hoped for the best. Sleep then became a bit of a problem for a few nights. I felt pretty vulnerable. In this way I spent the next few weeks entirely on my own in the middle of the jungle. Eerie! By that time however I had reached the stage of just accepting whatever happened. Kismet, I suppose you could call it. I think that we were all punch drunk, if not round the bend. I soon had made myself a platform, to keep the rice and me off the earth and a bed to sleep on. As long as I could keep a fire going, I could cook myself some rice and boil up tea. The working party each day were detailed to carry out rations and a hot meal for me when they went out to work. The bluebottles, mosquitoes and rats materialised out of thin air in large numbers. Luckily I still had some semblance of a mosquito net as I was the best target for mosquitoes for miles. I lived and slept alone for some weeks, alone that is, if you discount the rats, who arrived like filings to a magnet. The magnet was the rice. They came out at night, squeaking with delight, feeding, fornicating and defecating all over and around my threadbare mosquito net, as I lay on the makeshift bed, listening to the noises of the jungle and the river as a background. Someone appeared each day from the trace, bringing me some food and dry tea. If he was an officer I would get the headlines of the latest Griff. Otherwise it was a solitary life, but at least I was spared the Speedo on the Railway which was working itself up to a crescendo by then. The Railway construction was lagging behind schedule. This was a crime and totally unacceptable to the Japs; they became more frenzied than ever, if that were possible, lashing out in all directions, I was told. No Jap ever came near me. After a few weeks of solitude it was decided that the rice and I were in danger (someone must have had the tiniest shred of conscience) from the jungly Siamese at night and an officer was sent out with the evening rice to keep me company. I do remember one canoe with four or five hirsute, jungly Siamese paddling downriver like mad. I waved to them, there was no reply and I did not sleep too deeply for a few nights. On the other side of the ledger I had plenty of four-footed friends to keep me company at night. By the Grace of God, the rats were more interested in the rice than me. Perhaps they were vegetarians, though I doubt it. However, the experience of having hundreds of rats running around and over me as I tried to sleep is not one that I would care to repeat. How I survived I do not know. Being on my own has never bothered me, although I have never sought it, and I do enjoy the company of my fellow men. I am sure that it was the photographs (see under) and my determination to return home and see my beloved wife and miracle daughter, which kept me going. Also we all did then exist in a kind of limbo and time warp.

Eventually, the Jap Camp Commander, who seemed to have softened his stance since the move, was persuaded to make it official for me to have a companion overnight. This was a remarkable achievement and very welcome as far as I was concerned. So unpredictable are the Japs. My companion turned out to be Bill Watson, who had marched beside me and greatly supported me in the "ten-day march"; he brought out some better equipment for cooking and life and the cuisine improved considerably. He still had to report on the trace every morning for work; the original idea had been that we should take day about. He was however the world's champion wangler and had generally thought up a new excuse to go back to the main camp for something each day. He was a most entertaining companion, a fund of knowledge and most importantly the bearer of the latest Griff. He was a highly accomplished and inventive cook with a wide knowledge of the edible flora and fauna around us. As long as I did the tedious chores, he was happy to look after the cuisine and a vast improvement in the menu department materialised. He was also an accomplished angler and poacher; the odd muddy tasting fish boosted our diet.

The Japs then had another rush of blood to the head and produced meat-on-the- hoof, in the shape of the most extraordinary assortment of cattle I have ever seen. Some had humps, some had scimitar horns, some tight, narrow ones and one I swear was a unicorn. (Must have been hallucinating there.) All were little more than skin and bone, having been driven up the whole way from Bampong and no doubt enjoying the "benefits" of the Speedo. That was one thing the Japs could be depended on to be consistent about. Everything always happened at the double with the maximum amount of shouting and confusion together with a generous leavening of slaps and punches, but never any forward planning.

As the beasts were being driven up the track, from Chungkai, a few were dropped off at each working camp they passed through. The problem as to who was going to look after them here and where they were to be kept was easily solved by the

Japs. You've guessed it. They were left in my tender care with dire threats as to what would happen if I lost one; our own people would not have been too pleased either. It mattered not at all to the Japs that I knew absolutely nothing about cattle, but it did cause concern to our H.Q. I remained true to my code of neither volunteering for, nor avoiding any task. Probably Lochfield was an indirect result of this escapade. As an aside, I must tell you that the main camp gained a beast during the drive. One of the men working on the embankment knew a thing or two about cattle, got hold of a piece of rope and tied a laggard from the herd behind a clump of bamboo and kept it hidden, until the herd had passed well out of sight. Once the coast was clear the beast was expertly butchered, the inedible bits quickly buried in the embankment, and the rest cut up and smuggled back to the cookhouse. The Jap cowhands were so busy hunting the herd on, that they were none the wiser and on finding one short that night, just assumed that the beast had died, as so many had somewhere along the way.

Bill and I constructed a primitive corral out of bamboo and bark ties and shut the cattle in for the night. Bill was none too keen on becoming a cowhand and preferred to attend the working parties to keep in touch with all that was going on, not that he contributed a great deal to the work, usually finding a good reason to go back to camp for something. He was most persuasive and was one of the very few who could con the Japs without demeaning himself and get away with it. This suited me as he kept me informed of all that was going on in the camp and the outside world; and so I became the cowhand. This entailed letting them out to graze during the day and taking them down to the river to drink in the evening. This was quite exciting, since there was not a fence within hundreds of miles. Even on the trace, where the trees and bamboos had been felled, the elephant grass was high enough to conceal these scrawny beasts. Thus much of my day was spent in counting and re-counting them as they moved in and out of my vision. Luckily they were poor beasts with no great urge to head for the far blue yonder. There was ample food here for them and so they did not stray far.

They seemed to be able to eat and digest anything green and there was plenty of that. My most exciting moment came in the middle of one night, when a tropical storm struck. I suddenly woke up to see, in the lightning flashes, the cattle plunging and rearing against the bamboo corral, which soon gave way and off they went bellowing in terror. By this time the rain was coming down in torrents as it only can in the tropics. I could see nothing in the darkness by then, concluded that there was no hope of finding them or of repairing the corral, if I did, and went back to sleep, confidently expecting the worst in my usual way. Up at first light, I was much relieved to find them close by peacefully grazing. Thunder and lightning can be impressive at any time but to be in the heart of a tropical storm with trees being split by lightning all around was rather terrifying. The other possible problem for the cattle was tigers. We could hear them roaring away at night on the other side at the river. Fortunately the noise of the work on the railway must have scared them off, so keeping them on the other side of the river. They would have made short work of our cattle and of me too, I have little doubt.

A by-product of the cattle drive was a new-born calf which Bill found dying by the side of the bullock track. We put it out of its misery, skinned it and cut it up. This was all done with a broken-bladed table knife and a bluntish razor blade, which were honed on the wet inside bottom half of a coconut oil bottle (see above). These were all the tools available We fried up the liver, kidneys and heart, etc., to make a tasty evening meal, leaving the meat for the next day (about the limit in that climate). I was pretty horrified, when I looked down at the results of my efforts next morning, finding everything pitch black and feared the worst. All okay later, but quite a shock. The meat helped two days' rice go down. Fortunately the meat proper, so tender, did not have the same devastating effect, but it was good to be reminded of what real meat tasted like.

An amusing incident occurred as a result of the cattle drive. It happened to the Japs in charge of the semi-independent P.O.W. detachment, which erected the overhead wires providing communications for the railway. As a reward for keeping ahead of their time table the Japs had been issued with a bottle of beer per man and one of the beasts. Highly delighted, they tied the cow to a tree root at the back of their tent and caroused away at their bottles of beer. One bottle of beer was quite enough to send them "fleeing fou". On waking up, hung over, they staggered out of their tent to tell their P.O.W. squad to kill and cook their beast. But there was no cow to be seen, just a broken tether. They were not amused to be told that the beast had broken loose and disappeared so deep into the jungle that nobody could find it. The P.O.W.s were ordered back into the jungle to search again but to no avail. This was not too surprising as the beast had been butchered, cooked end eaten while the Japs were still in their drunken stupor. The Japs were so excited that they did not notice the "weel filled kites" of their slaves, nor the contented smirks on their faces. Neither did it occur to them that the ends of the rope were rather clean cut. It was another quirk of these extraordinary people that our regular camp Japs could look on with amusement while the P.O.W.s took the mickey out of another squad of their own people; something that they would have been made to pay heavily for, if their own slaves had done it to them.

All good things come to an end. (Good in this context is purely relative, of course.) The cattle and the rice finally were consumed and I had to return to the main camp to face the final viciousness of the speedo. This was unfortunate for me as I was far down with recurring malaria combined with a long period of continuous enteritis, never less than ten times a night, a frantic dash to the latrines and not always successful in making it in time. I was down to six and a half stone and finally admitted to hospital, which proved to be an outer fly of a tent, slightly isolated from the others. I was not really conscious for some days, until one evening dimly through a mist, I heard my C.O. and the M.O., as they stood at the foot of my bed discussing my case and the shortage of hospital beds. The M.O. said, "This bed will be free tomorrow—he will not see the night out." I said to myself, "The Hell he won't!" It was the finest medicine I could have had. I was up in three days and back at work in a week, still below seven stone, but mobile. Luckily the Jap engineer was the civilised one, who allowed me to ease myself back to work gradually.

We were halfway or more up the Railway and in the last camp of the first tranche. From now on the Speedo was in full flow and ever more vicious because the Jap army in the Arakan was being deprived of essential supplies by Allied submarines (see above); there was a lot of noise about that in Tokyo. The Railway, the only safe supply route, as they thought, was not up to schedule and I have no doubt that heavy pressure was being put on our Jap engineers to accelerate the work. We did not know that then, we only knew that the slightest thing threw the Japs into a frenzy and if one got through a week without a savage beating, that was a red letter week. Reporting sick was a farce! The Japs paid no attention, went mad and drove us to destruction. Our lives were totally valueless. If still breathing, you were passed fit for work for all the hours of daylight; our M.O.s were helpless. They got battered as much as the rest of us, but to give them their due, they never stopped trying to do their job. It would not have been so bad if the Japs had had any idea of organisation or forward planning. The whole operation was a classic case of crisis management, although I had not heard of that term at that time. Even though we got the beatings for their mistakes, we were damned sure we were not going to help them by showing them where they were going wrong.

That camp was where I had my second go of Dengue fever; probably that was what nearly finished me off. I think it was there that we had an eclipse of the sun. I, remembering the one at Cargilfield, filled a 4-gallon tin with water and watched the eclipse in it. No work for us that day, the Japs being too subject to their fears of the occult to risk their own skins. Eerie it was to hear the jungle noises slowly disappearing and reappearing as if operated by a rheostat.

Fortunately, I was working under a Jap Engineer officer of a type I had never met before, a real professional Mining Engineer, something most unusual. Fully trained, he had worked in the mining industry in China and was not a young man either. Things had to be done exactly right for him. He was also, for a Jap, fair, would listen to a genuine complaint unlike his colleagues and, if justified, would take the appropriate action. His sergeant also was fair, more like our regular N.C.O.s. He was just as ruthless in punishing his own men as he was ours. Quite untypical of his sloppy counterparts, he would march along the edge of the track smartly dressed with his rifle correctly at the slope and on coming to a halt for any reason, ordered arms just as if on parade; stood at ease, until he sloped arms again in order to proceed. That pair really were most untypical Japs. This was the time when I was in a pretty bad way. (See above.) Fortunately the Jap commandant was the one referred to above, who let me work myself back to work gradually.

The peculiar thinking of the Jap High Command was that all that mattered was that the time table be strictly adhered to. An order had to be carried out to the letter, however stupid or impractical it might be. Otherwise a senior officer would be made to lose face, something quite inconceivable to them. We saw a clear-cut case in this camp; it was no surprise to us that it was not possible to complete our part of the embankment up to his standards in the time allotted and make a proper job of it. Thus our bit of track was a week late and delayed the timetable of the track-testing engine. The two young engineers either side of us were also second lieutenants. Typically with them anything went in order to finish the allotted task on time. When the testing engine arrived it sank in several places on their hashed jobs and parts of the embankment had to be rebuilt, causing weeks of delay. On the other hand, our part of the embankment proved solid and never gave any problems then or later. The two young idiots were promoted; our man was not. He had more engineering knowledge and common sense in his little finger than the two of them had in both their bodies together. That cut no ice with the Jap hierarchy. The more I look back at their organising methods and standards of skill over anything more than a hashed job, the more amazed I am at their post-war trading success. I think the Yanks have a lot to answer for. The Japs that I met were so thick that you would not believe it; indoctrinated Military Fascists, unthinking obedience was all that was required.

The track-testing and rail-laying trains appeared at that camp and formed quite an ingenious set up. They had got hold of big dual purpose German Diesel trucks (probably Mercedes) with two sets of wheels, one for road and one for rail. These machines led the track-laying squad and followed hard on the heels of the completion of the embankments. They could come up to the end of the laid rails, hauling rails, ballast, sleepers etc., change to road wheels and lay out all the equipment for the next stretch of line ready for the rail-laying squad next day to lay and ballast. Back onto the rails and repeat the process. Ingenious, when you consider it was 1944, but still typically Japanese, so much Speedo frenzy all rough and ready.

Much depended on how well or badly the embankment had been constructed. Usually it was the latter and the track would subside under the weight of the engine. All Hell would then break loose, until the wretched engine had been jacked up, the embankment repaired, and the machine back on the rails. If the trucks went over, as they sometimes did, it was a real back breaking job righting them again. The engine could let down its road wheels and with the aid of some planks be backed onto a level bit, but not so the heavily laden wagons. Occasionally in their panic to fulfil the Speedo timetable they would make us tip a wagon into the river so as to get it out of the way. Here again, the inevitable shouting, rushing about and bashings by the Japs hampered us and everything took twice as long as necessary.

They never learned and we did not enlighten them. They had this extraordinary idea, that the more men they had on a job the quicker it would be finished. The reverse was often the case; we got in each other's way and created havoc. We revelled in that, while the Japs swarmed around shouting "Morea Men! Morea Men!" and lashing out at all and sundry. Promotion for the two whippersnappers but not for the competent Engineer. It does give you an idea of the ethos of the I.J.A. It was a bit pleasanter to work for this pair, quiet, meticulous and taking pride in the work.

Our tasks in the first Chungkai sector completed, 2 Group, leapfrogging the other groups, moved to a whole new area upcountry, entailing a ten-day march up the north side of the river. Conditions were appalling. Two full Monsoons almost back to back. Too many of the sick fell out and were left to die at the side of the track. I know what you are thinking, but the blows of rifle butts, the savage pricks of bayonets as we were hunted on and the memory of what the Japs were capable of, put self-preservation at the forefront of our minds.

Constant rain; atrocious going; a narrow track of mud, boulders and tree roots. No more were we on a level plain, but steadily climbing up towards the mountainous spine between Siam and Burma and the Three Pagodas Pass. Head down, at one point I looked up and fuzzily saw a pagoda hanging on the side of a mountain. This, added to our physical state, made the slog harder; finishing up each day at a Camp. This varied from the Dutch administered camps, appallingly dirty and disinterested, to the Australian, highly organised, remarkably clean and friendly, clearly making the best of a bad job. On the march, I fell in with Bill Watson (see under and above); one memory is very clear of him preventing me from treading on a yellow and black snake pretending to be part of a bush. Interesting, informative conversation and Society scandals fair helped the miles go by. I particularly remember an Australian camp we passed through, Hintok I think it was; very well run by the Aussies. They had constructed a masterpiece of Jungle plumbing using hollowed out bamboos to run clean water from a spring high enough up above the camp to be free of contamination. Even showers had been rigged up. We also got a fair ration of rice, a big contrast to our experience in the Dutch camps where we sometimes were left to sleep in the open. Bill, going one better, made friends with one of the cooks who got us a dry bed-space in a hut and produced a plateful of crisp fried pig's chitterlings. Ambrosia! I discovered the reason for the hospitality the next day. The cook was homosexual and Bill bisexual; they had evidently serviced each other during the night, right beside me; I knew nothing about it. I admit to being thick. I was so tired and overcome to have a dry bed under cover and some reasonable food, that I would have slept through Armageddon.

Numbers had shrunk so much, due to death and disease, that anyone not actually hospitalised, was forced to march. More than a few died during the march, just another example of the stupid and vicious spiral of dwindling numbers of so-called fit men being driven to ever increasing extra efforts to make up for the unfit. The rations were cut, according to the Japs' extraordinary morality. We of course did it the other way round by seeing to it that the sick got extra food, if they were capable of swallowing it; this of course meant that the rest of us got less; accordingly our health deteriorated; working numbers shrank and so on and on. The march went in this fashion. After breakfast consisting of what our temporary hosts chose to provide, usually pap, we would set off in a ragged procession to the next overnight camp, slipping and sliding under our burdens. You could not call it a march in the normal sense of the word. We just plodded on with our heads down trying to find possible footholds in the track. The fitter arrived at the destination just as daylight was fading and bagged any available accommodation, hoping to partake in that camp's evening meal. They would get some sort of sleep even in the Dutch camps, some of which actually refused us any form of shelter. If you are tired enough you can sleep in the open in mud and pouring rain. Take my word for it; I don't recommend it. The unfortunate sick and weaker ones, if they were lucky, got into camp just in time to start the next day's march. Some poor sods never made it; if they fell and could not get up, they were left to die where they lay. The Japs would not let us stop to help them die with someone they knew; they just battered us on and on. A rifle butt is a powerful persuader, the threat of a prod from a bayonet more so. A few got further and further behind and finished the march two days behind us. As long as most of us made it, the Japs were satisfied. They knew that the only escape open to us was death and that did not worry them one little bit.

We overtook many of the party ahead of us, just lying helpless at the side of the track, with no food and no attention. We tried to help them as best we could, but none too strong ourselves and hunted on by rifle butts and bayonets, could not do very much. How many died on that march I do not know, but it must have run into hundreds. It was bad enough for us, who had had some experience of the Japs and the Jungle but it was far, far worse for the unhappy F & H Forces, who, in order to make up the numbers of the workforce, had been dredged out of those who had been previously left behind in Singapore as being too unfit to travel and conned, like us, by the promise of Red Cross camps (one lot are reputed to have arrived at Bampong toting a piano!); they were forced to march from where the rail layers were working to Burma in a oner. Their death rate was horrific. Something like 50% dead by the time the rest got back to Singapore. They went past us; it was in their camps that the sick were carried out on stretchers and made to lie on their sides in the mud and rain, breaking rocks for ballast. They had had a soft life in Singapore compared to us and could not handle the situation mentally or physically. On the march, I fell in with Bill Watson (see under and above), a dead ringer for the old Barney's Punchbowl tobacco adverts. He said that he lived with a Tamil ballet dancer somewhere on the coast of Madras. Not married—I assumed that his companion was female. Society did some strange things in my book, but with hindsight, I may well have been wrong about the sex. The least I can say is that Bill was bi-sexual; not from personal experience, I assure you. He was a most interesting and individual man (see above). His father had been Curator of Kew Gardens, duly collecting a knighthood. There Bill grew up and so knew the names, Latin and English, of the flora and much of the fauna around us. He must have been a late child of a typical Edwardian family; seemed also to have been a bit of a rebel; had knocked about the world quite a lot, finally holding down some sort of pukka sahib's job in Southern India; a good companion; a fund of knowledge on all sorts of subjects, hitherto unknown to me. Twenty years older than me, and not looking it, he was very fit and kept me going through the ten days of the march. Interesting, informative conversation and Society scandals fair helped the miles go by. Probably I was ingenuous and easily impressed, but impressed I was. With his Empire Builder good looks and his U-accent, he could wangle almost anything. I was flattered by his attention; looking back, he did seem to take people up and then drop them, but we remained friends until he wangled a trip with the sick back to the Chungkai hospital at the end of the Railway. With hindsight, it is possible he tried to groom me, failed and settled for friendship.

On the march, as before, we had to carry everything on our backs including cooking utensils; now to help our sick who should never have been subjected to such a march, there were extra loads to carry. It was gruelling enough for us, who were in reasonable health by Jap standards. The theory was that we would be fed and put up in the camps where we were scheduled to stay overnight. By far the worst treatment we received was from the Dutch. After the war I met the Continental Dutch and found them totally different. In fact, it seemed to me that they disliked and looked down on their East Indian cousins. I particularly remember one Dutch Camp, when after a meal of rice and those disgusting, dried vegetables, I was bedded down in a fair sized puddle under the porous inner fly of a British Tropical tent, feeling so far down that I said to myself, "I hope that I don't wake up in the morning." It amazes me that that was the only night that I was so miserable that I prayed I would not wake up. The fact that it was lashing down and my bed-space was a tatty old groundsheet in a large puddle fed by the constant flow of surface water, may explain this. In the middle of the night I suddenly remembered that I had not made a will and therefore could not afford to die! I had seen all the problems that arose when my father died intestate. The troops had army paybooks; with the charming thoughtfulness of the War Office, the last page of the paybook was for the soldier to write his will on; no such provision for Commissioned Officers. I had stupidly never thought about it. Remembering all the odd not to say shady dealings, when my father died intestate, I decided that the only thing to do was to make sure I got back home to sort it out. I was not going to have that happen to Bette.

All of a sudden and a good bit further along the Railway in the second tranche we received letters. I was lucky enough to get quite a bundle, all more than eighteen months old but wonderful to get. I knew about Alamein by then, but still could see no quick end to our privations and Bette's letters did so much to raise my morale; it was the photographs in the second batch, further up the line which Bette had so wisely put in that really stiffened my backbone. Her father, being a professional portrait photographer, had done a magnificent job. Bette looked gorgeous in her embroidered house coat and Anne looked deceptively sweet in a little gingham dress. Butter would not melt! The only worrying thing was that the dear gentle girl that I had married had developed a chin at least an inch further forward than I remembered! No wonder, having to bring a child up on her own in wartime, not knowing if she would ever see her husband again. Strangely enough the photographs of Anne in swaddling clothes in the first batch did not make much of an impression, but the ones in the second batch of her standing beside her mother were electrifying; there and then, I decided that somehow I was going to get back to Scotland to see them in the flesh and hold them in my arms; nothing that the Japs could do, would prevent me. I treasured those photographs and the letters all the way up the rest of the Railway and down again and in the remaining camps. Bette wrote every week and my mother wrote once a month with an arrangement to avoid duplication, so I thus heard other family news, but nothing could compare with the photographs. I was so lucky to have such intelligent correspondents who only sent me good news. I think we did get another delivery of letters after the railway was nearly finished but also years out of date.

Someone in the Jap chain had clearly slipped up. The weirdest thing was that we found ourselves landed with a wind-up portable gramophone and two vinyl records; this in thick jungle, hundreds of miles from anywhere!! I remember Bing Crosby singing "Paper Doll" on one side and "Keep young and beautiful" on the other. Both were played to death. I knew from the photographs that I had a real doll of my own and a miniature one following on; I reckon that those photographs contributed more to my survival than anything else. In all the excitement of Liberation, they vanished, but George, my son-in-law, found copies amongst Anne's papers and very kindly made copies for me. Lee found the most remarkable double frame; how like her! First thing I see on waking, is Bette with Anne together and Lee on her Graduation day; such a wonderful feat after all that hard work in her shop.

Some were not so lucky. One unfortunate Lance Sergeant of my section, a joiner from Inverness, got a letter from his wife telling him that she had had another baby, clearly not his. He never really recovered and just wasted away. This was tragic as he was such a decent, hard-working tradesman. The mail must have come through the Red Cross. I can only suppose that the Japs only let enough through to keep Geneva quiet or perhaps they had no more room to store the letters. Red Cross parcels had been paid for and sent, but they never materialised. Sometimes parts of them would appear as a bribe or "presento" from the Japs, but not often. The rest they stole for themselves, even the bandages. There was in Bangkok, we were told, a Swiss representative, but the Japs pulled the wool over his eyes and never let him get near us; everything was done at arm's length. I have never since had the same respect for the Red Cross.

Finally, exhausted, we reached Takanun (I think), the first camp of our new stretch. The ten-day march was so Hellish that we saw the exhausted tail-enders being hounded into the camp we had spent the night in, and hounded out as we tackled the next stretch. It was every man for himself; stragglers were left to die; I would not have survived without Bill's help and encouragement. It was gruelling enough for us, who, according to Jap standards, were in reasonable health.

Eventually we worked our way up through the intervening camps (a repetition of our previous gruelling work), extending the track and arrived at our last camp of the second tranche, Krian Krai by name. After this life became less hectic. The rest and no Speedo must have saved some lives. There was always wood to be cut for the railway engines. This was cut in cords and stacked along the side of the track, like you see in old Westerns; passing engines picked them up, as required. Not that there were many trains to be seen. It certainly must have been one of the most ramshackle railways ever built and I doubt that it did much to support the troops in the Arakan; probably it was more used to carry wounded and sick back to hospital camps, as we were to see later on. Our bombers kept hitting the bridges and the Japs busy removing shattered rolling stock and repairing the track, bridges and culverts. Having managed to survive the Speedo, we knew we had experienced rock bottom and that nothing in the future could be any worse. The railway finished and having no orders for our future, the, Japs allowed us to celebrate Christmas as best we could. Largely it was a quiet day with a Divine Service and as good a meal as the cooks could manage.

The Japs had always tried hard to belittle the officers in the eyes of the men, which never worked. To this end, they grandly announced that New Year's Day would be a Sports Day. Their magnificent contribution to this was a few tins of Tuna Fish stolen from our Red X parcels, for prizes. My only contribution to the Sports was to be conscripted to the left wing of the officers' football team. It just shows how hard up we were for players! I thoroughly enjoyed the game, though being presented with an open goal at about 15 yards, I converted, but unfortunately only rugby fashion. The Japs organised a knockout competition, pairing the British and the Dutch O.R.s and the British officers and themselves, confident we would be easy meat and that the I.J.A. would make the final.

They had organised the draw so that we would play them first, and the British O.R.s V the Dutch, second. What they did not know was that a Signals officer, McDonald by name, had played a few games for Queens Park, in the days when they were a power in the game. I was detailed to mark the Jap right winger and was told that I could shoulder charge him as long as he had the ball. I much enjoyed the game, making sure that he got the ball regularly. My biggest problem was to get my shoulder low enough to knock him over; he spent quite a lot of time picking himself up. Of course our star ran rings round the Japs and we won handsomely. Our boys beat the Dutch O.R.s in a tense game. When their goalie was bundled through the "posts" by a hefty shoulder charge, there was a riot and the Dutch spectators rampaged onto the pitch. That charge was okay then in British football, but frowned upon on the Continent. An exciting ten minutes ensued while the pitch was cleared. The referee was Irish and never lived it down; our troops were kind to us in the final, got three quick goals in the first half, and lay back in the second to spare our blushes; we took second prize, a tin of Tuna Fish between eleven of us, such generosity! But what intrigued me was that McDonald, who won everything, steadfastly refused to accept his share of the prizes in case it affected his amateur status. How things have changed!

We organised horse races in which a stronger man carried a lighter one on his back over 50 yards. When the idea was mooted, one of my men, who ran a small newsagents pre-war and was accustomed to taking bookies' lines over the counter (illegal then) approached me and asked if I would fund him as an on course bookie. I fixed a limit, thinking, "Why the Hell not?" I got my education. On a sheet of paper, and where he got that from I know not, he kept a running total in columns of how much he would lose on each winning horse, and along the bottom how much he had taken in total stake money. By adjusting the odds, he ensured that, whichever horse won, he could not lose. No nonsense about place money; I was on 25% of the profit. The racing was a great success with the troops and the profits made it a success for me.

There was also a rugby match, Scotland versus the World. We won, not altogether unassisted by the fact that I was the only one with a pair of shoes (ex a corpse); very handy in the scrum. Ammunition boots were forbidden, but I won the technical argument that shoes were not. (Others barefoot.) My homemade socks helped too. So I can always claim *pianissimo*, that I played rugby for Scotland and won. The portrait of me was painted in Krian Krai by a red haired Aussie, who suddenly appeared and charged a few Bahts. It survives to this day; truly remarkable; he had to make do with what materials were lying about. Much shaving, hair-cutting and borrowing of respectable shirts went on. The original frame was made out of a piece of gas cape. Pity, a good friend with the best of intentions changed it.

We did get another delivery of letters, but years out of date. We had a bit of a laugh when one of our Kongsi read out a Post Card from his aunt posted from Blackpool where she was on holiday. It gave him the breathless news that it was raining in

Blackpool!! The monsoon was in full swing and we reckoned that the dear lady had no idea what real rain was.

We had been through such Hell that Krian Krai seemed like Paradise. No more Railway Speedo hassle, just a squad for wood cutting and a flying squad for emergency repairs, which got ever more work as our bombers got going.

The only excitement was that we were told that the Jap Top Brass would ceremoniously insert a gold spike in the sleeper, where the Siamese side of the Railway and the Burmese met. Golden my foot! If had been golden, it would not have lasted the night. However the "Flying Kampong" appeared one day behind an elderly Engine. An incongruous sight to see in the jungle, it consisted of a decorated flat on which lounged a couple of Top Brass Japs on wicker chairs, sweating freely, but determinedly flashing gold spattered teeth, all fankled up with their swords and even spurs, I seem to remember. Put on stage at the London Palladium, it would have fitted in with the Crazy Gang "nae bother".

One of the ways in which we maintained discipline was to keep the officers and men separate in different huts. Familiarity breeds contempt. In Krian Krai our hut was a novel concept; instead of one long hut with platform beds down each side, it was shorter and divided into four quarters and thus we could form little groups of like-minded folk. It was the dry season; quite cold; one threadbare blanket apiece; referred to by an irreverent mate as sainted because it was holey; the only way to keep warm at night was to make braziers out of 4-gallon tins (I doubt that Health and Safety would approve today). There were plenty of hard wood offcuts lying about, suitable for slow burning overnight.

Our bay was at one end of the hut, quickly named Sauchiehall Street; all Scots save two, both of whom were Regulars. One of them, I think Evers by name, was a really fine committed Christian, sincerely believing that, when he died, he would go straight to Heaven, so had no fear of dying. Absolutely genuine, not boasting nor proselytising, he was a sincere simple soul in the nicest sense of the word. We all respected him and many of us envied his rock solid faith; I certainly did.

The other Englishman in our bay, Brooke by name (also a Regular), was a different sort altogether. I was never convinced that he was the full shilling. Claimed to be the rightful king of England through being in the direct line of descent from some doxy of a Stuart or Plantagenet King. Issuing from the wrong side of the blanket worried him not a whit. He reckoned that he would not be the first king to come from there. He suffered a lot of kidding and never saw the joke. He took absolutely seriously our recommendation that he should raise his Standard in Strathfillan in true Stuart fashion, send round the fiery cross and raise the clans. He was so English upper-class that I doubt if anyone would have understood a word he said. We also discussed at length how many men he should bring. We all did go round the bend from time to time. He did however provide us with much amusement and helped to pass the time. We had him so confused that he never could decide whether Glenfillan or Monmouth's landing place on the south coast of England would be a better bet!

Apart from Dennis Smith, whom we naturalised as a Scot, George Haddow and me from Signals and Major "Dukey" Gordon, there were four Argylls. (Dennis was later shipped down to Chungkai with Amoebic Dysentery problems. The Japs had stolen all the emmatin. Are you surprised?) George Haddow was similarly shipped down with a really bad knee. Dukey or Major Gordon of the Gordon Highlanders was as fine a Regular Officer as I have ever met. A quiet man with inbuilt authority and a delightful sense of humour, he led by example. I was really pleased to hear that he later commanded his own battalion and had a distinguished military career. Most of us in captivity had encountered problems with some weird and wonderful colonels, but never any problem with him. We had too much respect for him. The Argylls consisted of Captain "Doc" Docherty Quarter Master, Captain ("Big Tam or take-a-chance") Slessor, also promoted from the ranks, a stereotypical swashbuckler, both good companions, Lts Rab later Rob Mundae, Jim McLean, and one, whose name escapes me, but known to us as "Clang Clang"(something to do with his civvy job with trams in the North East of Scotland). Rab, if born a generation later, would have given Faldo quite a run for his money. He was a delightful man and a very good amateur golfer. He had made up his mind that he would do no work for the Japs, if he could possibly avoid it; if we were stupid enough to do his share to get a job done, well and good. Not a lot different from the rest of us, but perhaps he banked on us being more pragmatic. He could develop raging toothache on the spot like no one I ever knew and was not always too popular; he could buckle to, if there was no other option and was genuine in his beliefs. On Liberation, he resumed his career as an Apprentice CA, sat the intermediate exam making it clear on his paper that he was a returned F.E.P.O.W. He passed on compassionate grounds, George Haddow told me. Realising that there was no chance of final qualification and enjoying his golf too much, he married the charming daughter of Carswells, the upmarket gentleman's outfitter on the corner of Renfield Street and Gordon Street, ultimately taking over the business and being most successful. Both were recommended to go for adoption on the grounds of his privations and wonderfully produced a brother for the adopted one within the year. You could not tell which son was adopted. Strangely, I heard in a Christmas Card that a similar miracle happened to Harry Bristow. I was delighted. Both Slessor and Docherty, the best type of promoted rankers otherwise Busty Stewart would not have tolerated them, were excellent companions and continued their careers in the Argylls. McLean, a Territorial like Rab, was a quieter type, did his fair share of the work and took an amount of ribbing due to his having previously been a Sanitary Inspector round about Greenock. Clang Clang lived up to his nickname; an ebullient character, he made sure that life was never dull and was good for morale.

Clearly we were a mixed bunch with diverse interests; it worked well. Having survived the Railway, we all knew when to get stuck in, when to keep our mouths shut and above all to be tolerant of our mate's idiosyncrasies. This fact will greatly surprise my family. Without good friends, survival was highly problematic. I doubt if any of them are still alive today (2010).

CHAPTER 17

BACK TO CHUNGKAI

HAVING made some sort of decision of how to deal with us, we had the doubtful privilege of being transported back to Chungkai on flats on the railway we had tried not to build. We all heaved a sigh of relief each time we survived crossing a bridge, remembering its Heath Robinson construction. It was forcibly brought home to me how quickly the jungle takes over an empty space. The deserted camps had been quickly swallowed up; only the lack of tall trees and above all the smell alerted me that we were approaching one.

Chungkai had become an enormous hospital cum rest camp and now held all that was left of 2 Group. Some had gone in Rustbuckets to Japan; thousands were dead. Half of the camp was taken up by the Hospital, which rammed home to us the enormity of the casualty figures. One complete hut was full of amputees, some double and two or three triple, another of Bacillary and Amoebic Dysentery patients. Of course no Emmatin was available, although the Red Cross had provided ample supplies; all stolen, like everything else by the Japs, whose cruelty to the sick still enrages me. To my mind they may strut about today in gold teeth and three piece suits, but they still are savages under the veneer.

I was able to bring myself up to date on my own men, who had been sent down sick during the Speedo. There were too many absentees. Amoebic kills slowly and seems to be incurable, but can be delayed given enough Emmatin, unlike Bacillary, where you either live or die quickly. The rest of the huts were filled with Malaria, Ulcerated and Beriberi patients. It was a sobering sight even to hardened eyes.

Our doctors and medical staff were beyond praise. I know that I could not have worked for long in all that filth and faeces, particularly in the Dysentery huts. It certainly brought home to me how lucky I was to be alive and mobile. Some had been sent to Japan; I think only one of mine (Finlay) survived. Packed like a double row of sardines on wooden shelves above a cargo of iron or copper ore with just one ladder for escape, it was a horrible death.

I had been so lucky to have been inoculated against tropical ulcers by my fall when playing hockey in Aloh Star and the subsequent M & B treatment. I, like the rest, got plenty of scratches and cuts; it was impossible to avoid them; thankfully none of them turned septic on me.

Unfortunately for the amputees, the surgeon then in Chungkai, one De Soldenoff, allegedly a White Russian, proved not a particularly skilled craftsman. Following our batch's return to Chungkai from up country, in another batch came a top surgeon from a London Teaching Hospital, Pemberton by name. He discovered that De Soldenoff, while having the time of his life sawing off bones, had cut them on the skew in such a way, that Pemberton claimed, no prosthetics could ever be properly fitted. The makeshift crutches in the camp did give a degree of mobility. But, for the future, the ends of the bones had to be squared off exactly. Pemberton then had the time of his life, trimming off the faulty ends. Not a lot of fun for the amputees though, having to go through it all over again. Pemberton was a most impressive figure, even managing to hold on to his short shiny operating Wellingtons throughout the Railway. I believe he was genuine and not motivated by professional jealousy, but I was very glad that he was not my M.O. He seemed to be not really interested in any branch of medicine except surgery and seemed to carry out the ordinary duties of sick parade rather perfunctorily, only to lighten up when he could wield his beloved scalpel.

The White Russian compensated himself later in our officers' camp by offering circumcision to all and sundry. (See under.) I did not avail myself of his kind offer, giving rise to much comment about a typical Scotsman being so mean that he would not part with anything for nothing. It was a remarkable sight to see a succession of stretchers issuing from the surgery every day, each supporting a naked body with a bloody bandage round its limp little willy. A camera would have kept me in clover for the rest of my life, using discreet blackmail. Ever since such close contact with them, I have had a strong aversion to surgeons. They are only too keen to get their scalpels out and cut you up. What is lost is gone for ever. Unfortunately I have no option nowadays.

We continued to suffer the equivalent of the Biblical plagues of Egypt. Bluebottles by day, mosquitoes by night; they tormented us in clouds and those who were able to preserve some semblance of a mosquito net guarded it like gold. I doubt that many of us escaped Malaria. Luckily it was mostly of the Benign Tertian variety, and not a quick killer like Cerebral. It just wore you down steadily, until there were not enough red— or was it white?—corpuscles to sustain life. It repeated itself; ten days malaria followed by ten days clear and so on *ad infinitum*. I had 23 goes of it, to the best of my memory; sounds impossible but that is how I remember it. Concurrent as it was with 18 months of enteritis, my life became a bit of a blur, but it is not far off the truth. By the last bout I was in rather a bad way. I remember the rigor hitting me when we were ballasting the track. Armed with hammer pickaxes, we stood side by side in pairs on sleepers and rammed the ballast under the sleeper, swinging in unison like the figures striking bells on Continental clocks. There was no way that I would be allowed to go back to camp and lie down before the work was finished for the day. That was a day I shall never forget. First freezing cold, shivering and shuddering with the rigor in the burning sun, changing to a temperature in the 100s and sweating buckets, I still had to keep swinging the pickaxe just the same.

I went on sick parade the next morning and by the Grace of God, a Scots M.O., Paddy McArthur by name who practised as a G.P. post-war in Inverness, had got some Atebrine (precursor of Mepacrine) from a Red Cross parcel that had slipped through the Jap's thieving hands. It was the new anti-malarial drug, invented by the Allies; fortunately the Japs did not know what it was; not too surprising as Paddy himself did not know anything about it and warned me, "In for a penny, in for a pound!" I chose to have a go and was lucky enough to be put on a course, which actually killed off the Malaria completely. I was left with a legacy of susceptibility to short fevers of a similar type for a few years but the virulent Malaria bugs must have been killed off. Fortunately, at the time, I was in Chungkai, otherwise there would have been no Atebrine and no me. It would have had to pass through too many sticky Jap hands for anything so valuable as that to have reached Krian Krai. Lucky again! Probably saved my life.

The other mosquito-borne fever, Dengue, was worse to suffer at the time, but did not repeat itself. It most resembled an extremely bad bout of flu and left the sufferer in a similar depressed state for a week or two. I only had two attacks; it really laid you low. Carried by a different type of mosquito to the anopheles; when you swatted one on your arm it left a striped mark like a child's transfer. "The mosquitoes in the football jerseys," we called them.

It was on a tree felling job that our Jap engineer cut off the branch that he was standing on. He was built like a Sumo wrestler (we kept our laughter for later); by no means the worst of the Jap engineers, solid ivory between the ears; he one day drew a rough map in the dirt, showing the intended route of the railway all the way to London including a bridge over the English Channel! His spirit level was calibrated to adjust to all the different gauges on the way! Another day, we were under a Jap sergeant who had killed a small snake, cut it open and swallowed its heart and lungs, still pumping. One of our men had cut his toe and rested it on the log, which we were trimming, to tie a rag round the cut. Some blood dripped onto the log: the Jap went berserk. Evidently the heart gave him great sexual potency, but blood on the log meant bad luck. Any bridge containing that log was liable to collapse without warning, causing hundreds of casualties. Such strange people! I managed to calm him down by telling him that in England (he had never heard of Scotland) blood was regularly dripped onto bits of bridge as they were built in order to bring good luck. He bought it and my man got off lightly: the snake was carried back to camp and added to the stew.

Maintenance of the track kept us occupied, due to the frequent attention it received from allied planes, concentrating on bridges. Enjoyable! Our Japs were so glad that the whole Railway escapade was over as far as they were concerned, that our treatment, but not our rations improved. Once our Group's bit was passed as completed, the next thing was that the Jap Top Brass would travel up by rail to insert the "Golden Spike" into the Border sleeper to mark the meeting of the Siamese and Burma ends of the track. If the "golden" spike had been real it would have been a race between the Siamese and ourselves to purloin it. Having been assured that the line was reasonably safe, a couple of flats, with atap roofs rigged as makeshift awnings, rickety bamboo tables and chairs, passed through, occupied by the Jap Top Brass, lounging about in their white uniforms and gold braid, trying to look nonchalant, as if this was the way to travel 1st Class in the tropics; their high boots of course were all tangled up with their silly spurs and clanking swords much too long for their little bandy legs. Talk about the Keystone Kops! The Crazy Gang would have made a wonderful sketch of it.

Finally the rest of us had the doubtful privilege of travelling back to Chungkai on flats on the Railway, which we had tried not to build. As I said, I heaved a big sigh of relief each time we survived crossing a bridge, knowing its Heath Robinson construction. Only the lack of tall trees and above all the smell alerted me that we were approaching an ex-camp site.

As for Chungkai, we found that it had expanded out of all recognition; really now more a Hospital than a Base camp; different huts for the main killers, Dysentery, divided into both types, occupied one, a complete hut full of amputees, many double and a few treble, another Tropical Ulcers, another Malaria, the fourth General. They were the "lucky" survivors.

I discovered that one of my drivers, who had been sent downriver as too sick to work with an ulcer in his leg, had lost the leg. I knew it was my duty to go and visit him. I did not look forward to it. He had not been in my half of the section and I had been quite glad not to have him with me. He was an inveterate moaner and I feared the worst. To my surprise he was bright and cheerful, full of plans to buy a little corner shop with a bell on the door, when he got home. He would sit behind the counter and serve the customers. He said the intense pain before, and the wonderful relief after the amputation had brought things into perspective and changed his whole mental outlook. He was just so glad to be alive and free from pain. His only trouble was that he could still feel his non-existing toes and could not stop himself from putting his non-existing foot out to stop himself from falling, which was rather sore on the stump. I knew that like a lot of undeserving men (like me), he had an excellent wife;

he moaned and she radiated sunshine. I trust that they made a go of it somewhere in the Midlands.

Two afternoons a week I went to the acute Dysentery hut to read to men who were too weak even to hold a book. I cannot pretend that I enjoyed it, but I could tell it was worthwhile. The stench of the faeces lying in the gangways, where the poor sods had been unable to get to the bamboo makeshift bedpans in time, stays with me to this day; it was overpowering. No blame attaches to the orderlies who were beyond praise for their dedication. They were walking skeletons like the rest of us. I never knew if the man, to whom I had been reading last time, would still be there this time. They preferred detective stories. The Saint books were the most popular. I shall never forget starting a new chapter one afternoon with the Saint escaping from a locked dungeon, 25 feet underground, using the "with one bound he was free" syndrome; this after being left, at the end of the previous chapter, handcuffed and in leg irons in the aforesaid cell with no chance of escape, my audience said with a big sigh, "I wish I was the Saint and could escape from here like that!" I have omitted some army adjectives, but that made it all the more poignant. We never did finish that book. Next week his bed-space was being scrubbed down for the next patient. The patients responded positively to my reading. How the attendants kept going was truly remarkable. The bedpans were hollowed halves of bamboo sections. Imagine holding that under a patient, cleaning him with jungle leaves, carrying it out and scrubbing it clean for the next poor sod. I was only there for an hour twice a week and found that hard work. Sadly I often found the bed-space empty and being scrubbed down for a new customer. As background music there was a chorus of screams as the ulcer sufferers scooped out their wounds in the river. I think I reached near rock bottom then and had a hard time forcing myself to realise that there were many far worse than I.

Later the doctors harked far back in history, I believe, and used maggots, which soon cleaned up the wounds relatively painlessly.

Malaria sufferers occupied a complete hut. I had been lucky enough to have been cleared of Malaria through Dr Paddy MacArthur (see above). I felt I ought to repay my deliverance in some way. The result was that after many appeals to donate blood, I volunteered and found myself lying on a bamboo bed, watching my blood, a droplet at a time being pumped by my heart up into a glass container (another Heath Robinson contraption) and ending up inside the poor soul lying beside me. I was most interested to note the change in his colour from cadaver-like to a healthy ruddiness. I felt really chuffed that I had saved some poor soul's life and was pretty pleased with myself. When I stated this, the MO soon cut me down to size by saying, "A few weeks maybe. Trouble is, genetically he cannot store the necessary vitamins to sustain life on our diet; a reprieve maybe, but not permanent."

My other job in Chungkai was to cut the lalang grass in the ever growing cemetery. For this I was issued with a spade, whose leading edge I sharpened with a stone and pushed it like a snowplough to hack down the grass. The result was rough and ready, but it did make the cemetery look cared for and I regret to say, a lot better kept than some I have seen in Glasgow recently. The cemetery was handy for keeping documents and drawings safe, sealed in tins and bottles and buried deep. These documents were not only useful evidence for war crimes prosecutions and records of deaths, but were invaluable medical records and drawings. The medics had an opportunity in Siam that was unique; no next of kin available, no Procurator Fiscals and no Coroners, whose permission to hold post mortems would normally have been necessary. The medics could and did open up many bodies for diagnosis and much valuable data was recorded, I was told. One day up country I was walking past the surgery, when a

333

bald skull top bowled like a hoop across my path. It shows how hardened we had become that I just thought it amusing.

Medical research under tropical conditions was undertaken on a scale previously unimaginable. A skilled artist was on hand to reproduce on paper operations, dissections and anything of medical interest. These, our doctors said, would be of enormous value to medicine. Where they got the paper from is a mystery; just a flying squad for emergency repairs was on standby. (I am glad to say it got progressively busier as our bombers got going.)

I was just getting into a new routine, when the Japs had one of their rushes of blood to their heads and realised that using our officers as gangers had been helpful to them during the construction of the Railway; but we officers had now become a security problem. Some dimwit had sussed out that the war was not going too well for the I.J.A. and if the fighting on land reached Siam as the Allies pushed towards Japan, large P.O.W. camps run under our officers would constitute a considerable security risk. They decided to move us away into a separate camp leaving the O.R.S. under the control of their W.O.s and some M.O. s. So we sadly had to say goodbye to our men, who had remained so loyal and who had stood by us and themselves under the most appalling conditions; at no time did they allow a wedge to be driven between us and themselves, however hard and long the Japs tried. Often my lot saved me from a beating; this worked both ways. A mutual hatred of the enemy and a cast iron determination to cheat and thwart them in every conceivable way, however small, united us. They were the best. Our only consolation was that some first class warrant officers and N.C.O.s would be with them and along with the doctors would look after them and keep the Hospitals and Hygiene up to scratch.

Off we were sent to Kanchanaburi, where the first officer's camp was to be. Our rest time in Chungkai had allowed us to recuperate to some extent and we were much more experienced;

so we took our time on the march. As we stopped for a Smokeo beside the track, a train made up of a few rice trucks halted and out came a dozen or so females of varying nationalities. No prudes, they leapt off the train and hurried to squat in amongst the bushes beside us (the Yanks would have called it a joint comfort stop). A very apt comment as these women were later described as Comfort Girls. It turned out that this was the Imperial Japanese Army's travelling brothel, under the charge of a Japanese sergeant. I reckon he had the best job in the I.J.A.: each girl had a truck to herself as her combined sleeping cum work place. No trade there I assure you. Perhaps that was why they were smiling. They were quite generous with more material comforts and we went on our way with cigarettes and small gifts. Their sergeant did not seem to mind, neither did our guards.

Coincidently we landed up in their base camp that night. That day's march went across unknown territory, finally finishing in the dark at a camp with unusual huts, containing a broad platform bed partitioned into ten-foot bays. It was a fairly long march that day so we sorted ourselves into groups and were soon fast asleep. We woke up next morning to find that we had spent the night in their empty brothel cum base camp. The floor was carpeted with used condoms, presumably more to protect the girls rather than the men: the Japs were fairly heavily polluted with VD and unsurprisingly pestered our doctors rather than their own for treatment. We were told by some of our troops from a nearby camp that Japanese R&R consisted of shipping in by rail a unit at a time and that they had been treated to the not so uncommon sight of a Jap unit getting its ration of comforts. Each man was issued with a large bottle of beer and a condom, one for each hand. Their numbers were divided up by the number of girls (???) available that day and formed orderly little queues outside each girl's room. Thus they could pass the time swigging the beer while studying and comparing the prowess of the man on the job at the time. By the time they reached the scene of action they were half cut. Time was saved by the next to be serviced being so aroused by the performance of the man in front of him that he was on and off in seconds. The result was, I was told, that the ladies could service a fair number of clients per session. Speedo must be the watchword for everything in the IJA! Our boys found it most amusing. I suppose when you read about the GIs in Vietnam, the Japs may have been cruder but there was not all that much difference.

The Japs gave us one last go of officer hate next day. We were ordered to clear the camp stores and load them onto rice wagons a couple of hundred yards up a slope. These stores consisted of metal bound tea chests, rice in plaited rice sacks, and solidified salt in weeping sacks which reminded me of carrying a huge lump of coal with a wee bit of dross. It would not sit on your back but rocked from side to side as you walked. The Japs had organised it for our maximum discomfort by making us carry the rice first so that our bare backs were liberally scratched by the rough matting of the rice sacks, next the tea chests so that the tin strapping made a real job of our backs, and finally the salt sacks to weep into the cuts. I can vouch for the verity of the old saying about rubbing salt into a wound. How they laughed and how we squirmed! As soon as the work finished we went down into a little mountain stream and lay in the icy water as it washed the salt out of our wounds. It was perishing cold, but sheer bliss and the sun soon dried us off.

The next morning, we resumed our march and carrying all our kitchen equipment etc., shambled across the new bridge over the River Kwai, not the one in the film, but a new one built of concrete and steel. What was left of the old one ran alongside. We were to spend the night in a camp at the other end of the bridge. Having established ourselves, we tried to find out what was what, from the local inhabitants, who warned us that the

Japs were in a permanent state of panic about air raids and sounded the alarm if a plane came within a hundred miles and we were not to worry as the alarms in daylight were always false.

It had been a short march, so after some rice we settled down to pass the time with a game of bridge. Sure enough the alarm went off and we sneered as the hut emptied and went on with our bridge. Suddenly we heard a plane coming in low, then a burst of machine gun fire followed by the whistle of a bomb. We did not wait to use the doorways, but dived straight through the atap wall and into the nearest slit trench. The Liberators, Canadian crewed, came in line ahead over the bridge seemingly heading straight for our camp. Each in turn gave a burst with the front guns, let off a stick of bombs and as they climbed away the tail gunner had a go for good measure.

I cannot say that I was ever frightened during the campaign. I was too busy or too stupid to give the matter much thought, probably a bit of both. But this was quite different. You feel very vulnerable in nothing but a G-string and no boots. All we could do was lie as flat as possible and wish for something to dig with to get even further down into mother earth. Personally I would have dug with my bare hands to get lower. The laterite however was sun-baked too hard. I called the episode a few names but "friendly fire" had not by then reached my vocabulary. There were at least four planes and each had two goes. I suddenly realised that I could get killed and did not much relish the thought, particularly after surviving the Railway. It seemed a long, long time before we heard them going away. We were not allowed to see what damage the bridge had suffered, but I was reliably informed that it had been damaged many times. Chastened, we resumed our game of Bridge, but I think our ears had grown larger.

We were pretty glad to put that camp well behind us and needed no encouragement to hasten to the new Officers' Camp and settle in at Kanchanaburi, where there were close by some O.R.s' Camps. Air Raids were becoming more common, but we were still forbidden to mark the roofs as P.O.W. Just another contravention of the Geneva Convention.

With the exception of some MOs, the camp now contained all the officers in Siam, British, Dutch, American and at least one Canadian. The latter and one American messed with us. Hank the Yank came from the Bowery and was anathema to the other Americans, who were from south of the Mason-Dixon line and had come from the Texas Artillery and the *U.S.S. Houston*. They had a most unusual pet, a parrot, which they had rescued after our delightful commandant had thrown it in the fire in a fit of rage after it bit him. We all prayed that the bite would go gangrenous but no joy. It was quite a sight to see a half bald parrot climb a pole with two sets of claws and a beak.

We had not realised how strongly the feeling was between north and south of the above line; they would have nothing to do with this red haired Yank. He ranked number one along with the Japs in their list of hatreds. If all that Hank was claiming was true, he had had a most exciting time, having escaped from Corrigedor, and was finally captured trying to cross into French Indo China. Big, brash and speaking almost a different language, he had nothing in common with his compatriots. The other strange bedfellows in this polyglot camp were half a dozen Chinese stewards off the *U.S.S. Houston*, whose officers refused to abandon them, knowing what the Japs would do to them.

We did think it strange that the Southerners would mess with Chinese but not with a fellow American. This was particularly intriguing, when we looked at the treatment of the coloureds by the other nationalities. The Americans and the Australians would not even speak to them; the Aussies called them Boongs (changed days now). The white Dutch never mixed with the coloured Dutch. We, the maligned Brits, were the only ones to treat all equally regardless of colour. There were many Eurasians with us, welcomed by us, but ostracised by the others. However, I must give the Americans their due; like us they never kowtowed to the Japs. I cannot say the same for many of the Dutch or Aussies. We did not trust the former; some Aussies were okay, but there were too many loudmouths among them.

We had acquired a new Interpreter, instantly also christened Hank the Yank, who had made the mistake of returning from the USA to Japan to sort out some family affairs after a bereavement and had been instantly whipped into the IJA. I remember him commenting one day as the Liberators went over, "Just you wait until our boys bring over the Flying Fortresses." He made sure there were no Japs within earshot. He did his best for us, which was understandably not much. His counterpart, our own interpreter, a very, very brave man, had previously been in our Diplomatic Service in Japan, had learned Classical Japanese, used only in the top circles of Japanese Society and spoke it fluently. This infuriated our Japs, particularly the Commandant. They could only speak ordinary Japanese and thus lost face when they could not match him in the niceties of grammar. He was with our then camp commander and put up a brave defence of our rights and both got heavily beaten up regularly. He was singled out for special treatment but refused to give in and after a particularly savage beating, in which he was partially crippled, was thrown into a kind of cellar at the main gate; originally intended as an air raid shelter for the sentry, but never used as it was permanently flooded. Even by Jap standards he was abominably treated and was on the point of death when rescued after the Japanese surrender. All protests by us were ignored. I am glad to say we were told that commander was among the first to be executed.

We were still getting the griff ex-Delhi thanks to the Webber brothers and the reserve trusted batteries. (Unfortunately the reserve proved damp and the Griff slowly dried up—no river, no Nai Boon Tat, no batteries.) We could sense that at last the tide had turned and that the war was definitely going our way. This was confirmed to us by the appearance in the evenings of 4-engined Liberators and the distant sound of bombs and finally by a 'Teeth and Trousers lookalike' roaring about the camp uttering wild curses and threats, waving his sword about, challenging the planes to come down on the level and fight him man to man. Our cheers did not go down too well and helped to maximise the foam round his mouth, till he began to look like one of the old Black and White Minstrels in a frenzied number. Seeing the rise in our morale, our new Jap commandant decided to make our lives still more uncomfortable if possible. Slit trenches were regularly inspected; piss patrols were instituted at night. The sentries had to count everyone in and out of each hut, and be ready with the numbers for Jap/Korean patrols. This was their way of getting at us, though they were highly conspicuous by their absence during active air raids.

Our new camp, called Kanburi for short, was very different. It was in a town and surrounded by a high fence, much more like a traditional POW camp, with regular searches, interminable roll calls and a real bastard of a Jap camp commander. He hated us and it showed. He did everything in his power to make our lives as uncomfortable as possible with regular searches, little realising that that was the best way to stiffen our resolve to make life as uncomfortable as possible for him without bringing the house down over our ears. We looked back if not with fondness at least with nostalgia at 'Teeth and Trousers'. He was thick; this one was anything but. He devised a new irritant in the form of air raid precautions. Slit trenches were dug; at night sentries were posted at the ends of our huts. These sentries (instantly christened the Piss Patrol) were checked at intervals by the Korean guards, who were very scared about being in the open at night and were conspicuous by their absence when planes were overhead; we were in mutual agreement that it was a good thing that the bombers had showed no interest in Chungkai.

We soon summed up the Yanks as reliable. As I said, I cannot say the same for many of the Dutch or Aussies. Lt. Col Toosey, whom I cannot praise enough, was a fearless Camp Commander, who stood up to the Jap Commandant and took therefore a lot of bashings and earned the respect of all of us for his integrity and courage.

As part of the general Japanese plan to punish us for the Allies overflying Siam, on the slightest hint of aircraft approaching, we were ordered into the slit trenches—generally at night; thus our beauty sleep was rudely interrupted. The above sentries had to keep a tally of the numbers traipsing out and back obeying nature's call. I found the hours spent thus in darkness spiritually exhilarating; first there were the stars to study; it was strange to see the Constellations moving so ponderously across the Heavens and the Southern Cross taking over from the Plough as the main "star"; also it was a great opportunity to recall some of the poems I had learned at school. Along with Henly's "Invictus", Hugh Clough's "Say not the struggle naught availeth" gave me the greatest uplift and strength. I was really chuffed to read later that it was Churchill's favourite too.

With little to do except the necessary fatigues, the rumour mill got more and more outrageous. One of the best was that a couple had got out of the camp and been hidden by some of the "ladies" and been put in touch with a small detachment of our troops located nearby. They stayed a couple of nights and were smuggled back into camp. I made good sure that I did not find out how. The "ladies" had offered them a long stay, but they knew the retribution that would befall the "ladies" in the inevitable denouement. We swallowed this story with a large pinch of salt hoping against hope that it was true. It *was* true, as we later found out, but our C.O. quite correctly rubbished it, severely cramping the style of any possible informant; some of the Dutch would have sold their granny for an extra dish of rice.

Much later we discovered that parties of four men, one officer, one sergeant, one medic and a wireless operator had been dropped in various strategic places in Siam in order to build up a Siamese resistance force. We were also told that a submarine had delivered a cargo of arms and ammo somehow in Bangkok harbour. This was possible but improbable; however a rising was being organised to chime with the planned Allied invasion.

We got used to the new set up and began to get organised to handle the tedium of life of a more traditional POW camp. Boredom had replaced physical exhaustion and was the new enemy. The books had all been read at least twice. For a while there was a rumour that shaving your head would prevent baldness, so a lot of "submariners" were to be seen. Then the beneficial effect of circumcision in the tropics was the thing. The flies buzzing about the pathetic, blood-stained willies of those who volunteered for circumcision were enough to put me off.

The Japs were everywhere in the camp, except during air raids when they became conspicuous by their absence. New rules were being enforced by the week; all designed to make our lives more restrictive and unpleasant. We juniors took our turn in the necessary fatigues, water carrying and so on. By then we knew that the war in Europe was over, that good progress was being made down Burma and that the Philippines were being recaptured, island by island, but had no idea how long it would take to shift the major war machine out East. Makeshift lamps fuelled by coconut oil allowed quite a lot of bridge to be played. Losers paid for the oil. We began to get organised to handle the tedium of the life of a more traditional POW camp. To compound our humiliation, the Japs decided that we would cultivate a big market garden. Knowing that the Japs would pick the best of any crop, we approached the work without enthusiasm. Some even planted the peanuts upside down (upside of a peanut?). The damned things grew anyway, so we encouraged colonies of ants, which seemed very enamoured of peanuts. I did warn you that we went round the bend now and then. In contrast beside our garden was another similar in size, but professionally worked by five Chinese, three male and two female. Their garden flourished; ours did not. Before Communism set in in China, I had often thought that a few thousand Chinese imported into the Highlands would soon have made that barren land flourish like the green bay tree.

It was on this gardening affair that I took part in my one and only mutiny. With so many Indian Army officers in the bag, there was a superfluity of Lt Cols, including the previously unfit for "promotioners". Their rank qualified them as Camp Commanders. This was not a bad thing as the shelf life of a Camp Commander was short; either they were weak and gave in to every whim of the Japs, thus receiving extra rations, cigarettes or delicacies; some were just plain intimidated by the threat of physical violence; others could not resist the bribes. Their removal from office had to be carefully engineered before the Japs got too strong a grip. We despised them and termed them as "Jap Happy"; others had immense courage and were prepared to stand up to the Jap Camp Commander even though they knew that the end result would be a severe beating. They were termed Slap Happy and had to be replaced for their own sakes. We were forced to allow one of the above "unsuitable for promotioners" to take us out to the garden and to be officially in charge. This was a mistake as by now we had assessed them on the Railway and categorised them as the real McKay and contrast them with the old school Regulars who regarded Subalterns as dirt, treating them with contempt, even going as far as taking the Jap side in a dispute. True! The out and out worst (Swinton) came off landed gentry in the North East of England. We had warned the "Powers that Be" that there would be trouble if he was put in command. All went well for a while. We quite enjoyed getting out of Camp, but I cannot say we did much damage to the ground. We did the minimum horticulture possible. We learned to enjoy life in the open, until one day this individual appeared to take charge and I found myself taking part in a mutiny. We refused point-blank to go out under his command; he tried every way to get us moving. We stood fast and refused to go under his command. He then threatened each one of us individually with court-martial for mutiny on our return to the UK. Legally he was in the right, but when we pointed out to him that any legal proceedings would reveal his conduct in the camps, with samples quoted and the promise of many witnesses, he backed down and we went off with another C.O. I suppose that I should not be too critical of these men, but they made sure that they got all the privileges and advantages of their rank and to Hell with their underlings. It would not have been so bad if they had accepted their concomitant responsibilities towards their subordinates. We did, for our men and would have been bitterly ashamed otherwise.

We had casualties once or twice when a Canadian pilot tried not too skilfully to shoot up the shunting engine, which the Japs, if there was any threat of air attack, had parked hard up against our fence. Yet another War Crime. One of the English officers had the most remarkable escape. He did not feel too comfortable lying in the slit trench and decided to turn over as if in bed. As he rotated his body an armour piercing bullet passed across his belly and buried itself six inches into the earth. I saw the red weal across his belly and inspected with awe the bullet, which he had dug out for a souvenir; it had a needle point, half an inch long. That man must have had a guardian angel.

With little to do otherwise, except the necessary fatigues, the rumour mill got more and more outrageous. One of the best was that a couple had got out of the camp, been hidden by some of the "local ladies of the night" and put in touch with a small detachment of Allied troops located nearby. They stayed a couple of nights and were smuggled back into camp. I made good sure that I did not find out how. The "ladies" had offered them a long stay, but our boys knew the retribution that would befall the "ladies" in an inevitable denouement. We swallowed this story with a large pinch of salt hoping against hope that it was true, but our C.O. quite correctly rubbished it, severely cramping the style of any possible informant; (some of the Dutch would have sold their granny for an extra dish of rice). The couple were full of all the local gossip, even to the effect that parachutists had been dropped round about; they were most optimistic about the way the war was going. I think that we wanted to believe it, but had been disappointed so often in the past that we kept our thoughts to ourselves. It all turned out to be true, as we found out later, but our British Camp Commander had wisely decided that he did not know how trustworthy the recent influx of officers from the other nations were and stamped on the rumour. Much later, we learned that parties of four men, an officer, a sergeant, a medic and a wireless operator had been dropped in various strategic places in Siam in order to build up a Siamese resistance force. We were also told that a submarine had delivered a cargo of arms and ammo somehow in Bangkok harbour. This was possible but improbable; however a rising was in fact being organised to chime with the planned invasion. In this camp we suffered more Jap anti/officer-demeaning. I almost enjoyed the work because anything was better than sitting about, wondering when and how the war would end.

In their stupid way, the Japs waited, until we had got used to the new setup with the gardening squad; circumcision and shaven heads becoming the new craze for bored P.O.W. officers Another rush of blood to the Japs' heads confirmed their growing concern that we officers were still too near to our men, posing a real threat in the expectation of an Allied invasion and must be shifted as far away as possible. As was my wont, I did not volunteer for the new camp, Nakom Nayuk by name (somewhere in the jungle, I honestly know not where), but believe it was about 180 kilometres north east of Bangkok, almost up to what was then Indo-China. I landed up there with the usual suspects in the second draft, just the same.

After interminable counts, recounts and searches of our miserable possessions, we were marched down to the local Railway marshalling yards, where we sat about in full sun all day. The Japs dared not move any trains in daylight. The number of shattered trucks and engines, which we saw, as we rumbled along later, proved that.

Beside us was a train of rice trucks, similar to the ones which had brought us from Singapore up to Bampong, containing about 200 Jap survivors from the Arakan, all that was left out of an infantry regiment of 3000 men. They were in a very bad way; mostly in the last stages of Malaria; some badly wounded. They were still dying; three bodies were thrown out of the trucks while we were there. We were deeply shocked by the treatment they received from their own people. A basket of pumpkins and some rice was slung at them; they were told to get on with it. This was the attitude of their Line of Communication troops, who had never heard a shot fired in anger, towards their own front line soldiers. We could not believe our own eyes when we saw these staff officers in spotless white shirts and breeches, wearing highly polished jackboots, spurs and their stupid trailing swords strutting about and treating their own people with contempt. They treated them worse than they treated us.

They, poor sods, sat on the rails holding out their hands to us begging for food just like monkeys at the Zoo. Some of us, not I, threw them hard boiled eggs, which they had saved for the journey and would be pretty hungry themselves by the time we arrived at our destination. It proved that those who withheld my Tommy gun and made me sign for ammo in Singapore were replicated in armies all over the world.

Clearly the Japs were on the run and it was imperative that I do all in my power to survive a little longer, so as to get home to my wife and daughter and check them out against the photographs; these I carried with me everywhere. Finally evening came and we were crammed into rice trucks to trundle off eastward under the cover of darkness. We passed through parts of Bangkok where the difference between the jungly and the city Siamese was very apparent. We only managed a fleeting glimpse, but could register the delicate beauty of the better class females. A faint whiff of nostalgia and then it was gone.

Almost immediately we had to disembark. A large bridge had been thoroughly destroyed and we had to cross, in single file on foot, a rickety bamboo and rope bridge carrying everything, our stuff, cooking pots, etc., the lot. This was quite exciting since the bridge swung from side to side as we crossed and it was a long way down to the river below. One look was enough for me. After the tedium of Kanburi it was quite energising to be on the move and on a track of which we had not botched the building. In the early dawn we were turfed out and marched for what seemed to me about 36 hours non-stop, just 5 minutes smokeo every hour. During the night, like many, I fell asleep while marching. Only momentarily, I suppose, otherwise I would have fallen. After the third time, I concentrated hard and managed to struggle on until daylight. It was an extraordinary sensation, dreamlike, more a nightmare. We all knew what happened if you fell. Thirst was the worst part; we were well used to extreme hunger. We even greedily drank the water out of a paddy field sluice, red with earth, but at least it was wet.

Marching along semi-conscious and still carrying everything, we took it in turns to carry the cats. They made it very plain as only cats can that they did not approve of being carried in a swinging 4-gallon tin and insisted on travelling on our shoulders. Those, who know me, can imagine how I felt when it was my turn. I can take cats or leave them alone and at that moment I would much have preferred the latter. Only the British could be so stupid as to carry two cats while on foot on a 36-hour march. The main disincentive to falling out was that the least bad thing to happen was to be left to the tender mercies of the Siamese peasants, and we doubted that they could read and understand the parable of the Good Samaritan. We may have been much fitter than when we tackled the long march, but this was some physical test for half-starved men. It was just a case of putting one foot in front of the other and keeping going. If your mate started to waver you gave him a hefty nudge and if that did not do the trick, you shared his kit around until the next stop, or he recovered.

When, finally, we left the metalled, not tarmacked road and started up a footpath to the camp, our worst fears were realised; it was under construction. That was why we were there. The area had only just been roughly cleared and the skeletons of a couple of huts were visible.

No more Griff now; no more Nai Boon Pong; no more river; no more dry batteries: water had seeped into our reserve batteries and rendered them useless, but seeing our aircraft flying with impunity and the leaflets fluttering down helped to keep our spirits up. They were aimed at the civilian population, but we had interpreters for any Eastern language and their contents were most encouraging. The very sight of them was enough to give us a boost. It was now abundantly clear that the war was going our way, but we had heard enough stories about 'hari kiri' to be pretty apprehensive about our future. Actually, in spite of all the boasting talk from the Japs, I never saw or heard of a single case.

We were fitter than when we tackled the ten-day march.

Ever more clearly, I realised that the Japs were really on the run and that it was imperative that I do all in my power to survive a little longer so as to get home to my beloved wife and daughter and check them out against the photographs, which I carried everywhere. After the tedium of Kanburi it was quite energising to be on the move and on a track, which we had not botched the building of. In the early dawn, we were turfed out and marched for what seemed to me about 36 hours non-stop, just a break for five minutes smokeo every hour. No food as I remember. During the night like many others I fell asleep while marching. Again only momentarily, I suppose, otherwise I would have fallen. As I said, if your mate in front of you started to waver you gave him a hefty nudge and if that did not do the trick, you shared his kit around until the next stop or he recovered.

After about 36 hours marching, we turned left leaving the metalled, but not tarmacked, road and started up a foot path to the camp; our worst fears were then realised; the Camp was just starting to be built. That, as I said, was why we were there. The area had only just been roughly cleared and the skeletons of a couple of huts were visible. Luckily it was the dry season, so we slept in the open until our hut was roofed.

There we were in Nakom Nayuk in the jungle, miles from anywhere; the nearest road not much more than a bullock cart track, possibly somewhere near the border with Indo China, or so we were told. It was down to earth time and we were back to slave labour; worst of all, the Jap commander was the bastard we had hoped to have left behind. He was enthusiastically supported by a poisonous Jap medical orderly, who was hell-bent on emulating his superior in making our lives Hell. In hatred terms he ranked close to his boss with us. Our administration showed little change—the same favourites got the best jobs. I remember particularly a middle-aged man who glumly stood all day with a thumb suspended from his neck. Another younger, freckle-faced and sporting a Glengarry often stood beside him. Neither contributed anything at any time as far as I could see. The first, I later learned from the media, was a regular cricket commentator on the B.B.C, which placed him on the right-hand side of God with the English. I believe that he was wine buff too. The other contented himself by trying to look important in a treasured Glengarry. As far as I was concerned, both were a waste of space; they ate up our rations and contributed zilch.

The food was not only worse; short rations prevailed. Communication systems were so non-existent that we were allocated some native hill ponies. These vicious little beasts were slightly bigger than Shetland ponies, sturdy but highly dangerous to walk behind or in front of. The reach of their hind hoofs at full stretch was remarkable for such a small animal and behind you, you could hear their teeth click. I made sure I had nothing to do with them; fortunately there were some keen horsy folk, mad enough to volunteer.

Until more of the favoured ones appeared in the next party, I worked at hut building. That only lasted a fortnight; it took a couple of days to accustom myself to working on a bamboo skeleton frame ten feet off the ground. It was like walking on bendy scaffolding in the open; the only comfort was the knowledge that bamboo does not break like wood does, but bends. Once I got used to it, it was quite enjoyable, but too good to last. The third tranche arrived and jobs went on the usual favoured-nation treatment basis; I found myself with the other usual suspects on the bamboo carrying party, which entailed about 12 miles a day consisting of five trips each way, in JapHappies and barefoot, half going to the dump and half carrying with a mate 3x30 foot bamboos back to camp. In full tropical sun, monotonous was not the word for it, and we needed no rocking at night. The food was about as bad as any we had previously experienced. Once we were cheered to see a load of shark arrive in a pick- up truck. Unfortunately it had been some days since they had been killed as our noses soon told us and I took a rain check. Those who did not wished they had copied my example, as a vicious attack of the trots made for a sleepless night. We were back to the days of the Speedo and were not even given any time to plant vegetables.

The occasional leaflets, encouraging as they were, were our only contact with the real world. We knew that they were propaganda and not to be swallowed whole; I began to get a little despondent. Our future seemed bleak. Every day the same, rice pap for breakfast, parade at dawn, listen to the guards doing their comical daily obeisance to Hirohito and off we went on the bamboo trail. The only light relief was Fritz, a red dachshund, belonging to a Singapore lawyer, who insisted on following his master on the trail, but by the time he had completed the last lap, Fritz was a good lap and a half behind. Dogged was not the word for him, he never gave up; a long way for his little short legs. One of the miracles on the Railway and after, was his survival through it all. As related above, the Japs relished a plate of dog stew and every now and then had a purge on all the dogs in a camp. Somehow the bush telegraph always alerted Fritz's owner and he got whisked away to another camp. Fritz was a real live mascot.

Quite a few did not relish the bamboo trail and selfishly reported sick, thus both getting an inside job and causing a cut in the overall ration strength. The Japs, in time honoured fashion, promptly cut our rations and piled more work on the "fit". This went on for a week or so, very boring and aggravating; after all we were not contributing to the Japs' war effort, but working for our own benefit. There were times when I did not like some of my fellow men.

Suddenly one morning, we bamboo trailers were left standing on parade, uncounted, not a Jap or Korean to be seen. After a while we drifted back to our huts, wondering what on earth was happening. The best part was that the favoured ones, who had stolen our camp construction jobs, were kept at work. We enjoyed that! The huts had to be finished and made watertight as quickly as possible.

Meantime, our C.O., Lt Colonel Toosey, a man of outstanding courage and leadership (his quiet demeanour belied the steel he was made of) smelt a rat, faced up to and challenged the Jap commander, which was exceedingly courageous of him, knowing what a bastard that one was. Rumours flew about like autumn leaves in a high storm. We began to realise that something shattering had happened to the Japs. We learned later that it was the dropping of the second Atom Bomb on Nagasaki and the implied threat of more to come. As he told us, our C.O. went at it hammer and tongs with the Jap Commandant for the best part of an hour and a half, our man insisting that the war was over and the Jap denying it again and again until he reluctantly said that there might have been an agreement to discuss a truce, whereupon our C.O., extremely bravely, ordered every Jap out of the camp immediately. Much to his surprise they cleared out and nary a one was ever allowed back. I suppose the surrender came as a bigger shock to the Jap Commandant than to our C.O. as he skedaddled so quickly that his written orders to machine gun us if there was an uprising, (due in about ten days) were left behind on his desk. This was a big shock too to the poisonous Jap medical orderly, who bounced up to the gate next morning only to be turned away and informed by our own guards of his likely future destination. Everyone enjoyed the opportunity to do a bit of kurrahing and buggeroing of our own.

By the time all the rumours had been dismissed and the truth had sunk in, it was dusk and we derisively cheered the construction detail as they returned from work. We then went mad and lit a huge bonfire; the flames rose about ten feet in the air. An ex-Shanghai policeman produced a smallish Union Jack, which he claimed to have taken down in the "Battle Box" in Fort Canning at the surrender and kept sewn into a little pillow, which he had carried all the way up the Railway and back. We were really chuffed by this, because the Americans, Dutch and Aussies took a few days to make up flags for themselves. We rigged the Jack to the peak of our hut and we never took it down. That sort of thing meant a lot to us.

We sang (God forgive me) "Land of Hope and Glory, there'll always be an England" and other patriotic songs again and again and again all night long. It was a highly charged emotional experience. Picture it—the jungle all round, the tropical night, moon and stars, flames rising ten feet in the air and a motley crew of emaciated unshaven pot-bellied skeletal men roaring out the words with tears running down their faces. It must have fairly shaken the Japs in their huts outside the camp, let alone the jungle creatures. We fell asleep eventually. We did not care. We just knew that there were to be no more parades, no more interminable counts and recounts, no more beatings, no more saluting, no more bowing to the scum of the earth and the possibility of some decent food sometime reasonably soon. We did not get a lot of sleep, waking up every now and then to convince ourselves that we were not dreaming.

Waking up the next morning to a non-alcoholic hangover, we had to start facing facts. The Japs were out of the camp—no doubt about that; we were still dependent on them for rations; we had enough for a few days but the future was unclear. No one had the foggiest idea of how or if we would be rescued or how the Japs would react to a sudden and abject surrender by their

God Emperor. Gods do not do that sort of thing. The general opinion settled on the determination never to do any f…ing physical work again as long as they lived. This was intermittently and very clearly expressed with the F-word punctuating each word and on occasion each syllable. Feeling that they had amply fulfilled their lifetime quota of manual labour, they decided that the only thing to do was to sit in the hut and pass the time playing bridge, until rescue came. I gave it a lot of thought, mistakenly supposing that we would be evacuated by sea and that the Gulf of Siam would have to be cleared of mines first and that this would take a fair time. I well knew that if I sat in a hut all day doing nothing but play bridge, I would go stark staring mad. I was completely wrong about sea evacuation. Being constitutionally thick, transport planes in quantity did not enter my brain. So I volunteered for the coffee making team. My Kongsi decided that I had finally gone completely round the bend. As a subaltern and a life member of the awkward squad, I would never previously have got such a cushy job; you needed friends in high places. I sometimes even thought you had to sleep with someone in authority. I was thus totally unqualified; this job ranked second only to the cookhouse for perks. Circumstances had changed so radically that a mug, prepared to volunteer for work, was received with open arms and mutterings of "I always knew that there was something not quite right about that man". It saved the "Powers that be" the unpleasant task of conscripting an unwilling bridge player, and risking a dusty answer.

My predecessors in the coffee racket, who had oiled their way all through captivity, had taken to permanent bridge as to the manner born. Coffee, you say! But you have spent pages emphasising your privations, so how come coffee? The alleged coffee was made by roasting rice until it was black, grinding it using a glass bottle as a rolling pin and then boiling it up in a 4-gallon tin. A dollop of Gula Malacca sweetened the concoction, which was hawked round the camp for a few cents a mug by my new mate shouting, "Hot Sweet and Filthy!" Note, not milky (Milk had not been seen since Capitulation) but filthy, no problems there with the Trade Descriptions Act; but not too sure about Health and Safety. It sold quite well as better than and a change from the issue green tea, which looked and tasted like trefoil.

It was a good job for me. Chopping up the bamboo, stoking the fire, boiling up the brew; working out in the sun suited me much better than sitting in a hut smoking and playing bridge; it kept me fit.

The fire was near to the RC padre's hut. He was a white Dutchman, a spare little man with a goatee beard. He had hung on to his black cassock, a sort of black dressing gown with silvery rope tied round the middle, making it obvious to the Japs that he was a man of religion, and so was treated with circumspection by them, a primitive superstitious race. He must have found wearing it rather hot in the tropics but was wise enough to twig that it impressed and even intimidated the Japs. It was a mistake to fit our padres out in officer's uniform. The different insignia meant nothing to the Japs and Koreans, who classed them as officers; they never got the same respectful treatment as the priest did. I asked this one if he was looking forward to going home to his family in Holland, now that the war was over. He replied that he just went where the Church sent him and had no idea where that would be. I found this remarkable, impressive and a bit troubling, considering the anti-Catholic culture of my childhood. He was a real character, thought nothing of shouting over one of his flock and berating him for not being at Mass the previous Sunday; all this in front of me! The coloured Dutch seemed in awe of him. One day he disappeared down the track, only to reappear the next day hauling behind him, at the end of a halter, a massive water buffalo. This was real meat on the hoof. We fair salivated at the sight. Somehow or other, it seemed that he had found a small RC parish nearby, something quite incredible in the jungle. He had gone to the village and conned them out of the beast by promising them any clothes we left behind. In fact we had little but rags. It was a bit like an etching from Don Quixote, this little figure in his black cassock, bent forward, hauling along the scythe horned, lumbering beast. He was a remarkable wee man and we had to respect him.

The problem about killing the water buffalo was how to stun it before cutting its throat. A full blooded swing with the back of a felling axe just made it shake its head. It must have taken the best part of ten minutes to get it down and off its feet. This looks bad in cold print, but to starving men, the end justified the means. We feasted that night as we had not since the wild pig episode. What made it even better was that the Japs, who were outside the camp, could smell it cooking but got none. The tables had been turned with a vengeance.

Much to my surprise, considering my upbringing, I could not fault the RC priests I met in the army. They seemed to me to be in a class of their own, utterly fearless, never failing to stand up for what they believed was right and often getting away with it. My only rather cynical conclusion was that they had nothing to lose, no wives, no children and no property.

Not to be beaten by the Dutch, our C.O., who was all man, borrowed enough bits and pieces of uniform from all and sundry to kit himself out as a pukka British Colonel and set off with an adjutant cum interpreter, similarly smartly dressed, to find the local Siamese Provincial Governor. Siam was still semi-feudal and the Provincial Governor was nearly as powerful as the King. As Toosey reported it to us, he introduced himself as being the personal representative of his Majesty King George VI of Great Britain, Emperor of India, Defender of the Faith etc., etc., and told the Governor, whom of course he complimented on being the representative of the King of Siam, that if his demands were fulfilled, he would on his return to Britain speak personally to his King, when he went to report to him at Buckingham Palace, and that King George would undoubtedly reward the Governor with a decoration suitable to his rank and of course commend him as one King to another to his fellow King of Siam.

He then presented the Governor with a lengthy shopping list and returned to camp. Much to our surprise the goods duly arrived the next day by bullock cart and contributed greatly to improving our standard of living. As I have said, Lt Col Toosey was quite a man. He controlled a camp of Bolshie Officers in highly unprecedented circumstances. All done so coolly and calmly; he was Number One for all of us. We were indeed extremely fortunate to have a leader like him at that time.

As an example of how mad the British are, the first celebrations of our Liberation took the shape of a Race Meeting using the wild mountain ponies. No power on Earth would have got me onto the back of one. However, there were enough lunatics to make quite a show. Not every rider reached the finish still mounted. What the Japs penned outwith our camp made of all the cheering and shouting, I cannot imagine. I expect too that the Dutch were confirmed in their belief that the British were constitutionally mentally unstable. It did use up three days of anxious waiting, one day planning, one day racing and one day mulling over. The initial euphoria tended to wear off quite quickly.

Another day the apparition of an U.S. officer manifested itself. He was not tall, but resembled a refrigerator (shithouse as the old sweats called it) on legs and was festooned like a Christmas tree, with the most impressive assortment of personal artillery. We gathered around, goggle eyed, to listen to this phenomenon. It appeared that he was a chemical warfare officer in the U.S. army, but thankfully, with no chemical warfare to wage, he had finished up commanding one of the aforementioned parties of four dropped at various strategic points in Siam. To us he seemed to have dropped from Mars. Either he was broader than his height warranted or he was not tall enough to balance his girth; the longer we gazed, the more he looked like a truncated Christmas tree, over enthusiastically decorated by an armaments manufacturer.

We felt that the age of miracles had arrived, what with the water buffalo, the Colonel's hoard of cigarettes and what seemed to us as luxuries, but were actually fresh meat, vegetables and bread of a sort. Here was this apparition straight out of a Western film, but much more heavily armed, promising to deliver anything within reason that we asked for. He departed with a long list and to loud applause, tinged with a certain amount of scepticism. Sure enough the next day a Dakota arrived overhead, opened the bomb bay and down came everything from boots to writing paper. The boots arrived at speed and a heavy thud. It would have been sad indeed for someone to have been brained by a pair of ammunition boots after having survived the Railway. It could well have happened as we milled about regardless, collecting what we could. Everything was shared out according to need.

All this time I was boiling away at my coffee to a band playing. The water was fetched from a well a couple of hundred yards away in which swam the biggest leech I ever saw; it swung like a compass needle as I passed a finger round taking good care to keep it airborne. One day at the well, I noticed some shaggy horses grazing nearby. We were surrounded, I was then told, by a complete Jap Army Corps; these horses were either their cavalry, or more likely, officers' mounts. They had marched all the way from China in order to provide reinforcements for the Arakan, fighting three battles on the way, taking them the best part of two and a half years. Their presence brought us down to earth with a bump and did not do much for our hopes of safety in the immediate future, knowing by then of the written orders referred to above. Fortunately they caused us no problems. Apparently another case of, "You run your unit, don't touch mine." We had been saved, I was later led to understand, by the second atomic bomb going off about ten days before the planned uprising and the implied threat of more to come. I just kept my head down and practised deep breathing when I went for water.

The Japs must have been in the same state of confusion and disbelief as we were at the fall of Singapore, just living in limbo. That second bomb saved our lives without a doubt; it convinced Hirohito that even Gods have to yield occasionally. How many more of his cities and their inhabitants would be obliterated if he did not?

The next thing we heard was that Lady Mountbatten had managed to get herself into Siam and was touring the P.O.W. camps in a jeep (we had never seen such a thing) and reporting back to her husband, who was Supreme Allied Commander Far East and rejoiced in the title of "Supremo". Factually or class based, it was decided that our camp was by far and away the worst and should be evacuated first. So you will never hear a word against her from me, whatever snash the gossip columnists and character assassins have written. She was a very brave woman to have crisscrossed the wilds of Siam virtually on her own. God alone knows how long we would have languished in Nakom Nayuk without her help. She did great work at the other camps as well, getting them food and medicines; an Angel as far as we were concerned.

The great day arrived and we were packed onto flat lorries and driven at, what seemed to us, breakneck speed to Bangkok Airport. It was a hair-raising drive, standing holding on to each other in order to stay on board; the side capes on my truck were almost six inches high. We were stunned to be on the move without continuous counting and re-counting and could not have cared less about safety. We were on our way.

At the Aerodrome we were allocated to the coolie lines with just enough room to sleep on the concrete floors, packed like sardines in a tin. We were given hot food with apologies for the poor choice available. It was ambrosia for us. Anyway we were overwhelmed by the sight of two British females dishing out tea and buns. This was very embarrassing after all those years, not helped by us being still dressed in rags. The pair (mother and daughter?) had been interned in Siam, a very different regime from that suffered by the women in Changi Jail. Strangely enough the daughter appeared some years later in the boarding house in Innellan during our family holiday. She had some connection with John Jennings, a crew member of our rowing boat of old.

Having been warned that it might be some time before we would be evacuated, we did not sleep much that night. Too much had happened in too short a time to take it all in. The only British presence in the aerodrome was a small invisible R.A.F. air traffic control team and one very visible Ghurkha, about five feet tall and armed to the teeth; he strutted about the buildings with his finger on the trigger of his Sten gun, (we had never seen one; it looked to us as if it had been made out of Meccano by a drunken plumber) putting the fear of death up any Japs he encountered. We delighted in the way the Japs jumped out of his way; he was having the time of his life, flashing a huge smile at us every time he passed.

The next morning we were told that this was to be the day the peace treaty was to be signed and the only plane to fly was a white one carrying the negotiators. We thought that we spotted it high in the sky. This caused much excitement, but nothing to our reaction when, all of a sudden, a complete Indian Army Airborne Division landed on the tarmac before our very eyes. They disembarked in battle order and formed up in immaculate parade ground style, headed by their General, who accepted the

Jap General's sword and turned his back on him when the Jap tried to shake hands. No one can imagine the pleasure that that gesture gave us! To see the Jap General humiliated in front of his own troops and lose face was the icing on the cake. We returned to our billet, very happy bunnies, to discuss it in detail.

Suddenly a R.A.F. Wing Commander (I think) pushed in the door and said, "We have been ordered not to take you back with us." Our hearts sank as we had put two and two together and hoped to fill the empty aircraft on its return journey. He then said, "But having seen the conditions you are living in, get in that plane!" We needed no second command but collected our pathetic bits and pieces and wasted no time boarding. You will therefore well understand that I will always have a soft spot for RAF Transport Command and Dakotas in particular. It was my first flight and I could not have chosen a better time for it. The pilot was a great guy and regaled us with some hair-raising accounts of his experiences, much of it about the Ghurkhas.

In Burma it was quite a job, after they had been overrun, to winkle the Japs out of their fox holes. The one sure solution, he said, was to sit a Ghurkha on top of the foxhole and let the Japs listen to him methodically sharpening his kukri. They could only stand the noise for so long, when out they would come with their hands up. On one occasion he was given the job of transporting some Jap prisoners back to HQ under a Ghurkha guard. On landing he was astonished to find that the guard was the only passenger. When questioned about his prisoners, he replied that he had kicked them out one by one; seeing no point in wasting good rations on them, and was very surprised to undergo a court martial. If we had sat on that court martial, he would have been given a medal and definitely found not guilty. As far as we were concerned the only good Jap was a dead one. Little has changed since to alter my opinion. The interior of the Dakota was pretty Spartan and it was quite chilly crossing the mountains; the seats, tubular and canvas, ran down each side of the fuselage; we were still dressed in rags.

The pilot was careful not to inform Rangoon of his cargo until we were past the point of no return. As I have said, he was quite a man and I remember him with much fondness. Coming into Rangoon, he asked if any of us had ever seen the Shwe Dagon Pagoda, a magnificent temple, its roof sheathed in gold. We said no; he banked the plane and did a full circuit; the gold roof reflected the bright sunlight and blinded us. Very impressive it was, but even more impressive to us was the number of aircraft parked everywhere, many 4-engined. We had no idea of the advances in aircraft design during our captivity and were greatly relieved to land safely and feel terra firma under our feet.

Given such short notice of our imminent arrival, Rangoon was totally unprepared; full marks to the "Forgotten Army". They did not hesitate and whisked us away in ambulances for a quick examination by an M.O. in a lamplit tent. This was where my stint on the coffee paid off. The others, who had spent their time in the huts playing bridge, looked pallid and unfit. I on the other hand was sunburnt brown and looked in good tid. After a brief examination the M.O. asked if I had any objection to going home on the first ship. This did not seem to me a very clever question; I said that I had no problem. After ascertaining that we were not carrying any contagious diseases and careful documentation, we were transferred to a pre-war stone-built anti-malarial hospital, which had never been kitted out and was very appropriate; many of us, not me thanks to Atebrine, were riddled with BT malaria.

There in quarantine we were fed and faced individual real beds. All the "Forgotten Army" had been on a week's half rations to provide food for us; for a few days we were better fed than the fighting troops. This was a notable contrast to the Jap's attitude and very British, very, very impressive. The 14th Army will always have a special place in my heart. It fairly showed up some of my companions. I have a vivid memory on the Railway of a Judge and a Postmaster General both in G-strings wrestling in the ashes of a fire in which a duck egg had been roasted, both claiming ownership. Roasting was the only way of cooking individually then.

Some of us had a hard time adjusting back to European food, but not I; my main problem was not to eat too much too quickly. That was hard work. It took a long time to believe that I would get fed regularly and there was no need to stuff myself like a camel filling up with water before a desert crossing. Even today after 60 years I am only just able to leave something on my plate and that is very seldom. That was hard work. It took years to believe I would get fed regularly and there was no need to stuff myself like a camel prior to a desert crossing. Poor Anne, I gave her such a hard time when I came home. Like many 4-year olds, she could be picky about her food; harsh rationing complicated matters. I was so unfair, but I am glad she forgave me for all my failings as a father the day before she died, when I had her to myself without the formidable crew of Crawfords, who obstructed me from seeing my own daughter as she was dying. I grew to love her to bits. Lee too, suffered from my failings as a father; I doubt her forgiveness, but I cannot fault her as a daughter. She has been so good to me since I lost Bette, that no way can I thank her adequately. Nothing can match my love for Bette, but she comes pretty close.

The beds were a big problem. There were clean white sheets and pillows to contend with, let alone army hospital mattresses. Some could not face it and slept on the concrete floor. I worked it out that I had no option, but sooner or later I would have to learn to sleep in a proper bed again. This was not too easy for the first few nights but over time my body accepted this new lifestyle. But what with that, all the excitement and no exercise, I did not get a lot of continuous sleep for a week or two.

Next morning, acting on principle, we all went on sick parade. It was mind boggling to report sick, knowing that I would get a proper examination, treatment and drugs instead of being bashed as an impostor. I had a few white spots on an otherwise mahogany brown chest and not wanting to miss out in this strange new world, walked in to the M.I. room peeling off my new jungle green shirt only to get the shock of my life. Remember this was 1945 and we had been out of circulation for three and a half years. The M.O. was not only a WOMAN, with three pips on her shoulder, she was as BLACK AS YOUR HAT. Things surely had changed, but a black woman doctor with three pips on her shoulder was a culture shock for me, if ever I had one. My shock was as nothing compared to that of Dennis who was looking forward to getting treatment and a cure for his perpetually inflamed and weeping scrotum. He charged in, in his usual headlong manner, all set to drop his shorts, took one look at the M.O. and came out like a rocket, his face as red as his scrotum. We thought it was the best joke in years. Give him his due, he managed a wry smile as he charged off looking for a male doctor, who sorted things out for him, no doubt with an inward smile.

After years in a G-string, we found clothes most uncomfortable against our skin and felt a lot of sympathy for those naked savages whom the missionaries forced to wear clothes. We much preferred a towel, worn as a sarong.

For the best of reasons, the anti-malarial orders were quite explicit. After dusk it was mandatory to wear long sleeved shirts, buttoned at the wrist, fold-down army shorts, which changed at the undoing of a button into trousers, socks and boots. In the tropical heat and humidity our skins rebelled and so did we. The night Sister, a nice wee Welsh girl, was appalled, on her rounds, to find us sitting round a table lit by a paraffin lamp clad in sarong type towels having a smoke and mulling over all the strange things that had happened in the last 48 hours. Deeply shocked, she gave us a right rocket, reminded us of Standing Orders and pointed out that it was only for our own good. Poor soul, she would have no idea that we had spent the last few years resenting and defying authority. To class us as Bolshie would have been an understatement. After taking a long slow look at her, the ex-Shanghai policeman, whose chest was covered in hair like an Oran-Outan drawled, "Not to worry sister, any mosquito rash enough to bite one of us dies instantly of Cerebral Malaria." The wee girl blushed to the roots of her hair; we never saw her again. Not fair, she was only doing her job, thinking of our welfare. We must have acquired quite a reputation. Next morning on her rounds the matron, a large and formidable lady carrying the rank of at least Lt Colonel, was horrified to find Fritz in the ward with his master. She was most definitely not going to have any dogs in her hospital and he, who was our mascot, a symbol of our will to survive anything that the Japs could inflict upon us, was ordered to be banished. As one man we stood up and informed the lady that if he went, we went with him. When she saw us packing up our bits and pieces, she realised we were in earnest and departed. Fritz stayed; we never saw her again.

The nursing staff must have been glad to see the back of us. They had never come up against our like in the well-disciplined British Army and had no idea how to handle us. We were considered unpredictable; an unknown quantity; a bit like an unexploded bomb. They were not far wrong. It took a long, long time to accept the civilised customs and rule of law. Indeed I am none too sure that my family think that I have been fully converted yet. Nor am I.

Next we were informed that the "Supremo", Lord Mountbatten, would address us the next morning. We were distinctly unimpressed. "Who the Hell is this man calling himself the Supremo? He must be a proper tailor's dummy with an over inflated ego." The troops on the ground, who worshipped Bill Slim, the General commanding the 14th or "Forgotten" Army, did not give the Supremo a good report. According to them Slim would arrive at the hot spots of the front line with the minimum of fuss or entourage, listen to what the men had to say and act upon it. Mountbatten on the other hand whizzed about in a motorcade like a US President and insisted that all other movements had to get off the road as he passed, no matter if it was ambulance, rations or an ammunition convoy.

We seriously considered boycotting the whole affair as a gesture, but curiosity got the better of us and we assembled in a low ceilinged room, wondering how long he would keep us waiting. Bang on time, this vision in the white tropical uniform of a very senior naval officer, sporting enough medal ribbons to paper a room, bounded in athletically, leapt onto a bench and proceeded to charm us totally. He was 100% charisma. Compared to him, even my son-in-law, good as he is, still has his L-plates on. He managed in some way to convince us that he could not have won the war in Burma against the Japs without learning the lessons from our disastrous campaign in Malaya. By studying our tactical errors he had learned how to beat the Japs. We almost began to feel like heroes, until we reflected on the facts.

There was a lot of truth in what he said. I am utterly convinced that if we had stood our ground every time the Japs appeared behind us and had actually fought to the last man and the last round, as the orders always stated, we would have caused sufficient delay to the Japs' headlong sprint down Malaya, to have saved the Dutch East Indies, and shortened the war considerably. If so, I would not be here to write this, but the ignominious collapse of the British Empire, which had many good points, might well have happened in a more orderly manner, much more favourable to Britain and to the benefit of the world in general. Instead, as I have often repeated, that order really meant, "Stand by to retreat another 20-30 miles at a moment's notice." I have little doubt that this contributed largely to the contempt in which the Japs held us P.O.W.s and our subsequent harsh treatment.

Mountbatten referred to that treatment, expressed his horror and disgust and promised that, if we provided the evidence, the guilty would be speedily brought to trial and any appropriate sentences promptly carried out. This went down well with us as we all had a tale to tell. He was true to his word and I am told that the executioner in Changi Jail did not have a lot of leisure time. As a matter of interest I met, in later life, a Forbes Sempill, who claimed to have been that executioner. He also participated in a tangled tale concerning English and Scottish law. When Lord Forbes Sempill died there were two Baronies at stake and no male heir. His cousin, a lady doctor in Fife, changed her sex and claimed the titles. When she/he died the titles were split, one according to Scots law, the other to English. My acquaintance got one and Anne the elder sister of June, my first sweetheart, got the other and took her place in the House of Lords. A strange character; very charming. When I met him in some Masonic order, he claimed to travel with a half bottle of champagne in each of his coat pockets. I saw one once, but empty. He and his wife arranged Seamus for Bette, a Scottie with peculiar front legs, but who proved to be a wonderful companion for her, giving her so much pleasure.

I supposed that my ship would be in Rangoon in about 10-12 days, time enough to get kitted out in the new jungle green, so much more practical for the jungle than khaki. I appreciated that the administration had to make sure we were not carrying bubonic plague or some other horrendous disease, something quite possible considering whence we had come. I have to say that the authorities did all in their power to keep us interested and make our transition back to civilisation as easy as possible. Mostly however we tended to hang about in groups, defensive against this intimidating new world, and marvelling at all that had been discovered and invented during our captivity. One night we were taken to an E.N.S.A. show in what had previously been Rangoon's Garrison Theatre. Dorothy Dickson and Dorothy Hyson, mother and daughter, were the stars, both great West End favourites pre-war. I remember the excitement of going, but little of the show. It was all too much too soon. One of us, ex-Indian Army, discovered a battalion of his old regiment and was whisked off to their mess, much to our envy. I think he was let loose in a jeep, went for a spin, wrote it off and put himself into traction, thus missing our boat and spent instead a couple of months in hospital. We had never seen a jeep before and had no idea that the combination of a powerful engine and light body made it a tricky beast when cornering at speed.

The rest of us sat around sweating profusely in our unaccustomed uniforms, waiting for the "Off". I must pay full tribute to the 14th Army. Considering that they were still winkling out pockets of Japs and nobody knew how the Japs in Malaya would react to the invasion then in progress, they could not do enough for us. It was considered highly probable that the Japs would not believe that the Emperor would surrender. Gods don't do that sort of thing. In spite of all the bullshit rammed down our throats by our captors, as far as I heard, when they faced the facts of life as opposed to mythology, there was precious little, if any, Hara Kiri going on. I never heard of a single case. Mostly they surrendered quietly just like we did. They were not completely daft.

We were highly impressed by how the Navy dealt with their few P.O.W.s. In two days they had them kitted out and off to Colombo on a fast minelayer. We only got half a kit; it was enough and we were grateful.

CHAPTER 18

HOMEWARD BOUND

THEN THE MAGIC ORDERS came through to head for the docks. I think that walking up that gangplank was one of the most moving experiences of my life. I faintly remember the name of the ship. (*Corfu?*) I think it was the one that I waved my father off in, on his final trip to Singapore. If so, that was her first voyage and this her last. The skipper, one of the best, was retiring and determined to go out on a high note by commanding the first shipload of F.E.P.O.W.s to get home to Britain. As we went on board, that wonderful smell of hot oil and fresh paint hit me and I was instantly back in the engines of the old Clyde Paddle Steamers watching the huge crankshafts rearing up and collapsing down, while an engineer dripped oil on them from an enormously-long-spouted oilcan. I had not smelt a whiff of oil or paint for so long. It was sheer magic!

We found our cabin had been converted from a 3-4 to an 8-berth by installing standees, metal two-high bunks. Then we discovered that the W.C. had a flushing system and nearly broke the mechanism queuing up just to flush it and watch the water swirling down the waste pipe. This was sheer luxury. Then, miracle piled on miracle, to sit on a real chair at a real table and have the food served to me by stewards dressed in white ducks! Real food too, three and four courses, not rice, not bully, not army biscuits. We knew from experience that this could not last and we were right. All forces personnel in a troopship came under an O.C. Troops, usually a dugout Colonel having a cushy war, free keep and cheap booze in the bar, as long as the submarines stayed away. We must have landed a right stumer. He had watched us boarding with his beady eye and decided that we needed smartening up and that a heavy daily dose of P.T. would do us a world of good. Most of us hated P.T. at the best of times and this was definitely not the best of times. I felt another mutiny coming on. However the skipper, a most astute man, had twigged the situation, summoned the O.C. Troops and explained to him that the war was over, that this was his ship and that there would be no P.T. on this special voyage.

You could have heard the roar that went up as far away as Singapore, when he announced on the Tannoy that there would be no P.T. on this voyage, but, that for our own sakes, we must attend with our lifejackets the daily boat drill every morning and would we please wear shirts in the dining saloon and not upset the Goanese (?) Stewards with our bare torsos and tattoos!! Otherwise he had decreed that we would be left severely alone. His ambition was to command the first shipload of F.E.P.O.W.s to get home to Britain. Off we set for Colombo in good spirits. There, some 14th Army personnel left us. We were, very wisely, not permitted to disembark. The sea was kind and our spirits were high as we resumed our voyage heading for the Suez Canal. Also on the ship were some time-expired 14th Army troops, the real heroes, going home to be demobbed, plus a detachment of Q.A.I.M.N.S, on their way home. They were under the command of a formidable matron, carrying the rank of Lt Colonel. She was large in every direction and we were told commanded the hospitals at Kohima and Imphal throughout their long sieges, armed with a revolver, which she was expected to use on herself if the Japs broke through. She was irreverently referred to, behind her back, by her girls as the "Atom Bum", which gives some idea of her silhouette. They reckoned that the reason that the Japs did not press home their attacks was that they knew that, if they did, they would have to meet her face to face. She certainly kept the Sisters in order. No fraternisation was the order of the day and strictly enforced. We could do with more of her like today in our hospitals.

The sea voyage did much to advance our rehabilitation. Good food, sea air and total relaxation were the best of medicines. The weather was good and the sea calm. Little beats leaning on the rail of a boat deck with a full tummy watching the tropical sun disappearing into the sea out of a cloudless sky. One minute it is a huge orange disc, the next it is gone. It was indescribable to feel clean and know that another shower was there at the twist of a tap and plentiful soap. Bliss! We had also been given forms to fill in and mugshots of Japs and Koreans to assist in the prosecution of War Crimes Trials. This, to us, was an enjoyable way to pass the time between meals. Being without glasses throughout my captivity made deciphering mugshots tricky, but I knew their names and hope that I assisted a few on their way to the gallows. I do not think that there was any shortage of evidence and indeed a Special Branch Inspector quizzed me further at home.

Our first port of call was at the foot of the Suez Canal, where we went ashore for a day to be kitted out with cold weather uniforms, largely manufactured in New Zealand; the best of stuff; it lasted for years. We were allotted German P.O.W.s as orderlies and a high spot for me was to have a large blond Africa Korps, Nordic, Hitler Youth type carefully swabbing down the lavatory seat before I condescended to lower my bottom onto it. That was a moment to savour and one indignity I never suffered.

We were also taken to a movie show in a huge Nissan hut. Unfortunately it had not been chosen for its acoustics. A turgid film in black and white, something to do with the life of Chopin. I would have much preferred to walk about instead, but the herd instinct was too strong. Still, it was a kind thought.

Back on board we steamed up the Red Sea and into the Suez Canal. The Red Sea certainly lived up to its name with a few palm trees here and there floating in the early morning mist. The Pyramids and the Sphinx proved all they were cracked up to be, as seen floating in the morning mist from the deck of a ship. At least the odour wafting across was a big improvement from that in the Far East. In the dusk and by moonlight we floated, as if in a dream. At the north end of the canal we were intrigued to see thousands upon thousands of Italian P.O.W.s guarded by Indian troops; every soldier had his rifle chained to his wrist, not so much for fear of the Italians breaking loose, as of the thieving Arabs. The Italians were presumably awaiting shipment home.

Once out of the canal and into the Mediterranean, it was flat out for Southampton. Our skipper was absolutely determined to be the first to bring home F.E.P.O.W.s. There was a very real race with another troopship, real neck and neck stuff. We followed the race daily, as the relative positions were posted on the notice board. However our rival, which was faster than we were, was directed for some unknown reason to Liverpool: our skipper, much to our and his satisfaction, achieved his ambition by a day. An amazing coincidence was that, after passing one of the majestic Queens on my arrival at Singapore roads on our way out, here was the other, berthed beside us and towering like a skyscraper above us in Southampton docks.

We disembarked to a hero's welcome and were bussed to a reception camp. I found it all rather embarrassing, when I realised that the men from the 14th Army, who had won the war in the East, filed off the rear gangway totally ignored, while we, who had ignominiously lost our drab little campaign, were fêted. They were so glad to be demobbed that they did not give it a thought. It was hot and sunny; the streets were lined with cheering crowds; even flowers were thrown through the open bus windows. At that time we did not take in the drabness of post-war Britain. We still had not got over Churchill losing the election. We could not understand the people turning against him. We took as Gospel every word he said, as related to us in the nightly Griff; we analysed everything carefully and found that he never promised anything that was not delivered. More than can be said for Roosevelt, Eisenhower or Montgomery. If it had not been for him and his dogged fighting spirit, we would today be under Nazi rule and there would not be a Jew, gipsy or handicapped person left alive in Europe. So little history is taught in the schools today, that there are two generations, including our terpsichorean P.M. (Blair) now who do not know that for over a year, Britain stood alone against Germany. Not for the first time Britain saved Europe from a Dictator. I sometimes think that many Europeans cannot forgive us for that; it was hard to find a Frenchman who did not claim to have been in the Resistance, or a German who admitted to have been pro-Hitler. Amazing how memories can manipulate facts!

Arriving at a nearby army camp, we were fed and drew some pay. I was pleased to note that my financial arrangements had worked okay and that Bette was still getting the surplus money every month. I had arranged with Cox & Kings' Bank, where my pay was lodged monthly, that any surplus from the preceding month would be credited to her Bank Account. Every now and then I get something right. I sent her a telegram to tell her that I was alive and back in Britain. She had not heard from me for well over a year and that card had taken over a year to arrive. We both had good cause to hate the Japanese. Even in small things they were loathsome. Looking back I do not know why I did not phone. Probably the telegrams were free and we were encouraged to use them rather than choke up the telephone system. Travel warrants were issued to whatever destination in the British Empire we desired. Those of us travelling north were put on a train for London to catch our night trains. Special seats were reserved for us—we were treated as V.I.Ps; even buses had been laid on to take us from and to our London stations. We greatly enjoyed the special treatment and decided that we would have no problem getting used to it. A few changed their names and headed for Canada, New Zealand and so on, their previous identities scrubbed for reasons known only to themselves.

The Glasgow train was packed solid, some standing, some sleeping in the corridors, but a seat was quickly evacuated for me and I could have smoked myself to death; so many cigarettes and hot drinks from thermosflasks were offered that I began to feel like a hero until I took a hard look at my inglorious military career. The real reason behind the amazing treatment was that I was a bright yellowy green after a long course of Mepacrine and thus easily recognised as a F.E.P.O.W.

I must have slept during the long journey to Central Station, Glasgow, dreaming of the reception I would receive. Judging by the recent hero worship, the least I could expect would be to be welcomed by a Brass Band, headed by Bette, the Lord Provost and cheering crowds lining the streets. I might have known Glasgow better. Not a sausage, no one! Just a depressed Ticket Inspector, and my fellow passengers hurtling off for trams home and a dull damp Glasgow Monday morning.

Disappointed but undaunted, I picked up my stuff and headed for a tram to take me to my in-laws and climb the winding stairs to their flat at 7 Downside Road. Unmindful of the time (all good Glaswegians were still a-bed) and desperate to see my love, I pressed the doorbell. Nothing happened. I pressed it again to be successful this time and was rewarded by the apparition of a panting mother-in-law in a plum coloured dressing gown, who took one look at me and burst into tears. In between sobs, the words "Oh Bette, oh Bette!" could be made out. What the Hell had happened to my wife? Was she dead? No, I would have known somehow. Had she found another man? Never! She was not that type. By this time into my fuddled brain had penetrated the words, "She has bought a house." I was punch drunk, astounded, gobsmacked and could only say "Where?" followed by "Where the Hell is that?" Eventually "above the boating pond" could be made out; without further conversation and my head in a whirl, I went back down the stairs, across Byres Road and broke the speed record to the tram stop at Botanic Gardens, leaped onto a green tram, willed the traffic lights to change and sat impatiently, until I saw the beginning of the separate tram track and knew that the Boating Pond was round the corner, jumped off before the tram stopped, hurtled across Great Western Road and started to climb, my head in a whirl.

How could she buy a house? Had my mother lent her the Deposit? Years later I worked out that she had squirrelled away savings all the time I was away. What a girl!! Far too good for me. All sorts of thoughts corkscrewed in my mind as I passed the bare outline of the block, destroyed by a landmine and saw the magic words "Winchester Drive" ahead. I walked up the middle of the road scanning each house and saw her in an upstairs bedroom plaiting Anne's second pigtail. Simultaneously, she looked out, saw me, dropped everything, tore downstairs, flung open the front door, ran out, hit me like a torpedo amidships in the middle of the road and nearly knocked me over. She had waited five years for me and had even bought a house for us!! Was I not the luckiest man in the world!

Lee arrived ten months later, to make our family complete and satisfy Bette and me that the Japs had not deprived me of my manhood. The Army Doctor was so keen to get me out of his Surgery before I raised the thought of a War Pension, that he told me that I would not see past my 40th birthday and never father a child. Clearly he had never met a Forbes before. I would have fathered more if the Spectre of Rhesus had not reared its Ugly Head.

I should be grateful for small mercies. Lee has always been there for us; we are so lucky; me specially so undeserving of two such exceptional women.

THE END